JOHN LYALL

A LIFE IN FOOTBALL

JOHN LYALL

A LIFE IN FOOTBALL

Dr. Phil Stevens

Foreword by Sir Trevor Brooking CBE

APEX PUBLISHING LTD

First published in hardback in 2014,
updated and reprinted in 2015 and 2016 by
Apex Publishing Ltd
12A St. John's Road, Clacton on Sea, Essex, CO15 4BP, United Kingdom

www.apexpublishing.co.uk

Copyright © 2014-2016 by Dr. Phil Stevens
The author has asserted his moral rights

British Library Cataloguing-in-Publication Data
A catalogue record for this book
is available from the British Library

ISBN 978-1-78538-492-9

Typeset in 10pt Baskerville Win95BT

Production Manager: Chris Cowlin
Cover Design: Hannah Blamires

Dedication

To the memory of John Lyall and Ron Greenwood

Contents

Acknowledgements

My aim in writing this book has been to construct John Lyall's life story mainly through interviews with his family, former players, colleagues and friends. It is an indication of Lyall's reputation in the game that so many people were keen to cooperate with the research.

Pat Holland, Phil Parkes, David Cross, Sir Trevor Brooking, Ray Stewart, Terry Venables, John Wark, Simon Milton, Mick McGiven, Chris Kiwomya, Charlie Woods, Tony Carr, Neil Burns, Alan Dickie and Dave Kingston were all generous with their time and willing to share their memories.

Jim Lyall deserves special thanks for his warm welcome and for patiently reading drafts of the early chapters. West Ham archivists, Steve Marsh and Stuart Allen provided invaluable assistance with important facts and figures. Particular thanks must go to Steve for providing photographs and match reports. Pat Godbold, long-serving Ipswich secretary and now club archivist, cast an expert eye over the chapters on Lyall's time at Portman Road. The distinguished Hammers' historian, John Northcutt, has been an encouraging and meticulous fact checker, saving me from errors, large and small. I am also grateful to John for allowing me access to a letter he received from John Lyall which is reproduced here in full. All of these people made my work highly enjoyable – writing the book felt like a real team effort.

The Ipswich Records Office and the East Anglian Daily Times kindly provided information and images from Lyall's time in Suffolk. I would also like to thank Chris Cowlin at Apex Publishing for supporting the project.

It is said that most of a writer's time is spent reading. In the preparation for this book I have read countless match programmes, newspaper reports and many of the excellent books on the history of West Ham United and Ipswich Town. The bibliography at the back of this book lists the standard works on the history of these two famous clubs and others I have found helpful for my research.

I would like to thank Sir Trevor Brooking for agreeing to write the Foreword and Murray Lyall for his poignant words about his father in the Preface. As always I am grateful to Mark Cripps and Linda Stevens for their warm interest and acute observations.

Finally, the book could not have been written without the encouragement and support of the Lyall family. I hope that Yvonne, Murray and Jim didn't find my constant questioning too much of an intrusion.

Preface by Murray Lyall

My dad and his great mentor Ron Greenwood were so much more than managers; they ran the club from top to bottom and stamped their personalities on it to such an extent that they became the very fabric of the club. Both brought unrivalled success to West Ham and without doubt they are the most successful managers in the club's history, but more than that they were responsible for creating many of the traditions that West Ham is renowned for. They were instrumental in West Ham being known as *The Academy of Football* with an enviable conveyor belt of home-grown talent and a free-flowing style of entertaining football.

After taking over his beloved West Ham from Ron, when he left to be England manager, doing things the *West Ham* way was something my dad had inherited and believed in strongly. By this he meant the style of play and the reputation of the club as a whole both on and off the pitch. He was the Boss and with the assistance of his backroom staff he managed every aspect of the football club, including players' contracts.

In the football world he was widely acknowledged as a perceptive, innovative and visionary coach, who simply had another dimension, and was honoured to have had the pleasure of coaching and working with some of the greatest names in the game. Every training session was different and if something didn't work, he would analyse it and improve it. John Lyall wouldn't accept technical faults.

His great teams of 1980 and 1986 played the simple game of pass and move, but he also encouraged his players to express themselves. There could be no better example than Alan Devonshire who, under dad`s watchful eye, developed from a promising non-League footballer to a West Ham legend and England international.

As a Hammers' fan I ask myself, when was the last time I was excited by a West Ham side and I find myself thinking back to the *Boys of '86* – biased because it was my dad's team maybe? What is certain is that it was a time when the team was good to watch. Things were done in a simple but thorough way. Players were keen to learn and develop through the sheer enjoyment of going to the training ground each day to learn how to play the West Ham way.

It was a privilege for him to be a football manager in an era of greats such as Sir Matt Busby, Bill Shankly, Jock Stein, Bill Nicholson, Brian Clough, Bob Paisley, Terry Venables, Sir Alex Ferguson and Sir Bobby Robson, who were all very special men in their own right and with whom he shared a great rapport, understanding and love of the game.

The John Lyall we all knew had self-respect and was highly esteemed in football across Europe. Although a disciplinarian in his approach to the game, John Lyall always respected other people and was courteous to everyone. He had a great regard for football and what it could do for people in their lives. The respect he had from players, coaches, directors and most importantly... the fans, was earned through his open and honest approach to things.

Our family is honoured by the fact that his memory and legacy will continue with the publishing of this book and it is important that the traditions and principles he, and many others, stood for in the game are maintained in future generations.

Foreword
by Sir Trevor Brooking

It is a great privilege to be asked to write this foreword about John Lyall. He was certainly a wonderfully gifted coach, but even more importantly he was a hugely respected and trusted friend. I was a player at West Ham United for 19 years and during that period had just two managers, Ron Greenwood and, of course, John. I was very lucky to have such a memorable career at the club I supported as a little boy, but even more fortunate that it coincided with two special talents at the helm as managers.

My first encounter with John was when I was being shown around the club. I was introduced to him when he was working in their offices after suffering a knee injury that curtailed his playing career. He was always a very approachable individual, but this early introduction revealed an immediate and strong link to each other as we both attended Ilford County High School for Boys. As Old Parkonians we enjoyed a quick exchange of familiar teachers and pupils who had crossed our paths, while also reflecting on how beneficial that quality academic experience had been for each other.

By the time I joined West Ham after I finished my O-levels, Ron Greenwood had already encouraged John into his coaching structure at the club and so my own progress as a player almost mirrored his own development as a coach. Throughout those 19 years from 1965 to 1984 I can honestly say my football experience was one of enjoyment, fulfilment and improvement. My assumption for most of that period was that all clubs and players received a similar programme of learning from their respective managers, but over time the feedback from other players highlighted that was often not the case.

John and Ron both believed in encouraging players to maximise their talents by expressing themselves creatively and technically. They gave us the individual confidence and belief to play to our personal strengths but embrace it into a team ethos which was entertaining for all watching fans. We were encouraged to think about the game too, and many of us did early coaching sessions in schools which made us appreciate how different the game can appear from the touchline.

If there was one clear distinction between the two managers then it was definitely John being firmer and stronger with players than Ron. As time has moved on, players have tended to challenge authority more, especially with the extra money and profile coming into the game. I thought John dealt with that transition superbly and his excellent man-management provided a perfect balance between clear decision-making, alongside fairness in the manner of keeping people informed.

When I stopped playing in 1984 I naturally kept in touch with John's remaining spell at West Ham, plus his impact which followed at Ipswich. The large numbers of players from both clubs who attended his Service in 2006, reflected the massive respect we all had from our football time together.

At that Service I will always remember that Sir Alex Ferguson flew down to speak, even though his club, Manchester United, had been knocked out of the Champions League the previous night. He eloquently conveyed how John had helped his early managerial years at Old Trafford by always being a reassuring voice to speak to for guidance. It was a friendship John himself kept very private.

My final thanks to John is on a more humorous note. When I shook hands with him in May 1984, following my last game for the club, he punched me lightly in the stomach and said, "I can see you putting on a load of weight now you are not going to have me on your case!" I naturally defended myself and said that would not happen. But in all honesty, during the years that followed, John's words often ticked over in my head whenever my trousers started to feel a bit tight. So even now I am still listening to his wise old words because for me he is someone to whom I will always remain indebted.

Introduction

John Lyall was one of the most successful managers in English football in the 1980s. The former West Ham full-back, forced out of the game by a horrific knee injury at the age of 23, showed immense courage and determination to become one of most admired coaches of his era. Lyall led the East London club to their highest-ever top-flight league position, won the FA Cup twice, once against the mighty Arsenal, and took the club to the final of the European Cup-Winners' Cup. But Lyall's career did not progress effortlessly from one triumph to the next. It was full of crushing lows and extraordinary high points which he met with good humour and a healthy dose of Scottish stoicism. As Kipling might have written, *he treated the imposters of success and failure in exactly the same way.*

The Upton Park faithful loved him, not just for his success, but for encouraging his teams to play football the *Hammers'* way. To take this unfashionable club to within a whisker of winning the old 1st Division title in 1986, only to be pipped at the post by Liverpool, was a remarkable achievement and a tribute to Lyall's outstanding leadership and inspirational coaching style. Many of his ex-players and colleagues talk about Lyall's excellent man-management style. Professional football clubs are rife with rumour, intrigue, vendettas and cliques. Lyall would have none of this and inspired a common purpose in his staff, players and crucially, the fans.

Cruelly sacked by West Ham in 1989, Lyall spent 18 productive months working with Terry Venables at Tottenham, before being snapped up by Ipswich Town, who were then languishing in the lower half of the old 2nd Division. Lyall achieved a minor miracle with the *Tractor Boys*, leading the Suffolk club into the newly-formed Premier League in only his second season at Portman Road.

John Lyall's influence as an innovative and perceptive coach extended beyond East London and Suffolk. It is not widely known in football that England managers, Sir Bobby Robson and Terry

Venables, regularly turned to Lyall for advice and guidance, as did the younger Alex Ferguson. The story of how these top football brains shared their considerable expertise makes interesting reading for all football lovers.

Lyall's chief battle cry was excellence. He insisted on high standards and expected his players to follow his example of studied professionalism, attention to detail and exemplary personal conduct. At Upton Park he was astute enough to gather around him a dedicated staff team and a core of high quality footballers who understood exactly what their coach demanded of them.

As the appointed successor to Ron Greenwood, Lyall slipped quietly into the manager's job at the Boleyn. But, as the former England manager was quick to acknowledge, Lyall was very much his own man. Greenwood acknowledged his successor was a stronger character, despite his outwardly genial nature. At once amiable and tough, Lyall possessed a fine football imagination and feel for the modern game as his West Ham side very nearly swept all before them.

Former players, colleagues and fans all agree that Greenwood and Lyall were special. Neil Burns suggests the pair had,

'... a rare ability to touch both hearts and minds across big communities. Despite being no longer with us in person, the quality of their example continues to impact on many people's lives, both in the world of football and beyond.'

If Lyall was a highly respected public figure, his family and friends paint a picture of a much-loved and sorely missed husband, father and companion. He was a devout family man and in some ways, despite his success, unsuited to the crass, commercial world of the Premier League. Lyall is part of the DNA of West Ham United, his values and achievements are buried deep into the claret and blue soul of this once celebrated football club. While Lyall was at Upton Park the poetry of the Hammers' football was protected.

Despite his undisputed allegiance to West Ham it never surfaced at Ipswich, where he led the *Tractor Boys* into the Premier League in its inaugural season. Ex-players and coaching staff from Lyall's time at Portman Road continue to have a deep regard, almost reverence for their former manager.

No one who knew Lyall failed to like him or to respond and engage with him. He never compromised his deeply held values and dignity, despite the professional temptations that came his way – the beliefs instilled in him by his parents were too deeply ingrained. Early in his managerial career he promised his wife Yvonne that he would retire from the game he loved in his mid-50s. Needless to say, he kept his word, only too aware there is a life outside football.

As he led his team out at Wembley for his two FA Cup wins, the Hammers' manager had the appearance of a very proud man. Tall, confident and immaculately dressed, Lyall provided an impeccable example to his players. It is now just over 30 years since Lyall took his West Ham side to the summit of the English game and Ipswich Town into the Premier League. This is the first biography of John Lyall and is offered as a warm tribute to his outstanding contribution to the history of two great football clubs.

www.apexpublishing.co.uk

Chapter 1
A happy childhood

Today's West Ham fans must look back on the club's golden age with tremendous affection and longing. In the years between 1975 and 1986, under the leadership of the saintly John Lyall, the Hammers came close to winning the 1st Division Championship for the first time in their history, while twice winning the FA Cup. Following the first West Ham manager, Syd King, and his successors Charlie Paynter, Ted Fenton and Ron Greenwood, Lyall was only the fifth manager of West Ham in just over 80 years. He represented the very best traditions of the Hammers pioneered by the club's founder, the East London shipbuilder, benefactor and moralist, Arnold Hills. With the peerless Bobby Moore as his captain, Greenwood won the FA Cup in 1964 and the European Cup Winners' Cup in 1965, but it was his prodigy John Lyall who led the Hammers to their highest-ever league position, glorious European campaigns and two unforgettable FA Cup triumphs.

The Hammers have a special place at the heart of the English game. The West Ham way of playing a fast-flowing, attacking football, full of bewildering exchanges and great goals, gave a grateful nation Moore, Hurst and Peters, and some of the most exciting football ever seen in this country. John Lyall was one of the creators of the West Ham Academy and a true pioneer of all the good things the club came to represent. His record places him alongside legendary historical claret and blue figures like Hills, King, Greenwood and Bobby Moore himself. As a young man Lyall played with the great West Ham names of the late 1950s, and if it were not for a career-ending injury he might have developed into a decent international defender. But it is as an exceptional coach that Lyall is best remembered both at the Boleyn Ground and at his second club, Ipswich Town. He was part of the 50s' generation of

Malcolm Allison, Noel Cantwell, John Bond and Malcolm Musgrove, yet many years later he was a thoroughly modern manager full of ideas, well-prepared, and in his early days, desperately keen to learn. Lyall had a great teacher in Greenwood and learnt from older players at the club like Allison, Bond and Cantwell, but he was always very much his own man and as a coach had a decisive influence on the club's reputation for playing exciting football. As a manager Lyall would have much preferred to lose a highly entertaining game 4-5 than grind out a 0-0 draw, although he would have had some harsh words to say to his defenders after the game.

The impression I have gained of Lyall from conversations with fellow coaches, managers, ex-players and friends was of a deep thinker about the game of football. Here was a man who combined a true love for the game coupled with a genuine respect and affection for all his players. A born leader, from the outset this inspirational coach had a serious interest in improving individual players and developing successful teams. Lyall's qualities included sound judgement and a keen sense of timing. Throw in a lifelong ethic of hard work, persistence and forensic attention to detail and you have all the personal attributes required for a successful football manager. There is one other quality which marks out Lyall from most other managers. It is difficult to define, but can best be described as a certain presence. Player after player has spoken of his command on the training ground and in the dressing room – he commanded respect by his sheer presence – a rare quality indeed.

John Angus Lyall was born in Ilford, Essex on 24 February 1940. His mother, Catherine was from the Isle of Lewis in the Outer Hebrides and his father, James hailed from Kirriemuir, near Dundee in north-east Scotland, a birthplace Lyall shared with Sir James Barrie of Peter Pan fame. Kirriemuir is set in the rural vastness of the Braes of Angus where young John acquired his life-long devotion to fishing. John's dad was the son of a ploughman and the second oldest of eight children. Lyall's mother, Catherine, was born in the crofters' village of Back, near Stornaway, on the Isle of Lewis, bordering the Minch, one of the most testing stretches of sea around the British Isles. She was one of six children and on leaving school entered domestic service. Life in the Outer Hebrides for its 25,000 or so inhabitants was tough and challenging in the early part of the 20th century. Despite its awesome beauty, the cold, inhospitable weather and remoteness the Hebridean Highlands were no place for young people with ambition.

For John's mother, staying to work on the island meant digging potatoes or helping to cut the family peats, none of which appealed to an ambitious young girl with her entire life in front of her. So, like many others of their generation, young Catherine and her brothers and sister left the island to find a future on the mainland. Remarkably, all became successful in their chosen careers. Older brothers, Angus and Donald left for the United States to become successful businessmen, while Roderick followed and built a career for himself in the car industry of Detroit's motor city. Angus did eventually return to Lewis, but retained his entrepreneurial spirit buying out the local bus company with his younger brother, John, who later became the local village Postmaster.

Catherine's sister Kate also returned to Lewis, and not to be overshadowed by the boys, set up her own successful dressmaking and tailoring business. In many ways Kate reversed the trend of young girls on Lewis as John points out in his autobiography *Just Like My Dreams: My Life with West Ham (1989)*. It was a long-standing tradition on the island for girls to go into domestic service, primarily on the mainland. At the time, service offered a respectable career for young girls throughout the United Kingdom. Working class parents were delighted if their daughters secured a job in a comfortable household where they would be secure, looked after and reasonably clothed and fed. Perhaps lacking the same spirit of adventure as her brothers and her sister's latent entrepreneurial skill, John's mother, who was the youngest in the family, chose the only available route open to her, which was to go into service. She quickly obtained a position with the wealthy Glenmorangie whisky owning family based in Edinburgh, where she steadily worked her way up the household ladder and became assistant cook to the head chef, a formidable and highly qualified woman from Paris.

While working in Edinburgh, Catherine developed a close relationship with the Glenmorangie family's handicapped son. When the company created a new export division in London, the family relocated to Putney and the highly valued Catherine was asked to join them. But instead of working in the kitchen she was offered the position of personal carer to their handicapped son – an opportunity she happily accepted. It was in London that she met her husband-to-be, James Lyall, who hailed from the Vale of Strathmore area in the rugged Glens off Angus in the north east of Scotland.

With most of the grain mills closing down due to a harsh recession, work was increasingly hard to find and John's father, who trained as a millwright and carpenter, made the inevitable decision to leave the Kirriemuir area. Now widely known for the excellence of its game fishing, walking and shooting, this part of Scotland was a harsh place for young people back in the early 1900s. Just like the Hebrides, most young people left for the potentially richer pastures of Glasgow, Edinburgh, or even as far away as London. John's father was a bright student who did well at school and was expected to take up a place in one of Scotland's excellent universities. His Headmaster was horrified when, as a result of extreme family hardship young James, perhaps sensing the future, gave up Latin for a more practical subject. In such difficult financial times, university was never a realistic prospect for a boy like James. Instead he qualified as a carpenter/joiner and worked in the mills and factories dotted around Kirriemuir, before the work gradually dried up leaving him with little choice but to move away.

James left Kerriemuir and worked his way down to London, arriving with few possessions and fewer prospects. But, ever resilient, a characteristic his sons were to inherit, James ultimately joined the police force and enjoyed a successful career, reaching the rank of sergeant in the Essex Constabulary. James would probably have rather used his joinery skills to earn a living, but in the gloomy depressed late 1920s, the Police Force provided a solid and secure start to his new life. This was important for the young Scot who knew that work in the construction industry was generally poorly paid and terribly insecure. Initially, the life of a serving police officer was something of a culture shock for James. Living in a Section House in central London, although largely occupied by fellow Scots, was a long way from the peace and tranquillity of the Glens of Angus, but James did find time to represent the Metropolitan Police at football, as he slowly settled into his new London life.

New home in Essex

Catherine and James eventually met at a Scottish social function in London. A romance subsequently blossomed and the couple married in December, 1935 at St Columbas Church of Scotland, Pont Street in London's West End. Catherine and James began their married life together in Leyton in East London, before moving a few miles to the relatively prosperous suburb of Clayhall in Ilford.

Ilford was a good choice for a young couple setting out on a new life in London. The flat, above a shop in Claybury Broadway, was just a few miles away from the Ilford Palais where Bobby Moore famously met his young wife, Tina. John's future wife Yvonne, had a very strict father who flatly refused to allow his daughter to go anywhere near the Palais. But at that time the glitzy dancehall provided a great night out for the young and not so young in Ilford and the surrounding area.

In the 1950s Ilford was in general a quiet suburb, but only a few miles from the tougher environment of the East End. To the north lay the well-heeled, leafy boroughs of Havering, Barkingside and, to the west, Wanstead, where John's father was finally stationed. In the 1950s, factory work was plentiful, if poorly paid. The defence and electronics contractors, Plessey, who produced prototype TVs for John Logie Baird, employed over 15,000 people in nearby Vicarage Road in the '50s. In addition to the Plessey plant there was work at the Marconi television firm and the nationally known, Ilford Films.

The more attractive option for generations of local young people was to make the short commuter trip to Liverpool Street to work in the City or the West End. The Stock Exchange, banks and finance houses provided attractive employment for generations of bright young people from the area. These jobs were well paid compared to those in the local factories and a position in the City was seen as some kind of status symbol. In the early years of their married life Bobby Moore's grammar school-educated wife, Tina actually earned more from her City job than her famous husband did at West Ham. Or she did until the 1966 World Cup changed things forever for the Barking boy. If the young John Lyall had not shown so much promise as a footballer, he might well have left school for a job in the City or an apprenticeship in Plessey or Marconi. Fortunately, John's parents were happy to indulge the youngster's insatiable love of sport and football in particular.

A good start in life
James and Catherine Lyall were both from solid Church of Scotland stock and carried with them cherished memories of a happy childhood. Their own parents had taught them the meaning of hard work, integrity and responsibility. James and Catherine were determined to pass on the values of Lewis and Angus to their own children. They had left the comfortable and warm environment of their close-knit Scottish families to seek a better life hundreds of miles away in London. This took courage, determination and resilience, qualities John and his two brothers subsequently inherited in abundance.

Partly because of their early, challenging experiences, John's parents were understandably cautious people and were never tempted to purchase their own home for their growing family. Flat 12a, Claybury Broadway was rented from the outset, not an unusual occurrence in the 1950s. James and Catherine understood the value of money and would have been wary of getting into debt, a family trait they passed onto their children. While James was carrying out his constabulary duties, Catherine stayed at home to look after the boys, as was the tradition in the 1950s. Though careful and very private, it would be a mistake to see the Lyalls as a stereotypically high-minded, austere Highland couple. James and Catherine were warm, loving and highly supportive parents but, with their own tough Highlands upbringing, could be strict disciplinarians if the occasion demanded.

John's brother, Jim, now a fit 76-year-old, lives in comfortable retirement in Norwich, where he still enjoys cycling, walking, trout fishing and weekly games of squash. Jim recalls his childhood with great affection and fondness, but remembers testing his father's patience from time to time. One evening Jim cycled over to Hainault Lakes to do some fishing. For hours the fish refused to bite. Just as darkness approached he sensed a change in the atmosphere. He waited an hour for dusk to settle around the lake. His patience was rewarded when he eventually landed a huge tench. Jim remembered a neighbour in Clayhall, once said to him, "If you ever catch a big tench let me have it. It will clean out all the rubbish in my pond." Jim tucked the prized catch into his shirt and cycled home at breakneck speed, stopping on the way to deliver the prized tench to his delighted neighbour.

Although extremely late, Jim was relieved to be home, but began to worry when he found the front door locked. He tried his key, but was mortified to discover the door was bolted on the inside. Accepting his punishment, Jim resigned himself to a night in the coal shed. But within a short time his father appeared. After the appropriate scolding, James was finally allowed back into the house and the safety of his bedroom. That night young Jim learned a valuable lesson – if you have done something wrong, own up immediately and take your punishment, and with no excuses.

'Wait till your father gets home,' is a familiar warning from fractious mothers to badly behaved children at the end of a difficult day. On one particular evening the boys waited silently in their room for their father to come home from work. After what seemed an eternity dad appeared at their bedroom door in full police uniform, truncheon in hand.

"I understand that you three have been messing around and playing up mum all day," said the angry police sergeant to the boys cowering in their bunk beds. He reminded the boys of his position in the community and how they needed to show responsibility and set an example to other children. The three troublemakers learnt their lesson that day and it stayed with them for life.

Born in 1936, Jim was the only brother to do National Service. After a spell in Portsmouth he was posted to Egypt. To his parents' surprise, he returned home unannounced late one night from the Middle East, following a long and tiring flight across several countries. Jim remembers still having the sand of the desert in his pockets. When the young serviceman knocked on the door of the family flat his dad welcomed him as if he popped out to the shops 10 minutes ago, calling out, "Mother there is someone here to see you." This was not a lack of affection, more a sign of James Lyall's complete unflappability.

Jim spent the last few months of his National Service in Liverpool where he worked as an RAOC army ammunitions clerk in the famous Liver Building. During his short spell on Merseyside, Jim, a decent footballer, turned out a few times for Everton's A team. After one particular match, the coach turned to Jim and said rather rudely, "You're the wrong Lyall – we thought we were getting the other one." Fortunately, Jim was not offended by the remark and loved his time in Liverpool, before returning to the normality of civilian life.

Occasional boyish misdemeanours apart, the young family settled easily into life in Ilford. James spent time on his allotment and did a few odd carpentry jobs to earn extra money. John remembered traditional Sunday lunches at home, with dad insisting on one of the boys saying Grace and doing the washing up – you can almost smell the roast lamb and mint sauce. The boys took their turn at the wringer when mum was busy with the ironing, or dad was sleeping after a night shift. The household was modest but happy. John, Jim and Rod were always encouraged to follow their sporting interests, and grabbed every opportunity to play football and cricket or cycle out to fish in the lakes of Hainault, Highams Park and, especially Abridge, where John subsequently bought his first home.

Despite never owning a car, the family took the occasional summer holiday to Hove in Sussex or breezy Dovercourt on the Essex coast. When the children were older there were regular summer trips to the Hebrides, which the boys loved. During the war they were evacuated with their mother to Lewis, staying very close to Catherine's birthplace. More than anything, it was the wartime years in Scotland that gave the elder Lyall boys such a close and firm connection to their parents' Scottish roots. John has fond memories of this part of his childhood, and in 1990 wrote:

'My family used to go to Scotland each summer. My mother took the three boys for a month and my father followed us for the last two weeks. The journey to the Isle of Lewis could take almost two days by train and boat, but I loved going back to the island and still do.'

The boys were steeped in Highland life and today brother Jim retains a good grasp of Gaelic, while John's lifelong passion for fishing dates back to the many happy hours he spent with his brothers in the delightful rivers and lochs surrounding Stornoway.

Growing up in post-war East London
As a London policeman, James was required to remain in Ilford while his family were far away in the Scottish Highlands. After the war he continued to work long and unsocial hours, but occasionally found the time and energy to take the boys to watch local sport, including speedway at West Ham. It could not have been easy bringing up three boisterous young boys in a crowded flat in East London at a time of austerity and hardship. It is a great tribute to John's parents that all three boys became successful in their different ways. Four years older than John, Jim qualified as a banker. He then worked for the Ford Motor Company for several years, before becoming the Managing Director of a local Car Retail Distribution Group. In the mid-50s, despite his business commitments, Jim found time to play several matches alongside his more famous brother in West Ham's A team. The youngest Lyall brother, Rod, worked in construction and established a flourishing building business.

The Lyall boys totally embraced the family values handed down by their parents and forged in those war-time Stornoway summers. They were to serve John throughout his life, and especially in his career in football, as he readily admitted:

'I've always been positive, determined, perhaps a touch stubborn at times. As a manager you have to develop a degree of resilience, but obviously many of my characteristics were inherited from my parents.'
(1989)

John was so drawn to his Scottish roots that, late in his West Ham career, he found time to visit Kirriemuir during the busy schedule of the annual pre-season tour of Scotland. Lyall remembers his father's home town with great affection. He wrote in his autobiography,

'...we would travel across Scotland to my father's home town of Kirriemuir, where we would fish in the trout streams.'
But even in those days, football was never far away:

'Even there we would watch football... my dad used to take us to watch Dundee or Dundee United. I can remember seeing some great Scottish players like Bill Brown, Billy Steel and Doug Cowie.'

In the early 2000s, Jim and John spent an enjoyable week together in the Perth area, where they caught up with many distant relatives and a few ex-West Ham players, including Scottish international, Ray Stewart, a formidable full-back in his West Ham days.

Buy an ice-cream or take the bus?
If a first floor flat, with little or no garden, was not the ideal place to bring up three lively young lads, in some ways, it was the perfect place. Encouraged by their parents, John and his brothers loved nothing more than playing football and cricket for hours on end in the local public parks which abound in this part of East London. Their parents had no need to worry about their whereabouts or safety. For a child growing up in the 1950s, life was fairly straight-forward as John remembered:

'You went to school, you played football or cricket, and maybe you went

to the cinema on Saturday mornings. There were few other options.'

The biggest decision for a boy like John at that time was:

'If I walk to the cinema I'll be able to buy an ice-cream, but if I take a bus I won't.'

Or, as Jim Lyall remembers:

'The same applied to our visits to Upton Park – if we went by bus both ways, we had no money for a programme. If we walked one way, then OK.'

What could be simpler? Decisions like that provided a clarity that remained with John throughout his life. Young people today face a bewildering and not necessarily wholesome, range of choices. What cool young teenager today would be content with a handmade kart fashioned out of a set of old pram wheels as a Christmas present? Or, as in my case, a lovingly crafted toy fort which must have taken my father months to secretly assemble.

For young John, at that time, whether to take a bus or buy an ice-cream was the biggest decision of the week. Today's children demand X-Boxes, PS3s, iPhones and all the other must-have techno toys. A senior Apple executive recently claimed that 'children today are either asleep or online'. An exaggerated boast perhaps, but one many of today's parents will recognise. In his autobiography Lyall wrote,

'...on balance our upbringing was a far easier, less fraught, process. We didn't face the temptations that children face today. We created our own entertainment. We created our own Wembley in the little alleyway at the back of the shop...'

But it would be a mistake to view the 1950s through rose-tinted glasses. John and his brothers, like many others at the time, could have chosen a different path. They could easily have joined up with a group of tough teddy boys who terrorised Ilford High Road on

Saturday nights, or drifted into crime. The activities of the notorious Kray twins stretched from the Mile End Road out to Ilford and there were plenty of wannabe Krays who were keen to stamp their authority on the local snooker halls and drinking clubs. Fortunately the youthful Lyalls dutifully accepted their parents' kindly, but firm, authority and their passion for sport kept them well away from trouble.

John Lyall was of the same generation as Brian Clough, Bobby Robson and Alex Ferguson. These great football figures inherited their parents' values of self-sacrifice, hard-work and loyalty. Lyall's generation learned their trade in the late 1950s, but needed to adapt to the new world of the '60s, ushered in by the Beatles in 1962. They had to negotiate a difficult path between the old ideals and the ever-present vanity of the modern celebrity-obsessed society. Only the remarkable Ferguson has succeeded in bridging the old standards and the new, less-predictable world of modern sport.

Of course, it is always a mistake to generalise about people or try to fit them into convenient boxes. Thousands of young people today continue to enjoy impromptu games of football and cricket in the parks, or play for their school, District or County just as the Lyall boys did for Ilford. Modern school sport is far healthier than its critics suggest. Most of these people haven't the slightest idea what goes on in the PE Department of Ilford High, John and Trevor Brooking's old school, or on the playing fields of Barkingside, Clayhall, Wanstead Flats or West Ham Park. Having said that it remains true that today's young people don't enjoy the same freedom to play outdoors as those growing up in the 1950s.

As a boy, John Lyall would regularly come home from the park, after hours of playing football with his mates, covered head to foot in mud. On such occasions his mother would plunge him into the bath, where he would sit until he was clean enough to have his tea. Mrs Lyall was a wonderful cook, famous for her delicious apple pies. She was old school, but extremely proud of her sons and even went to the extremes of washing and ironing their football boot laces for District and County matches. One memorable day in the early '50s young John received a brand new pair of Arthur Rowe boots for his birthday. The brand was fitting as Rowe was responsible for Spurs' famous push and run style, the basis of the adult Lyall's own football philosophy. John would have known the boots were expensive and could hardly contain his excitement. Every other football-loving boy in the street would have been envious.

Jim Lyall recalls a similar story. He played regularly for his school team and represented Ilford District on many occasions. Jim knew the family had little spare money, so when his first pair of boots wore out he was forced to borrow a pair from a school friend, Frankie Bell, in return for repeatedly running irritating errands. One day Jim's mum asked him, "Why are you so fed up, that's not like you Jim?" He told his mum about the condition of his ancient boots and that he was fed up with fetching and carrying like a skivvy for his wealthy friend.

Mum said, "OK, I'll ask dad to nail some studs into an old pair of shoes for you." When this didn't work, Jim became increasingly frustrated. Catherine saw Jim was clearly upset, so one afternoon after school she told her eldest son:

"Come on we are getting the bus up to Cranbrook Road."

"What for mum?" replied the surprised youngster.

"To buy you a new pair of football boots, that's what," said Catherine

When they arrived at the prestigious Cranbrook Sports Shop, Catherine asked Jim what kind of boots he wanted. "The Hotspur ones please," Jim replied immediately. On the way home the delighted youngster asked his mum where the money for the boots came from.

"I used the coal money Jim, but you really needed your new boots." It would have been a little chilly in the Lyall household for the next few weeks and Jim will never forget his mother's generous gesture.

Both parents made extreme sacrifices to support the boys, as most parents did at the time. Oddly, John's dad was a heavy smoker, which seems strange when you think how careful the couple were about money.

One day in later life, Jim asked his dad, "You are an intelligent, smart man. How come you smoke so much, dad?"

His father was ready with his answer. "When I was your age we lived in a tied cottage on a farm and were restricted primarily to a diet of rabbit and turnips and, as a result, were often hungry. A packet of ten Weights were cheap and if you had a cigarette in your mouth you were never hungry."

Of course, this was at a time long before smoking was recognised as the dangerous and anti-social activity we now know it to be today. It also explains why John refused to eat rabbit.

Like most parents, James and Catherine wanted the best for their children. Although they were always keen to encourage the boys, they showed little enthusiasm for attending matches. John and Jim would run home to tell their parents they had been selected for the district side or the Essex Boys' team, only for mum to say, in her understated way, "Well done dear, just make sure you always do your best." This understated support should not be seen as indifference, as Jim remembers,

'...it merely reflected their view that making a determined and successful effort at everything in life was a reward in itself.'

The Lyalls knew that John was a real prospect in a neighbourhood which was and remains a hotbed of football activity and they were keen to do all they could to encourage and support him.

A few years ago, out of the blue, Jim Lyall received a letter from his brother, John. In the letter John reflected on the tremendous influence their parent's had on their lives and how fortunate they had been. The brothers are very conscious that James and Catherine rose from very humble origins. They taught their children the traditional values of honesty, courtesy, respect and the importance of good manners. They lived their own lives by way of example. The brothers have never forgotten their parents' advice; their values have provided the watchwords for their entire lives.

One of the Lyall family's neighbours in once fashionable Ilford was the respected football journalist and TV presenter, Peter Lorenzo. In those days Lorenzo, who wrote the notes for the programme of the 1965 West Ham v Munich European Cup Winners' Cup Final, was learning his trade at the *Ilford Recorder*. John remembered kicking a ball against the wall of Lorenzo's flat for hours on end, first his left foot, then his right, in his determination to be as two-footed as possible. The budding reporter was patient with the noisy youngster and even encouraged him, won over by John's sheer enthusiasm. The pair later became great friends and John was later devastated to hear of Lorenzo's untimely death at the age of 58.

Practice makes perfect

Legend has it that the great East London rock band from the '60s, the Small Faces, based their song Itchycoo Park on the old Essex county ground at Valentine's Park. Others argue that particular honour belongs to Manor Park a few miles away. What is beyond dispute is that back in the 1950s the great West Indian batsmen, Worrell, Walcott and Weekes flayed the Essex bowling attack to all parts of Valentine's Park. To the delight of the locals the celebrated Hollywood actress, Jayne Mansfield opened the annual fete at the Park around the same time as the boys from the Caribbean were lofting sixes into Cranbrook Road.

Nigel Benn, Nasser Hussain, and the Essex and England cricketer, John Lever were all born and brought up close to the park, with its smart rows of terraced houses and even smarter villa-style mansions. Valentine's Park and Clayhall Park were the beating heart of the area. Like the Lyall boys and their friends, these great sporting figures would have spent their summer evenings and school holidays playing football and cricket in the park, where Trevor Bailey, Keith Fletcher, Graham Gooch and Hussain entertained the locals during the Ilford cricket festival. The park has been the home of Ilford CC for over 100 years. Lever, Hussain, Gooch and Stuart Turner were all junior club members and attended the Trevor Bailey-owned, Ilford Cricket School under the tutelage of the legendary coach, Bill Morris.

Close to Clayhall Park was Parkhill Primary School where John passed the 11-plus and like Trevor Brooking after him, won a coveted place at the local grammar school, Ilford County High. John was never in the same class as Brooking, either academically or in football terms, as he later admitted, but he was happy to play football morning, noon and night. As young as seven-years-old, John tagged along with his brother Jim to the regular Sunday morning matches in the local park. Initially nothing more than a ball-boy, young John had to wait until he was nearly 12-years-old before being allowed to play regularly for his brother's Sunday morning side. He simply couldn't wait for a game. He was a strong, tough-tackling, sturdy lad and refused to be intimated by the older boys. As Jim observed recently:

'John was a quick leaner at everything and even as a youngster he tackled fearlessly, like a Sherman tank.'

Playing all sports well above his age group toughened up the youngster and was an ideal preparation for the physical demands of professional football. He remembered,

'...one Sunday they let me play in goal and, then finally the moment came when I was a fully-fledged team member.'

Anybody who played in these types of games at the time will know how serious they were taken, not just by the players, but sometimes the whole neighbourhood as Lyall testified:

'It was like a cup final every week, and by Friday all the local lads were speculating about the outcome of the big Sunday match.'

Playing in these games on rock-hard pitches in the summer or mud-baths in the winter toughened up young players – although strong, often brutal tackling brought serious injuries and may have been the root cause of Lyall's later career-ending knee problems. In his autobiography My Manchester United Years, Bobby Charlton talks about the full-bodied games of football played in his local park in Ashington when he was a boy.

"We all played football – that's all there was," Charlton remembered. These pick-up games were played out in every city park the length and breadth of the country. You rarely see these kinds of informal encounters in the sanitised, safety-conscious municipal parks of today.

In his early life John was totally immersed in his favourite sport of football, but still found time to play cricket in the summer months. John and Jim regularly travelled up to Gidea Park for practice sessions with the Essex coach, Ken Preston. But football was John's first love. Back in the 1950s many East London football fans liked to watch West Ham, Leyton Orient or Tottenham on alternate Saturdays. John and his dad would take the 144 bus along the North Circular Road, passing the London Rubber Company, the LEB headquarters and the infamous Cooks' Ferry Inn, on its way to the Angel, Edmonton. From there it's a short walk down the High Road to the Tottenham ground. Back in the '50s, Tottenham High Road was a quiet place, even on match days. Spurs' supporters would sleep overnight on the pavement while queuing for tickets to see their heroes play European ties against Eusebio's Benfica or the great Italian sides of the early 1960s. Spurs' manager, Bill Nicholson, who later became a great personal friend of John Lyall, lived in White Hart Lane most of his life. In his spare time he loved nothing more than tending his allotment just down the road from his neat, but modest, semi-detached house. Gun crime, gang warfare and full-scale riots now blight this deprived, but once undisturbed part of London.

Fortunately, his dad's Tottenham allegiance was never going to sway young John away from Upton Park. Next-door neighbour, Frank Whale, was an avid West Ham fan and regularly took John and Jim with him to Upton Park, where they stood on the sacred North Bank. The boys had strong local loyalties and West Ham was their local club. A lifetime commitment to the claret and blue of West Ham United had begun. However, the youngster's heart was not in standing on the terraces watching football, but out on the pitch playing. He later wrote,

'... there was no substitute for playing the game. Every spare minute of each day was devoted to playing football.'

This level of enthusiasm combined with his undoubted ability soon got the Ilford youngster noticed. John's teachers quickly recognised his sporting potential. One of the most important influences on John's development at Parkhill Primary was his form teacher, Mr Tom Carter, who was largely responsible for John passing his 11-plus. Lyall remembered his old teacher with great affection:

'Mr Carter was a big influence on me in those days, and years later we were friends. He wrote to me regularly as manager of West Ham, until he died a few years ago.'

With supportive parents and teachers like Mr Carter, John was given every encouragement and opportunity to succeed. He was not going to let anyone down. The great lesson Mr Carter taught John, he later recalled, was the power of positive thinking. Young John was not allowed to play football as long as he told Mr Carter during Maths lessons, "I'm sorry sir, I just can't do it." With sympathetic teaching John quickly learned how to solve mathematical problems and duly passed his 11-plus. At the same time the reluctant mathematician became the best footballer his school had seen for a generation, with apologies to older brother, Jim. The promising young striker's impressive displays for his school soon caught the eyes of the Ilford District selectors. John Lyall's life in football was under away.

Boyhood dreams
James and Catherine were delighted when John won a place at Ilford County High School. To see their son leave the modest flat in his smart new uniform would have made them very proud indeed. With a name straight out of a Carry On film, Mr Roy Percy Pyman was John's PE teacher at the High School. He was a qualified referee and coached the boys in football and cricket. John

remembers Pyman as a conscientious teacher who noticed his new pupil was extremely left-footed. He told John he needed to work on his weaker right foot if he was to have any chance of fulfilling his dream of becoming a professional footballer. John was quick to take advice. He worked hard over the next few years to improve his right foot, testing the patience of his neighbours to the limit. His single-mindedness was quickly rewarded and before very long John could take penalties and corners confidently with either foot. At 12-years-old, he was determined to fulfil his dream of becoming a professional, preferably with West Ham United. For a very brief moment, John did consider a career as a PE teacher, but he really had no Plan B such was his obsession with football.

Former class-mate Dave Kingston, who remained life-long friends with Lyall, offers us an interesting insight into John's emerging character:

John was a hard worker who moved from C stream in our first Year to B stream in our second and A stream in the third. His progress was unprecedented.

Kingston played football and cricket alongside Lyall at Ilford High and has some vivid memories of their schooldays together. John played inside-left for his school and Dave recalls one particular match in their second year:

John picked up the ball in his own half, ploughed through the mud leaving the opposition in his wake, before unleashing a screamer into the top corner.

At school John played two years above his age-group and as a strapping 13-year-old scored a memorable hat-trick against a team of 15-year-olds. Dave Kingston remembers, "At school John stood out as an outstanding young prospect." Young Lyall's sporting talent was not restricted to football. He excelled at cricket and represented Ilford District as a batsman. But, as Kingston explains, it was a school boxing match which brought out the true side of John's character:

'John was never captain of the school cricket or football teams. That honour belonged to a lad called Johnny Mitchell. In their second year the two fought against each other in a school boxing final. They went hell for leather for three rounds before John was given the decision on points.'

The boxing incident reveals a great deal about John's 'never say die' attitude to life. As Kingston remembers, he was very much a leader at school, extremely popular and a real good bloke. The thought of re-introducing boxing into schools today would have friends of the nanny-state chained to the school railings, although that view might change following Team GB's success at London 2012.

Like Lyall, Dave Kingston was also a good student. The Barking boy was sent to Ilford because his local grammar, Barking Abbey, was full. He said later, "It was the best thing that ever happened to me." Dave became a PE teacher rather than a professional footballer, although as a youngster he did have a trial with West Ham. To this day he retains in his possession a letter from Ron Greenwood stating, in the most polite terms, that he wasn't going to be good enough for the professional game. Kingston enjoyed a distinguished career in education, gaining an MA before moving to teacher-training. The two old friends kept in touch for most of their lives. A few weeks before John's death, the Lyalls were due to stay with Kingston and his wife at their home in Kent. Sadly, the reunion never took place.

John continued to represent Ilford Schoolboys on a regular basis while at High School and particularly enjoyed the training sessions of District coach, Stan Frankland. Men like Mr Frankland, who was involved in Essex school football all his life, were the heart and soul of school football. Teachers gave up their free time to provide outstanding young footballers from schools across the area the opportunity to play at a higher level. The young Lyall loved Frankland's training sessions and felt honoured to play for Ilford against other districts across London and Essex. John always appreciated the support he received from Mr Frankland, as did his brother Jim. When Stan Frankland passed away, just before John's own untimely death, both brothers attended his funeral at Cranham, Essex along with other remaining members of the Ilford District Old Boys team.

Sadly, District school football has largely disappeared. The best youngsters are now recruited by the professional academies that refuse permission for contracted players to represent their school or district. Deprived of the best players, school football has seen a rapid decline in standards that has nothing to do with the quality and commitment of PE teachers, but is a consequence of the hard-nosed approach of the professional academies. What is good for the top clubs can be disastrous for school sport. In fairness to West Ham, the Hammers' highly respected Youth Academy Director, Tony Carr, does allow his youngsters to play for their school, providing there is no clash with academy games. The West Ham academy issues 12-month contracts to youngsters as young as eight-years-old. These budding professionals play five a-side matches against other professional academies until the age of 11, when they progress to full-size pitches. The harsh reality is that most of these youngsters, full of hope and expectation, eventually fall by the wayside.

But in John Lyalls' schooldays, district matches attracted scouts from all the big London clubs. Top managers and coaches would turn up at Hackney Marshes or Wanstead Flats hoping to spot the next Jimmy Greaves or Johnny Byrne. I remember one Saturday morning in the early 1960s standing close to Spurs manager, Bill Nicholson at the George White Sports Ground, close to the Walthamstow dog track. The legendary Tottenham manager was there to watch the Walthamstow Boys under-16 side, which in 1962 came very close to winning the English Schools Trophy. Bill *Nick*, as he was affectionately known, was often seen at the George White enjoying a steaming hot cup of tea outside the old tea hut. In the star-studded Walthamstow side that day were Ian and Roger Morgan, Derek Bellotti, Denis Bond and Mick Leach – all of whom went on to play top flight professional football. In his own quiet way Nicholson would have been excited by the football on show, served up by some of the best young footballers of their generation.

Wally St Pier, the West Ham scout, would have shared Nicholson's excitement after first seeing the 15-year-old Bobby Moore play just a few miles across East London in Leyton. Outstanding schoolboy footballers, held in awe by their contemporaries, often fail to achieve their potential and the transition to the professional game. Moore was never going to make that mistake. Clubs in the 1950s and 1960s knew that local boys were the future of the club and gave them every opportunity to succeed. It was Danes school teacher John Cunningham who first recognised the real potential of the teenage John Lyall. Cunningham had seen Lyall play for Ilford Schools and was impressed with what he saw. He had a connection with West Ham and recommended the young striker to manager, Ted Fenton and Wally St Pier. One Saturday morning Fenton and St Pier drove up the North Circular Road to watch Ilford schoolboys play Walthamstow Boys at the same George White ground where Bill Nicholson did his scouting for Tottenham. John's performance that morning confirmed Cunningham's initial assessment and convinced the West Ham duo that the 15-year-old had a future as a professional footballer. Fenton had made up his mind – Lyall was a fine prospect and he wanted the Ilford youngster at the club. The Hammers' manager was a very determined and persuasive character, as John's parents were about to discover.

Forest Gate-born Fenton eventually persuaded James and Catherine that professional football was a worthwhile career. Initially, James and Catherine had other ideas. With their Scottish safety first instincts, they were not convinced that football was a suitable career for a grammar school-educated Ilford lad. The Lyalls were keen for their son to complete his education before considering a future on the risky road of professional football. Mr Lyall went to see John's headteacher who reminded him of the benefits of a good education and sound qualifications, along with the financial commitment they had made when John was awarded a scholarship. John's parents took some time to make their decision. Eventually, they gave their consent for John to leave school and sign for West Ham, probably against their own better judgement and financial interest. James and Catherine also felt

John might never forgive them if they turned down Fenton's offer. They were also persuaded by John's single-mindedness and commitment to football and believed he would make a success of his chosen career.

To his credit, Ted Fenton listened to John's parents who, after exerting some pressure on the West Ham manager, were reassured when Fenton offered John a job in the club's offices as part of his football apprenticeship. The club also gave the Lyalls an undertaking that they would enrol John on a sports' journalism course. This would not only supplement his income, but would provide John with some interesting on-the-job training as well as providing an insight into the operation of a professional football club. Fenton's persuasive manner finally won the Lyall's over and John was free to sign his contract. The new West Ham apprentice had achieved his ambition and was delighted with his princely starting wage of £4 a week. For the youngster, years of working hard on his game and achieving good results at school, were more than simply worthwhile – he was close to having all his teenage dreams come true.

Chapter 2
A very happy teenager

Lyall left the comfortable world of park and school sport behind for the very different, often ruthless, world of professional football in the tough environment of the East End. Happy with Fenton's offer, Lyall's parents signed John's contract in May 1955. He was just 15-years-old. The Ilford boy's career was up and running. But there was one tricky obstacle to overcome before he could take up his dream job. As John was an 'A' stream pupil, Ilford High School demanded a leaving fee of £10, a sizeable sum at that time. The Lyalls paid up without a second thought. It was a small price to pay to launch such a promising career. The youngster was confident he had made the right decision and couldn't have been happier as he took his first tentative steps on his new life as a professional footballer. John's parents would have been a little more apprehensive, but their 15-year-old son was clearly thrilled to bits,

'So, I left school and, shining brightly and full of enthusiasm, reported for duty at Upton Park in June 1955.'

In the club's offices John was fortunate to work closely with secretary Frank Cearns and his assistant, Pauline Moss. Across the room was that great club servant and former player, Eddie Chapman who joined West Ham shortly after being demobbed from the army. But his real mentor in the office at the Boleyn was Mrs Moss as John testifies:

'She taught me virtually all there is to know about office administration.'

According to the Hammers' former goalkeeper, Alan Dickie, Mrs

Moss was a consistent and benevolent presence at Upton Park and proved a great source of support and encouragement to young players. She undertook to teach the teenage Lyall every aspect of the club from making the tea to making up the wages.

Lyall was blissfully unaware at the time just how the much the kindly advice and guidance of people like Chapman and Mrs Moss would help him in the future. Working with skilled administrators and great football people would have been an invaluable experience to a young man with an enquiring mind. John enjoyed working in the office where he gained valuable insight into how a professional football club functions. Frank Cearns became secretary at the Boleyn in 1946 and his family had been at the heart of the club following W. J. Cearns' appointment as chairman in 1935. The young apprentice could not have wished for a better team around him than Cearns, Chapman and Moss and he was a quick learner. Geoff Hurst said later about John Lyall, "He knew the club from top to bottom." He was to experience every single facet of West Ham United over the next 34 years.

Young John revelled in the office environment, knowing that on most days he would be out at Grange Farm in Chigwell training with the other young professionals. Dickie, who enjoyed a few years at Upton Park in the late '50s and early '60s, tells a story about the pre-season training at Chigwell. Ted Fenton introduced something called the Pudding Lane run, a tortuous cross-country trek which ended back at Grange Farm. Lyall loved training almost as much as playing but even a madly enthusiastic youngster might have winced at the prospect of Pudding Lane.

Dagenham-born Terry Venables, who eventually chose to sign for Chelsea, has better memories of training with West Ham. Venables played in the same Essex and London schoolboy teams as Ronnie Boyce – the pair were born on the same day in 1943. The two 15-year-olds were invited by Bill Robinson to join the juniors for training. Venables remembers Malcolm Allison's evening sessions in the car park in front of the ground with great affection. Lyall was a little older than Venables, but also attended Allison's lively masterclasses. Young Terry was one of a number of outstanding young local footballers that slipped through the Hammers' net.

Courted by Tottenham, Venables assumed rightly that with Danny Blanchflower and Dave MacKay in the Spurs midfield, his first team appearances would have been limited, so he plumped for Chelsea, to the great frustration of Robinson and Wally St Pier. But Venables must have picked up something during his short time at West Ham. The Dagenham boy took his FA Coaching badges early in his career and gained Distinction at both levels – Malcolm Allison would have approved.

Training at West Ham could be fun for the young pros. John particularly enjoyed the company of three professional cricketers who, like Graham Gooch and Neil Burns in later years, were invited to join the club's training sessions. Frank Rist from down the road at Walthamstow CC, Surrey's Mickey Stewart and the Essex and England batsman, Doug Insole all trained with the juniors at Chadwell Heath. Rist had a distinguished amateur football career before signing professional terms for Colchester United under their young manager, Ted Fenton. Insole played in the winter months for many years with Walthamstow Avenue and Pegasus, alongside his great friend and colleague, Trevor Bailey. Stewart was also a useful footballer who played briefly for Charlton Athletic and, like the other three, was a terrific example to a young professional learning his trade. Young John loved his cricket and the company of these great cricketers, but understood the need to focus on his football if he was to make a success of his new career.

We never had it so good?
In the world outside football John Lyall's generation experienced the privations of the immediate post-war period, but were still young enough to be excited by the huge social changes of the 1960s. As John set out on his career, the world suddenly seemed to become a very different place, new and exhilarating and best of all, alive. The 1950s were fogbound, dark and dreary by comparison. Park railings had been ripped out during the war, shops were shabby and unattractive and crime rates were soaring. In 1938 there had been 58,000 violent crimes in England and Wales; in 1948 there were 130,000. Post-war Britain was a difficult, uncertain

and often dangerous place.

What was called at the time 'a modern matrimonial landslide' saw divorce rates soar in the decade immediately following the war, as wives struggled to cope with returning soldier husbands. There is a great deal of nostalgia for the 1950s: the decade of family values, Ladybird T-shirts and Saturday morning pictures. The reality was rather different. In the great smog of 1952, 12,000 people were killed in the capital within just four days, but little fuss was made of the disaster. Holidays were spent on windswept resorts getting soaked to the skin, with little to do but the occasional donkey ride. Not much to get nostalgic about there.

Football helped to relieve the boredom and monotony. Huge crowds were attracted to Football League matches in the 1950s, entranced by the sublime skills of Wilf Mannion, Tom Finney and Stanley Matthews. Just to indicate how popular professional football was at this time, in the 1953/54 season an average of 7,000 people attended lowly Accrington Stanley's home matches. Throughout the '50s the Hammers regularly attracted crowds of 25,000-30,000 to Upton Park when they were stuck firmly in the 2nd Division. Of course there was no 'footie' on TV and matches always kicked off at 3.00 pm on Saturday afternoons. There was little else to do aside from watching wrestling or horse racing on tiny black and white TV screens.

Rapid change occurred in sport as in other areas of life. The minimum wage in football was abolished in 1962 thanks to the persistence of Jimmy Hill and the courage of George Eastham. The professional/amateur distinction in cricket was removed at a stroke, although the great all-rounder, Trevor Bailey claimed that Essex treated every player with equal respect whatever their background. Other sports followed cricket's example, although a little more reluctantly where class prejudice was more deeply ingrained. In 1960, when John Lyall and his great friend, Bobby Moore were setting out on their careers, the patrician Harold Macmillan was Prime Minister. In March of that remarkable year, Elvis Presley returned from US Army duty in West Germany and promptly hit the top of the charts with 'It's Now or Never'. While Elvis was enjoying his return to civilian life, the newly formed Beatles began a 48-night residency in a Hamburg night club, as a prelude to changing popular music forever.

This was the sporting and social context for the start of the most successful decade in the history of West Ham United. Bobby Moore and John Lyall narrowly missed national service but, as well-educated grammar school boys, they would have been aware of the changing world around them. These two footballers, who were to make such an impact on the game, bridged two worlds. They were part of a new generation excited by change, but steeped in the values of hard work and family life instilled by their parents. But some things were slow to change. Up to the early '70s you could still buy a steaming hot cup of Bovril in the shed behind the West Stand at Upton Park and stir it with a dirty old spoon bearing the club crest fixed to the counter by a piece of string.

A new life at Upton Park

Lyall had experienced success as a teenager. He had excelled at school in football and cricket and had achieved high academic standards. He was a key member of the West Ham side which reached the FA Youth Cup Final in 1957, before losing 8-2 on aggregate to a very strong Manchester United team. The club was not happy with the defeat and the players were bitterly disappointed. But for the coaching staff at Chadwell Heath, reaching the final confirmed the success of the club's youth policy. Within a few years the Hammers produced a host of wonderful young players, including Bobby Moore, Martin Peters, Geoff Hurst, Andy Smillie, Tony Scott, Ronnie Boyce, Johnny Sissons, Harry Redknapp, John Cartwright and later, Trevor Brooking, to name just a few. Not all these budding stars progressed as the club would have wished. Ron Greenwood once described the young Cartwright as the 'white Didi', he was that good. Didi was the star of the great Brazilian side of the late '50s and coming from Greenwood, this was high praise indeed. Greenwood sold Cartwright because he was not convinced the youngster would fulful his considerable potential. He was right. Cartwright's playing career stalled after he left Upton Park, but unexpectedly, the inside-forward became an outstanding coach of talented youngsters. Lyall did have the right attitude and was in some very good company. Ted Fenton's youth policy looked to be paying dividends. His young stars had tasted success and wanted more.

Young John's solid performances for the junior and A teams at Upton Park came to the notice of the England selectors. During the 1955/56 season the striker scored eight goals in 30 Metropolitan and Eastern Counties League matches. The following season he scored three goals in nine Metropolitan League appearances and, in addition, played 30 games for the junior side, scoring nine goals. This was a decent return for a young striker and it was no surprise to Robinson when Lyall received his England call-up.

He was thrilled to be chosen to play for England Youth in the game against Luxembourg in 1957, the same year he played in the FA Youth Cup Final. The undoubted star of the Luxembourg match was not the newly-capped forward from West Ham, but the youthful Jimmy Greaves who scored four goals that day. Back in their flat in Ilford, John's parents were brimming with pride at the news – their faith in their son had been justified.

Encouraged by his family, John was making good progress in his new job. He had achieved his boyhood dream of playing professional football for his beloved West Ham and his selection for the national team was a wonderful bonus. He became popular around the club with players and staff alike and was dedicated, organised and a keen listener. Lyall was desperate to take his chance and would do everything necessary to achieve his full potential.

A bright future in the game seemed assured for the young Hammer, but sadly, his England Youth cap against Luxembourg was the only international honour in his shortened playing career. But for the moment life was good. John was settled at Upton Park, was learning every day, loved his job and had achieved international recognition. One of the great careers in the club's history had begun.

Back in the top flight
The club was firmly rooted in the 2nd Division when John signed

for West Ham. Despite their lowly League position, club skipper Malcolm Allison led a strong side whose fortunes were soon to change. In 1957 Ted Fenton recruited Vic Keeble to join John Dick up front and the pair clicked immediately. Their goals secured the club's promotion at the end of that season. In one of the best years in Hammers' history, Fenton's team ran away with the 2nd Division Championship with a record number of points. But with John Dick still at the top of his game and his new partner Keeble proving an instant hit with the North Bank, there were few opportunities at Upton Park at this time for budding young strikers like John Lyall. He would have to wait his turn.

Lyall was a patient youngster and knew he had everything to learn from the manager and his team of internationals. Ted Fenton is almost a forgotten figure at Upton Park and his influence on West Ham's success in the 1960s is barely recognised. It is scandalous that Fenton's entry in the rightly respected *West Ham United Who's Who* amounts to no more than a cursory paragraph. Before Fenton secured promotion in 1958, the club had been out of the top tier English football for 26 years. Contrary to popular belief, Fenton was a thoughtful and modern football manager. The former England international played a decisive role in establishing the important qualities for which West Ham became known throughout the world of football – an attacking, exciting style of play and a commitment to developing local young players. Despite his huge influence on the Hammers, Ron Greenwood was not the originator of either of these two fundamental features of the club's football philosophy – its roots go much, much deeper.

Local boy Fenton pioneered new training techniques. He asked weightlifting champion Bill Watson to lead training sessions, an innovation which also assisted players to recovery more quickly from injury. Fenton even acquired a trampoline to liven up the week, a novelty which must have produced a few comic moments in training. Fenton was thorough. He tinkered with the players' pre-match meal, introducing steak lunches and lengthened training time to four hours in an effort to make his team the fittest in the League.

Once in post at the Boleyn, Fenton set about the task of getting West Ham back into the 1st Division, an aim he achieved within seven years. He put together a formidable team and by the end of the decade had achieved his target. As an apprentice, John Lyall would have observed his manager at first hand. He would also have rubbed shoulders with Fenton's players, trained with them, and occasionally be invited to join their Allison and Cantwell-inspired tactical discussions in their famous Barking Road café.

A thoughtful young man, Lyall had joined the right club. West Ham has been a thinking footballers' club throughout its history. In 1923, when the Hammers lost the ill-fated White Horse FA Cup Final to Bolton Wanderers, the East Ham Echo wrote on 4 May:

'West Ham United, of whose fine performances on the football field everybody is talking about ... are confidently being named as certain winners of the English Cup in the first final at the great new stadium at Wembley.'

The Wembley pitch, churned up by horses' hooves and narrowed by the encroaching crowd, suited Bolton's direct style as the Hammers' natural passing game became stuck in the mud. Manager Charlie Paynter was devastated by the result but never abandoned his commitment to the West Ham way. Fenton, Paynter's successor, took the claret and blue football philosophy onto another, more professional level.

With the great Ernie Gregory in goal, Cantwell and Bond at full-back and the young Ken Brown succeeding Dick Walker at centre-half, the defence, with Bobby Moore still to come, was arguably the best ever seen at Upton Park. For Fenton, the most important thing about this group of defenders was that they could all play and loved to attack in the classic West Ham manner. In midfield Fenton had Bill Lansdowne, Malcolm Pyke and the underrated Andy Malcolm, who many good judges regard as one of the best midfield players ever to play for the club, and that includes Johnny Byrne, Martin Peters and Trevor Brooking. Fenton's '50s side included two outstanding wingers in Malcolm Musgrove and Mike Grice, both were quick, tricky and in Musgrove's case scored hatfuls of goals.

The formidable John Dick, Harry Hooper and later Vic Keeble provided the spearhead of the attack.

Good as this side was, Fenton knew there was something missing. He found the missing ingredient in inside-forward, Phil Woosnam. In 1958, Fenton bought the Welsh wizard from neighbours Leyton Orient for a record fee of £30,000. As Fenton wrote in his autobiography (1960):

> 'For a long time I had been Phil Woosnam's number one fan. Many a time I had watched the Leyton Orient inside forward, and each time I had been more and more struck by the likeness to Len Goulden.'

Goulden graced the midfield at Upton Park in the 1930s with his vision, exquisite touch and immaculate passing. With 14 England caps, Goulden, a former teammate of Fenton at Upton Park, was one of the best inside-forwards of his generation. To compare Woosnam with such a distinguished West Ham legend was rare praise indeed. Fenton explains:

> 'Here was the same subtlety, the same football intelligence at work. When Goulden, one of the best inside-forwards I ever saw, and BSc schoolmaster Woosnam, were at work, you could practically hear them thinking as they sized up their moves.'

Fenton loved thinking footballers and Woosnam provided the Hammers' manager with the creative influence he believed his team lacked. The Welsh international, who gave up his teaching career to join West Ham, became a dominant influence at Upton Park with his superb touch and incisive passing. Woosnam was the kind of player Fenton cherished and for young apprentices like Lyall he was the perfect role model. Working with players like the Welsh wizard and absorbing Fenton's innovative methods, would have contributed enormously to the young apprentice's football education.

Left-back – me?

The West Ham staff recognised that, despite John's undoubted progress, the youngster would have few first team opportunities with Dick and Keeble scoring 50 goals a season between them. Sensing his potential and aware of young Lyall's competitive instincts and physical strength, assistant manager Bill Robinson decided the youngster would make a decent left-back. John was a pragmatic young man and accepted Robinson's suggestion with enthusiasm, rather than sulking and requesting a transfer as might happen today. John had no problem moving back into defence – he really just wanted to play football and had the greatest respect for Robinson and chief scout Wally St Pier. Lyall also trusted Ted Fenton's judgement. The Hammers' manager had taken to the young apprentice. Both loved cricket and Fenton invited Lyall to join him at his club, Clayhall CC. The two clearly had a good rapport which progressed beyond the usual manager/player relationship.

The converted full-back worked tirelessly to improve his defensive positioning, tackling and heading. His hard work brought dividends when Lyall became a regular in the A team. Fortunately, at Upton Park he had people around him who were prepared to assist a young player starting out on his career. The legendary centre-half and former captain, Dick Walker was an enormous help to the young apprentice. Dagenham-based Walker retired in 1956 but not before he passed on some invaluable advice to the young full-back as Lyall acknowledged:

'He taught me a great deal and was a big influence on my early career as a player... he would tell me, "John, if you don't pass the ball quickly and compete, you won't have a chance."'

Young John lapped up this sort of advice, as did his teammate, Bobby Moore. The two friends spent a lot of time together and with other young players at the club like Tony Scott and Joe Kirkup. Moore, a year older than Lyall, attended Tom Hood School in Leytonstone and his parents' Barking home was a short bus journey from Ilford High Road. After training Moore and Lyall enjoyed nothing more than sitting quietly with the senior players in Cassetari's, that old East End crucible of football. The players would sit upstairs listening to Allison, Cantwell, Sexton and Woosnam discussing the latest developments in the game, using salt and pepper pots to illustrate their ideas.

England had been destroyed by Hungary at Wembley in 1953, the first defeat of the national side on home soil. Despite the defeat the dazzling Hungarian football excited the senior players at Upton Park. Led by the colourful Allison, they were keen to emulate the fresh, new playing styles of continental clubs like Honved and Real Madrid. Ted Fenton reflected on Hungary's 6-3 humiliation of England in typically graphic style:

'On 25 November 1953, the first nuclear test was carried out in football. The Hungarians came to Wembley and exploded their own pet atom bomb under England's record of never have been beaten at home by a continental side.'

Fenton knew that football had entered a new era. He continued:

'No footballer, manager, official I have spoken to had seen a performance to compare with that put up by the Hungarians. It was brilliant, legendary...'

In a sense Fenton welcomed the England defeat and the resulting wake-up call. He knew that at Upton Park he had encouraged his players to play in a style similar to that of the Hungarians – he had been vindicated. His players were gripped by what their manager described as the new 'smart, super-fit chromium-finished Hungarians'.

The ideas that came out of Cassetari's players' meetings heavily influenced the Hammers' playing style through the 1960s, as Fenton gave way to Ron Greenwood. The latter was equally excited by the new continental style of close passing and quick movement. But West Ham's success in the 1960s was largely founded on Fenton's commitment to the beautiful game and those long

34

afternoons in the Barking Road café where Malcolm Allison and Noel Cantwell thrashed out their new ideas on coaching, tactics and football philosophy. Bobby Moore and John Lyall, the future of the football club, listened intently to every word.

First team debut at last

Lyall made his reserve team debut against Plymouth Argyle on 28 September, 1957. In his three seasons with the club prior to his first team debut in 1960, he made 52 appearances for the reserves. Today most Premier League clubs have scrapped their reserves teams, thus denying young players the opportunity to play alongside experienced professionals. With the Metropolitan League, the London Midweek League and the London Combination League, there was no shortage of full-bloodied, competitive matches for young players to learn their trade. The London Combination was a prestigious league back in the 1960s and attracted decent crowds. London football fans would scrutinise the Sunday sports pages to check the result of their reserve team's Saturday match. The Hammers' 1st and reserve teams played at the Boleyn on alternate Saturdays – a practice that ceased with the advent of the benighted Premier League.

John Lyall's first appearance in the West Ham first team might have happened as early as December 1958. Fenton had thought of giving John his debut at Maine Road against Manchester City, but the young full-back was suffering with a knee injury at the time and Joe Kirkup played instead. Northumberland-born Kirkup was a decent full-back who played nearly 200 games for West Ham, including the highlight of his career, an appearance at Wembley in the 1965 European Cup Winners' Cup final. He was an interesting character who trained as an engineer after passing nine GCEs at school. When Fenton signed the young full-back he failed to convince Kirkup's parents that he might do better finding a career more suited to his considerable academic abilities – the youngster would have none of it. In a moment of unexpected thoughtfulness, Fenton said about signing young players:

'I cannot help thinking how much a successful career means to the

parents of these boys. In most cases they have probably devoted most of their lives to giving their sons an adequate education.'

The injury that gave young Kirkup a chance in the first team was to plague Lyall for the next few seasons as his seemingly trouble-free journey to the first team came under threat. In the following season Lyall was chosen by Fenton to make his first team debut against Millwall in a Southern Floodlit Cup match. An excited Lyall woke that morning full of anticipation, but as he began his preparations for the match, John was told that his father had suffered a heart attack. Naturally, John withdrew from the match and left to join his mother in Scotland, where his parents were attending a family funeral.

At this difficult time for the Lyall family, Ted Fenton showed genuine compassion to the youngster, which to some might appear uncharacteristic. In his autobiography Lyall wrote:

'Typical of Ted Fenton and the club, my wage packet that week contained £38. My usual wage was £14, but they had paid me the first-team appearance and bonus money.'

Ted Fenton provides a contrast of the life of the professional footballer in the late 1950s with the mega-rich lifestyle of today's Premier League players:

'At West Ham the boys get £20 a week when they are in the first team. They have meals found for them and those who need houses are provided with them at very reasonable rentals.'

And in a moment of incredulity:

'Quite a lot of them drive cars.'

Fenton's simple act of generosity towards Lyall won the respect of the youngster and when things began to get difficult for the West Ham manager, Lyall was able to return his manager's kindness and support. When he finally made his first team debut, the fledgling left-back impressed both his manager and his teammates. Fenton had prepared his young players well and had no reason to doubt that young John would let him down. As he explained:

'When a boy joins West Ham he will play essentially the same type of football as the first team. Right down through the club the theme is the same, the only difference being in the rise in the performance the closer you get to the first team.'

Consistency was all important and so much easier to achieve with the pick of the home-grown talent. All the club's young players were educated in the Hammers' style, even the very best:

'Now a boy like Bobby Moore, a teenage youth international, steps into the League side and feels comfortable at home because the players around him have the same background and approach.'

In their first season back in the 1st Division the Hammers had made an encouraging start to the season, although their form had tailed off in mid-season. So when the moment arrived Lyall was ready. In a 1st Division match against arch London rivals, Chelsea on 6 February 1960, West Ham's converted half-back came head-to-head against the England winger, Peter Brabrook, a swift and wily outside right, who later had a spell with West Ham. Lyall would have been all too aware of the England man's ability. Brabrook had represented East Ham and Essex Schoolboys a few seasons before Walter Winterbottom awarded the winger a full England cap. In the dressing room before the Chelsea match, Lyall received some timely advice from Noel Cantwell. The Irishman told the fledgling full-back:

'If you don't get a good tackle in he will run you off the park.'

Not the kind of advice you would expect from an Irish football philosopher, but it stuck in Lyall's mind. A hefty challenge early in the second half kept Brabrook quiet for the remainder of the match. To Ted Fenton's delight, the debutante defender, after a hesitant start, came out on top in his personal duel with the England man and the Hammers won the match 4-2. The Stratford Express reported:

'Brabrook at his England best utterly bewildered an unhappy Lyall but the fine covering of Moore and Brown averted disaster and long before the end the courageous Lyall had turned the tables.'

But not before Brabrook waltzed past three defenders in characteristic style, rounded Dwyer in the West Ham goal, and scored a breath-taking solo goal. Later Lyall claimed, along with Blackburn's Bryan Douglas and Cliff Jones of Tottenham, that Brabrook was among the most difficult opponents he ever faced. Fenton also awarded young Tony Scott his debut in the game against Chelsea and the boyish and leggy winger was a big hit with the home crowd, as the Express report informs us:

'Tony Scott ... one of the lesser-known of Hammers' talented youngsters stole the show from his much-lauded opponents.'

But Scott's promising debut that day was overshadowed by an unlikely hat-trick from stand-in centre-forward, John Bond. Old Irons supporters will remember the crowd-pleasing full-back was christened *Muffin the Mule* by the North Bank, his awkward running style resembling that of the children's TV puppet. The following match Bond was back attending to his more familiar defensive duties, his moment of glory stored away to be retrieved for the later benefit of his grandchildren. Jackie Dick added the Hammers' fourth goal glancing in a smart header from Bond's cross.

Young Lyall had impressed the 29,000 Upton Park crowd on his debut. Despite their lowly League position this was a strong West Ham side which included internationals like Phil Woosnam and Dick, the emerging Geoff Hurst and Hammers' legends Mal Musgrove and Ken Brown. Chelsea fielded a young team which included Jimmy Greaves and a 17-year-old Terry Venables, making his debut in the Blues midfield. Ted Fenton was encouraged by the young full-back's performance. He had remained calm and confident throughout, while his positional play and tackling was first rate. John came off the pitch that night feeling ten feet tall.

He remembered thinking:

'Well, maybe I've arrived at last...'

If the young full-back thought he had arrived he was quickly put in his place by his manager. Fenton taught Lyall a lesson he was to put to good use in his own managerial career 25 years later:

'Ted Fenton put all that euphoria into perspective. I had done well enough, he said, but no more than that.'

That night Fenton gave Lyall a masterclass in how to nurse young players through their career. But, for now, all that practice in the alley behind the family flat in Ilford seemed to have paid off and John was now a full member of the first team squad. The young full-back had made a confident debut in a tasty London derby where he came face-to-face with a tricky opponent. In addition Lyall was popular with everyone at Upton Park and the fans had taken to the Ilford youngster. His future in the game seemed secure, although Noel Cantwell swiftly recovered from his injury and was eager to get back into the side. So despite his encouraging debut, Lyall had to wait until the following season before he was assured of a regular place in the side.

Following his confident debut, Lyall returned to the reserves for the next match, with Noel Cantwell regaining his regular first team spot against Newcastle United. John was brought back by Fenton for the following game – a 1-3 defeat by Nottingham Forest. In contrast to Lyall's debut match this was a dreary non-event. The Stratford Express summed the fan's frustration,

'... this drab, uninteresting affair was agony. It was like watching two ageing fighters in the ring struggling to regain the touches that once made them great.'

Fenton continued with the failed experiment of Cantwell partnering Woosnam, Hurst and Malcolm in midfield. Only Woosnam played to anything like his best. After his Chelsea hat-trick, Bond retained his place at centre-forward, but without Moore the defence was sluggish and exposed. Towards the end of the first half things went from bad to worse for the away side when, as the Express reported:

'Only seven minutes of the first half remained when Lyall, twisting in full flight to help a half-hit clearance on its way, fell to the ground and was carried off on a stretcher to take no further part in the match.'

A last minute goal from Malcolm Musgrove brought little consolation for Fenton's men on a miserable day for the Hammers. The bright promise of early season seemed a dim and distant memory. The sight of young Lyall being stretchered off at the City Ground was distressing to Ted Fenton and the travelling Hammers fans. John was distraught and realised his injury was serious enough to keep him out for the remainder of that season. In his first season as a first team player he had played just two games, his encouraging debut against Chelsea and the away game against Forest, in which he sustained the first of a series of frustrating knee injuries which began to threaten a highly promising career.

1960-61 – My best ever season
In West Ham's first season back in the 1st Division, Fenton's side finished in a highly creditable sixth position. At the end of the following season, during which John Lyall made his first team debut, the Hammers frustrated their loyal fans by ending the season in a lowly 14th position, losing 20 of their 42 fixtures. A heavy January defeat at the hands of Huddersfield Town in the 3rd Round of the FA Cup added to the fans' sense of disappointment. Fenton sold the highly promising inside-forward John Smith to Tottenham in return for goal-scoring centre-forward, Dave Dunmore. There was a sense of change in the air at the Boleyn. The side that won the 2nd Division title so emphatically was

beginning to break up and despite the odd convincing performance, Fenton was struggling to come to terms with the standard in the higher division. To add to the sense of change, the great Ernie Gregory played his final game for the club against Leeds United in September 1959, although he was to remain at the club in a coaching capacity for many years.

The Hammers' third season in the 1st Division brought further poor results, including defeat in the 3rd Round of the FA Cup and an early exit from the League Cup at the hands of lowly Darlington. The influential skipper Noel Cantwell departed to Manchester United, and most importantly Ted Fenton left the club he loved to be replaced by the Arsenal coach, Ron Greenwood. The 1960/61 season was a turbulent one in the history of West Ham United. The only constant was the ever-impressive John Dick, who yet again ended the season as the club's top scorer. Amid the turmoil there were three encouraging signs for the fans. Firstly, 17-year-old Ronnie Boyce made his first team debut in the 5-2 win against Preston in October. Secondly, the team showed what they were capable of hammering Arsenal 6-0 at Upton Park on Guy Fawkes Night, courtesy of a Dunmore hat-trick. Such fireworks were rare but lit up a dark November night at the Boleyn. The third reason for optimism was the slow return to fitness of young John Lyall.

Lyall's knee injury responded well to treatment in the summer of 1960 and by September he was relishing the prospect of a full season in the first team at Upton Park. However, despite the Hammers uncertain start to the new campaign John had to be content with a place in the reserves for the first two months of the season. Ted Fenton knew young John was a promising full-back and knew how hard the youngster worked on his game. He also respected John for accepting the coaching staff's view that he would make a better full-back than a centre-forward. Fenton knew Lyall was impatient for the first team and wanted to help, but one man stood in his way, Noel Cantwell. The swashbuckling Irishman had formed a classic full-back partnership with John Bond, which was the bedrock of the famous West Ham promotion winning side of 1957-58.

Cantwell was a larger than life character and a huge influence on the young John Lyall. The Irishman's revolutionary ideas on football made a deep impression on the young apprentice which stayed with him for life. He later wrote:

'In a way I was sorry to see him go. He was captain of the Republic of Ireland, a superb professional, full of life. I used to play cricket with him in the summer, and sometimes we'd enjoy a drink together... it was sad to see him leave Upton Park, but his departure opened the door to the first team for me.'

It was inevitable that Cantwell would move to a bigger club sooner or later – he had simply outgrown West Ham. When Manchester United made a princely offer of £29,500 for Cantwell in September 1960, the Hammers could hardly refuse. United's offer was a record price for a full-back at the time. The move to Old Trafford was a great personal success for Cantwell. He captained the 1963 FA Cup-winning United team and in the following season led the Red Devils to victory over holders Tottenham in the European Cup Winners' Cup. When his playing career ended Cantwell enjoyed success as a manager with Coventry City and Peterborough United and had a spell as player-manager of the Republic of Ireland. He became chairman of the Professional Footballers' Association and won 36 caps for his country. Cantwell was highly respected in the game and widely admired for his judgement of players and was persuaded by Sven Goren Eriksson to leave the comfort of retirement in 2002 to join the England manager's World Cup scouting and assessment team. Noel Cantwell died in September 2005. His death was marked by an emotional minute's silence before the Hammers' game against Aston Villa later that month.

Lyall lapped up every word of Noel Cantwell's advice and as a young professional, could not have had a better mentor. But Cantwell was ambitious and Fenton did not want to stand in his way. The Hammers' manager knew that in Lyall he had the perfect replacement for the Irish international. When Cantwell picked up an injury that September, just a few weeks before the Irishman departed to Old Trafford, John was brought back into the side. This time he was determined to keep his place.

Internationals, Cantwell and Phil Woosnam were left out for the 1st Round Football League Cup tie against Charlton in late September and replaced by Lyall and John Cartwright. The Hammers won the match 3-1 in front of just 12,000 spectators who witnessed the rare sight of a Bobby Moore goal as the young no. 6 hammered in the home side's third goal from 25 yards. Lyall had a decent game and looked forward to an extended run in the side.

A home league match against Blackburn Rovers on 1 October provided Lyall with a further opportunity to show his manager he was ready to replace Cantwell. In front of 17,519 lively fans, John came face to face with an opponent who was a far tougher proposition than Peter Brabrook, the man he faced in his testing debut match the previous season. Bryan Douglas, the experienced England international, was one of the most exciting and feared wingers in world football. With his low centre of gravity, pace and shoulder-dropping trickery, Douglas was the classic winger. He was part of a very good Rovers side which included three England internationals, the great England defender Ronnie Clayton, outside-right John Connelly and himself. Douglas made 36 appearances for England, scoring 11 goals and played in both the 1958 and 1962 World Cups. He was also a member of Sir Alf Ramsey's victorious 1966 squad. In the moments before the team ran out onto the Upton Park pitch, Lyall would have remembered Noel Cantwell's advice about the need to make an early physical challenge on his opponent. But, although Peter Brabrook was a useful winger, Bryan Douglas was world class and had played against the world's best defenders. But Lyall was not to be intimidated and waited for his opportunity which came early in the game. However, the challenge hurt Lyall more than Douglas as the full-back later recalled,

'After just six minutes I challenged Douglas for a high ball, we clashed heads and I broke a tooth. I was knocked out. I had a bruised lip, throbbing gum and slight concussion.'

Physiotherapist, Bill Jenkins was swiftly on hand to work his magic. Fortunately, the youngster recovered quickly and kept Douglas relatively quiet for the rest of the game, earning him the following day's headline, 'Lyall Dims England Star'. Thanks to John Dick's winning goal the Hammers won a pulsating match 3-2, leading one observer to remark that the result could have easily been 9-9. Lyall left the field admitting he was, 'the proudest man on the pitch'.

Awarding Lyall a commendable 8/10 for his performance, the Stratford Express reported:

'John Lyall, West Ham's young left-back, playing his first league game of the season, played England's Bryan Douglas out of the game for long periods.'

There was further praise for the returning youngster in the club's next match programme:

'After a somewhat hesitant start John Lyall came into his own in the closing stages of his first League game of the season.'

Playing against the likes of Douglas and Brabrook so early in his career was a tough test for the Hammers' young full-back. But Lyall was up to the task. He showed real composure, his defending was solid and sure, and in true West Ham tradition his distribution was excellent. During the Blackburn match, Lyall even found time for some surging runs down the left wing, much to the delight of the fans crowded into the Chicken Run.

By coping well with the dazzling skills of top international wingers, the strong-tackling Lyall convinced Ted Fenton that he was a more than adequate replacement for Noel Cantwell. After frantic dental work to repair the damage done in the clash with Douglas, and despite Cantwell's recovery from injury, John kept his place for the next game against Birmingham City, a game which the Hammers won 4-3, with goals from Musgrove, Dunmore, and Mike Grice. Lyall was now full of confidence and optimism for the rest of the season.

With more diligent physiotherapy, Bill Jenkins successfully patched up the young defender's knee so that Lyall was ready to challenge for a long run in the first team. The season was a turning point for the Hammers. The influential duo of Cantwell and Malcolm Allison were gone, although Malcolm Musgrove, John Dick, Ken Brown and John Bond remained first team regulars. Despite losing key members of his most successful side, Fenton was confident he had the right blend of youth and experience to cope with the 1st Division. Bobby Moore made 13 appearances in 1959-60 and 38 the following season. The young defender was the undoubted star of the first two matches of John Lyall's come-back season against Charlton and Blackburn. With his impeccable tackling, clever interceptions and immaculate passing, Moore was well on the way to one of the most glittering careers in sport.

With youngsters like John Lyall, Geoff Hurst, Martin Peters and Andy Smillie banging on the first team door, Fenton had high expectations for the future of the club. Phil Woosnam settled quickly into the side and developed a fine understanding with Musgrove, Boyce and the ever-consistent, Andy Malcolm. However, during the early part of 1960-61 there was growing speculation about the great Welshman's future, including that Woosnam was on his way to Wolves, although this was vehemently denied at the time by chairman, Reg Pratt. But with Johnny Byrne soon on his way to the Boleyn from Crystal Palace and Hurst and Peters ready for the first team, the future for the West Ham manager looked bright indeed and John Lyall was at the heart of his manager's thinking.

The young full-back was now established in the first team and continued to produce competent performances. He was popular with the North Bank and his strength and enthusiasm more than made up for the loss of Cantwell. Lyall was clearly enjoying his season and for the first time in his career could look forward to the future with confidence. But unfortunately, the side's form fell away after Christmas with just three wins in the second half of the season, as the Hammers slipped down the League. With the club gradually becoming engulfed in transfer rumours about Woosnam and speculation about the future of their manager, John Lyall was just happy to be playing football. Despite the side's poor form the left-back could look back on some real highlights, together with one or two less distinguished moments.

The 6-0 defeat of Arsenal at Upton Park on 5 November 1960 must surely go down as one of the most remarkable performances by any West Ham side. In what became known as the 'massacre in the mud' nearly 30,000 passionate fans witnessed the humiliation of the North London giants. The Hammers, with our hero at left-back, systematically took the Gunners apart from start to finish. Phil Woosnam dominated midfield and crowned an outstanding performance with a goal, while a Dave Dunmore hat-trick and further goals from Malcolm and Dick ensured an emphatic victory. Arsenal manager George Swindon looked a picture of misery as the goals flew in. His mood worsened when Tommy Docherty was taken off after receiving a knock. The tough-tackling right-half later returned, but only as a limping passenger out on the left wing, much to the delight of the mocking fans in the West Stand.

The Hammers defence that day were majestic with Ken Brown and Bobby Moore in unbeatable mood, and young John Lyall making regular surges down the Gunners right flank. Cheered by the sight of the hapless Docherty the home supporters were in dreamland when their beloved Hammers scored four times in the last 20 minutes. Happy days!

A superb defensive display at Maine Road on the 11 November helped the Hammers towards an unexpected 2-1 victory against Manchester City. Moore and Brown, ably supported by Lyall and Bond, were again outstanding in defence. Moore was at his most commanding as he skilfully marshalled the defence while keeping a close eye on the ever-dangerous Denis Law. Goals from Dunmore and the quixotic young winger Mike Grice sealed the victory.

In the run-up to Christmas young Lyall was a regular in the side but was about to experience the frustrating inconsistency that has dogged West Ham down the years. By the end of November Lyall had become a crucial part of a strong West Ham defensive unit and dovetailed neatly alongside Moore, Bond and Brown. Ted Fenton would have been delighted with his young defender. But tougher challenges than Arsenal and Manchester City lay ahead. Champions-elect, Tottenham were the visitors to Upton Park on Boxing Day that season and in front of a capacity crowd showed just why they were, by some way, the best team in the League. Spurs' international stars, Blanchflower, White and MacKay produced a masterclass of midfield magic. But the Hammers were far from humiliated that day and played their part in an enthralling encounter, but the home side were simply outclassed by one of the best teams in Europe. John Lyall played his part as the Stratford Express reporter noted,

'... the 'keeper threw clear to Lyall who alertly spotted another crack in the visitors' defence and made a great run through to put Musgrove away.'

Sadly, Muzzie fluffed the chance and the stunning victory over Arsenal back in November suddenly became a dim and distant memory.

Lyall missed the whole of March due to persistent knee problems and the excellent form of Bond and Kirkup. However, he returned to the side in April, making a further three appearances prior to the end of the season. In the final game against high-flying Burnley, Lyall showed his enforced break had not affected his form. The disappointing crowd of nearly 18,000 were in for a rare treat. In the first half the two sides produced 45 minutes of breath-taking football. The Hammers went ahead in the 11th minute courtesy of a Woosnam left-foot rocket into the top corner. Burnley surged forward for an equaliser but:

'The West Ham defence had tightened considerably. Kirkup and Lyall tackled so effectively that Rhodes had an easy afternoon in goal...'

After a string of missed chances the Hammers failed to build on their lead and the inevitable happened. Burnley equalised and then Pointer secured victory for the away side late in the game. For the home fans it was a cruel end to another disappointing season.

For John Lyall it was his best spell for the club to date. With just two appearances in the first team in 1959-60, Lyall had made a frustrating start to his career. He had his first ligament operation at the age of 17, but it failed to improve the condition of his troublesome knee, as he later recalled:

'I spent most of the next three seasons in and out of the reserves, in hospital or on the treatment table at Upton Park.'

Club physiotherapist, Bill Jenkins worked hard to get John on the field and fit enough for 90 minutes. Some of the opposition were less sympathetic. In one particular come-back match John had some unwelcome opposition,

'...against Arsenal in the Southern Floodlit Cup, a Tommy Docherty tackle sent me straight back to the treatment table.'

Despite the Doc's unwanted attention and thanks to Jenkins' good work, Lyall's knees improved sufficiently for the full-back to make 25 League and Cup appearances in the 1960/61 season. Naturally his confidence improved and with it his form. His career was back on track and at the age of 21, he was still very much a part of his manager's plans. But to put Lyall's best season in perspective, Ken Brown, Mal Musgrove and Andy Malcolm all played over 40 matches that season, while alongside them a youthful Bobby Moore chalked up 38 appearances. Even Mike Grice, the Hammers' gifted, but inconsistent forward made 26 first team appearances in Lyall's comeback year.

If he could not yet be considered a first team regular, at least Lyall made substantial progress. He was healthy and his troublesome knees were holding up. Both Ted Fenton and new manager, Ron Greenwood began to trust the young full-back enough to pick him ahead of Joe Kirkup, whose partnership with John Bond had been so effective. Throughout his injury problems Lyall remained positive, believed in his own ability, refused to become disillusioned and fought hard for his place in the side. There were no question marks about the courage and tenacity of the young full-back.

Farewell to Ted Fenton

In the 1960/61 season humiliating Cup defeats opened deep wounds in the Hammers' football psyche, which have failed to heal right up to the present day. What happened next reflected badly on all those involved. Despite his success in 1957/58, the Hammers' disappointing results back in the top tier meant that Fenton was now tainted with failure. There were also unanswered questions about his personal life and the way he conducted himself professionally. An earlier players' revolt led by Allison and Cantwell undermined his authority and credibility with the board. On 13 March 1961, club chairman Reg Pratt announced, with the manager's agreement, that Fenton had been placed on 'sick leave'. It would have been no coincidence that the announcement followed a 4-0 defeat by Preston, hard on the heels of early FA Cup exits and an extremely poor away League record. Fenton left the club under a heavy black cloud, perhaps of his own making, but the fans knew that the club had mishandled the whole sordid affair.

Ted Fenton had put together a highly promising group of young players at Upton Park which should have coped comfortably with the demands of the 1st Division. But the manager was unable to turn a group of highly talented individuals into a collective unit. Fenton's side seriously underachieved in the two seasons following promotion and he paid the ultimate price. The man who signed John Lyall as a young apprentice, brought him into the first team, transformed a gawky centre-forward into a sturdy and useful full-back, and generally provided support and encouragement to both John and his parents, had left the club. Lyall was loyal to the man who,

'...had been a great help to me.'

But like the rest of the playing staff, Lyall was kept in the dark about Fenton's exit from the Boleyn:

'As is often the case, the players rarely know the real reasons behind a manager's departure. I was just 21 and as surprised as anyone... I remember a story in the 'Ilford Recorder' at the time stating that he had

been allowed to resign rather than be sacked.'

The club issued the following statement:

'For some time Mr Fenton had been working under quite a strain and it was agreed he should go on sick leave.'

The hint of a compromise allowed the club to retain its proud boast that they had never sacked a manager. Inevitably, Fenton saw things differently:

'They gave me no money and sacked me.'

Fenton's management divided players at West Ham. Lyall and one or two others supported the manager who had given them their first chance in football. Others, notably Malcolm Allison, were contemptuous of the man and his alleged outmoded training methods and tactics. Ted Fenton left the club he joined as a young centre-half in 1943 with his tail firmly between his legs. He made 176 appearances for West Ham, winning a Football League War Cup Final medal in 1940. His distinguished playing career included playing five times for England and as a young manager he took minnows Colchester United to the 5th Round of the FA Cup in 1947/48. At West Ham he succeeded the legendary, Charlie Paynter and eventually returned the Hammers back to their rightful home in the 1st Division. But the man who guided John Lyall through his early days as a professional was gone and the youngster would have to adjust to life with a new manager who could not have been more different to the old school local boy. Fenton went on to manage Southend United before retiring into the pub trade. He later opened a sports shop in Brentwood, passing on the business to his son Alan, who played a few A team games for West Ham in the 1950s. Ted Fenton died tragically in July 1992 following a road accident near Peterborough.

Chapter 3
A new dawn at Upton Park

In the early 1960s, John Lyall's life unfurled in ways he could not have imagined when he started out as a 15-year-old apprentice professional. Firstly, the arrival of Ron Greenwood at Upton Park in May 1961 was a defining point in Lyall's career. Secondly, despite the best medical treatment available at the time, the full-back's troublesome knees worsened and finally brought an end to a promising career. At the age of 23 he was forced to face a future without the game he loved so much. A career-ending injury is difficult for any professional sportsperson to accept – at the age of 23 it must have been almost unbearable. In such cases adversity can provide an opportunity for an individual to dig deep and show their true character. Fortunately, John Lyall was a strong personality and accepted his fate with surprising, but typical, good grace. It helped to have his young wife, Yvonne, by his side at this difficult time.

A fine romance

Lyall's faltering football career must have been a terrible frustration for the young full-back. But he would have been more than consoled by events in his personal life. Early one morning, in the week prior to the Young England match against Luxembourg in 1958, John arrived at his usual Ilford bus stop to make the short journey to the Hammers' training ground at Chadwell Heath. In the queue that morning, like every other morning, was a pretty young girl on her way to work in the City. For weeks the shy young footballer tried to pluck up courage to speak to his attractive young neighbour. This morning was different. Tucked in his pocket was a letter from the FA confirming his selection to play for the England Youth team. His confidence, boosted by the letter burning a hole in his jacket, John seized his moment.

"Good morning," he said, "how are you today?" Having broken the ice, he whipped out the letter from the FA and announced. "I've been selected to play for England." What girl could resist that killer Ilford chat-up line? His neighbour knew very little about football, but showed enough polite interest to encourage her mildly embarrassed pursuer. One thing led to another and the couple became engaged on John's 19th birthday in February 1959 and were married just over two years later in May 1961.

Yvonne lived with her parents and two sisters just around the corner from the Lyalls in Marlborough Drive. She was a middle sister just as John was the middle brother in his family – *the jam in the sandwich* – as she later recalled. Like John, Yvonne came from a respectable working class family; her dad had a thriving building firm down by Blackfriars Bridge. He was very strict with the girls, but Yvonne remembers him with great affection. She recollects spending the whole of one Saturday taking in a pair of slacks until they resembled fashionable Teddy Girl trousers, only for dad to declare, "Don't think you are going out in those," before throwing them in the dustbin. Later in life, Mr Webb achieved his dream of retiring to the peace and quiet of Holland-on-Sea out on the Essex coast. Yvonne's mum was from Walthamstow and one of nine children, a large family, even by East London standards. If John and his family had to endure occasional caravan holidays on the breezy Kent coast, Yvonne's family enjoyed touring holidays to Italy and France and regular day trips to Southend.

Yvonne and John were in the same year at Parkhill Primary School, but Yvonne went to Clark's College in Ilford for her secondary education. Clark's prepared bright girls like Yvonne for a job in the City of London or down in the West End. Like her friend, Tina Moore, Yvonne was a bright Essex girl and on leaving school soon landed a good job in the London Stock Exchange. The two families became great friends and Yvonne remembers John's parents with particular fondness. "It was like having another mum and dad," she recalls. Like all John's friends she loved Mrs Lyall's wonderful cooking and, much later, used to spend Saturday afternoons at the Lyalls while John was away with West Ham. The couple's relationship got off to a good start despite not having a car – no Baby Bentleys or WAG sports cars back in the early '60s. It was a while before the couple could afford any sort of car. However, in those days local transport was cheap and accessible and very few young people in East London had the luxury of owning their own car. With John settled as a professional footballer the couple could look forward to a bright future together.

One summer's day John was playing cricket for Billy Wright's X1 when he was invited onto Clayhall CC's end of season tour to Westgate-on-Sea. John wanted to take Yvonne, but first had to seek permission from her dad, who fortunately, gave his consent. That's how things were done back in the late 1950s.

The couple married in May 1961 and moved out to the quiet Essex village of Abridge, where they paid just £3,675 for their first home together. The newly-weds bought the house from local builder Roy Lowe, who John knew from his involvement with Billy Wright's charity team. The couple lived modestly and, like many professional footballers, John had a summer job to supplement his off-season wages. Using his building skills, he worked as a plasterer off-season, while early in their married life Yvonne left her City job for temporary secretarial work in Ilford – temping as we used to call it. The couple were careful with money and saved hard. They bought their first car, a Morris Traveller Estate, although John continued to take the short bus journey to Grange Farm for training as Yvonne needed the car for work.

Only son, Murray was born in April 1962. Yvonne went into labour in the middle of the night, but John was prepared and left nothing to chance, even to the extent of keeping the car's battery on charge all night – he made it to the hospital with minutes to spare. Yvonne settled quickly in Abridge with her friends and family around her. She eventually gave up the temporary job in Ilford and took on clerical work from home, often working late into the evening. With the support of Yvonne, his family and West Ham, John could face the future with cautious optimism. The young full-back had got his career back on track in 1960/61, married and became a proud father the following year. Lyall had come a long way in a short time. He could not have imagined at the time the challenges that lay ahead.

Back at work

Lyall later described 1960/61 as, "my only good season as a player." Although his knees were improving, in reality he had only featured in half of that season's fixtures. But Fenton showed patience, took the young defender under his wing and the youngster responded to his manager's encouragement. He trusted and respected Fenton as he disclosed in his autobiography, "He was an excellent trainer...an innovator who tried to vary training routines."

Both Fenton and Lyall must have been bitterly disappointed when, just as things began to look up, his knee problems knees flared up again. A series of operations and Bill Jenkins' skilled physiotherapy provided only temporary relief for the youngster. In a recent biography of Brian Clough the author analyses the emotions and behaviour of the 26-year-old, goal-scoring sensation, just before his career was brutally ended by similar knee injuries to Lyall. Clough took it badly. He was scoring goals in a Sunderland side on the verge of promotion back to the 1st Division and became a regular in the England side. Newly married, Clough was aware of his family responsibilities and naturally, the stricken centre-forward was bitterly disappointed. He was desolate, felt discarded and began to drink heavily. It is to West Ham's great credit that John Lyall reacted to his injuries more positively. Instead of self-pity he showed great courage. Instead of bemoaning his luck, Lyall chose to fight back. In adversity he revealed his true character. Ted Fenton and Ron Greenwood were sympathetic and provided unwavering support in his struggle – an indication of how well-regarded Lyall was at West Ham.

The Hammers completed the 1960/61 season in lowly 16th place, a whopping 30 points behind the legendary double-winning Tottenham team of Blanchflower, White and MacKay. The Hammers' defence, rarely reliable at any time, conceded 88 goals in that campaign, losing 19 out of 42 games in the process. A 1st Round exit from the FA Cup at the hands of Stoke City and an embarrassing defeat by Darlington in the League Cup were the low points in a disappointing season. The thumping 6-0 win against Arsenal at Upton Park in early November brought brief respite, but Fenton's side fell away in the second half of the season finishing in 16th place in the 1st Division. In summary, a frustrating campaign for the club's loyal and passionate fans, but one which gave their young left-back real hope for the future.

The Reverend Ron

Around the time young Murray was born, Ted Fenton left the club he first joined in 1933. Within a month of Fenton's departure the board appointed Ron Greenwood as the new Hammers' manager. Greenwood proved to be a seminal influence on Lyall's career and in the early 1960s the pair began a close and enduring partnership that brought trophies and glorious football to Upton Park. No biography of John Lyall would be complete without acknowledging the man who became his great friend, teacher and counsellor. It is generally accepted in football that Ron Greenwood was a very special coach and his record confirms his reputation as he guided the Hammers to glory.

The Greenwood/Lyall project almost never got started. Greenwood had real doubts about joining West Ham. In his role as assistant manager at Arsenal he built a reputation as an inventive and forward-thinking coach. Greenwood was also manager of the England Under-23 side and appeared destined for a dazzling career. If Greenwood was John Lyall's coaching mentor, the Arsenal man looked to the England coach, Walter Winterbottom for advice and guidance. Aircraftsman Greenwood and Wing Commander Winterbottom had met during the war and became good friends and respected colleagues. The England man later said of his protégé:

'Ron Greenwood has always believed that attacking football and good sportsmanship are not obstacles to success. He has been a strong, positive influence on the game – and only a small and distinguished number of men can have that truly said of them.'

As Winterbottom admitted, he had been asked by the West Ham board to sound out Greenwood about the manager's job at Upton Park. He wrote:

'It...fell upon me to play a part in Ron's appointment as manager-coach at West Ham.'

The West Ham board had clearly done their homework and were keen to make the right appointment. Winterbottom was generally regarded as one of the most influential figures in world football, but his words failed to convince Greenwood who initially refused the job point blank, telling his friend and mentor: "I'm happy at Arsenal. In any case, if they're going to sack people like they did last night, it's obviously not a happy club."

OUCH!! Why would a man with such a bright future in the game leave Highbury and move across London to a club whose 1st Division status was hanging by a thread? Fortunately for West Ham, Greenwood became unsettled at Highbury when he was overlooked in the Gunners' search for a new manager in favour of George Swindon, who succeeded the former England captain, Billy Wright.

Feeling undermined, Greenwood began to have second thoughts about Reg Pratt's offer to join the East End club. He met Pratt and vice-chairman, Len Cearns, accepted their offer, but not before demanding full control of all team matters and no interference. The offer was generous. Greenwood had been earning £1,500 a year at Highbury and West Ham raised this to the princely sum of £2,000. True to character, Greenwood took his time before making a decision. But really his mind was made up and within a few days he told Pratt, "I would be delighted to be your new manager."

Greenwood took to West Ham like a duck to water. He was impressed that in Syd King, Charlie Paynter and Ted Fenton, the club had had only three managers in nearly 60 years. He trusted the board and was confident enough to begin his new job without the restrictions of a contract.

Unlike John Lyall, Greenwood was not a local boy. He grew up in a small terrace house in the Lancashire village of Worsthorne, close to Burnley. His father was a painter and decorator, while his mother worked in a local mill. Again, as with Lyall, he remembers a happy childhood with football at its heart,

> '...the village in which I was born, is at the heart of the game, two and three-quarter miles of honest Lancashire above the town of Burnley; and that was the road I first took to League football. I was five-years-old and my father, Sam, used to carry me down the hill to Turf Moor, perch me on a barrier, and let me get on with my hero-worship.'

Greenwood's childhood was very similar to Lyall's early years in Ilford as he explains,

> '...we used to play football until dark on the local recreation ground at the top of the village... coats acted as goalposts and the weather never mattered. Football was an obsession to me.'

Greenwood's parents moved south to Wembley when young Ron was just 10-years-old. Within a short time he was captain of his school side and the Wembley Boys district side. Like most outstanding young footballers, Lyall included, he regularly played two years above his age group. The youngster left school at 14 and took up a five-year apprenticeship with a Wembley sign-writing firm. As luck would have it the firm had a contract with Wembley Stadium and young Ron spent many a weekend writing new signs for the stadium. Much to his delight, one of his tasks was writing up half-time scores on a blackboard, which he then held aloft and carried around the ground.

As a teenager Greenwood never gave up his dream of playing professional football. He had a trial with Chelsea and joined their famous youth scheme. But the war intervened, as it did for most professional footballers of the time. He spent the war as an RAF radar technician and saw action in France. At the end of the war, Chelsea sold Greenwood to 2nd Division outfit, Bradford Park Avenue for £3,500 where he was quickly made club captain. At Bradford he had the good fortune to play alongside the legendary inside-forward, Len Shackleton, before Shack left for fame, if not fortune at Sunderland. Greenwood's greatest moment at Bradford came at Highbury in 1948 when he captained his team to a 1-0 FA Cup victory over 1st Division champions, Arsenal. The Burnley lad had developed into an accomplished centre-half as this report of the Arsenal match illustrates:

'Towering like a giant over the whole fantastic and fanatical game was the figure of the Bradford centre-half Greenwood. Every Bradford footballer was a hero. But Greenwood was the greatest of them all.'

Greenwood moved back to London in 1949 where he joined Brentford for a record fee of £9,000. Like Hammers' legend Johnny Dick after him, he enjoyed three happy years at Griffin Park. His outstanding leadership skills were again recognised at Brentford when he was made club captain. Alongside him at the Bees was the soon-to-be famous Jimmy Hill and, for a spell, the great Tommy Lawton. Greenwood and Hill later took their FA coaching badges together and remained life-long friends. After his spell at Brentford, Greenwood returned to Stamford Bridge where he was a member of Ted Drake's championship-winning side of 1955.

Greenwood moved from Chelsea at the age of 33 to complete his playing career with Fulham at Craven Cottage. Although the move involved dropping a division, Greenwood was attracted by the thought of playing out his career in the company of Johnny Haynes, Jimmy Langley, Bedford Jezzard, Bobby Robson and his old friend, Jimmy Hill.

There was little doubt that Greenwood would turn to coaching when his playing days were over. He had his FA coaching badges and was a profound thinker about the game. During his late career spell with Fulham, Greenwood was close to being offered the manager's job at Craven Cottage, but in the end the West London club chose the experienced Vic Buckingham over the undoubted potential of their centre-half. The Fulham rejection was a blessing in disguise, as Greenwood later explained,

'My apprenticeship as a coach and manager was long, varied, eventful, often frustrating and sometimes maddening, but in the long run it was immensely rewarding.'

It certainly was varied,

'It involved England's Youth and Under-23 sides, Ealing Grammar School, Eastbourne United, Oxford University, Walthamstow Avenue and Arsenal. I learnt the trade trick by trick and, inevitably, mistake by mistake.'

In his time at Green Pond Road, the Avenue won the Isthmian League and in 1954 achieved a famous 4-0 FA Cup victory over Queen's Park Rangers – to that point his proudest moment in football. At Walthamstow he was fortunate to work with such great amateur internationals as Jimmy Lewis, Len Juliens and Vic Groves. While at Eastbourne, Greenwood was appointed chief coach of the Sussex FA, an indication of the high regard in which he was held at the FA. During his time on the South Coast, such was the strength of his growing reputation he received at least six offers from Football League clubs. But, for now, he resisted the temptation to join one of the big clubs chasing his signature. People in the game were also impressed by the Burnley man's work with the Young England side of Bobby Charlton, Jimmy Melia, Jimmy Greaves and of course, Bobby Moore. Outside of his club responsibilities, Greenwood was working with some of the greatest young players of their generation.

The young coach was a quick learner and benefitted greatly from Winterbottom's FA courses at Lilleshall as he admitted:

'Walter and his coaches gripped us with their ideas and opened my eyes to a brand new world of coaching...they seemed to take us right inside the game.'

In his playing career Ron Greenwood won a championship medal, captained every club he played for with the exception of Chelsea and took his coaching badges while still a player. A rock-solid, competent centre-half, Greenwood missed out on international recognition, although he did captain the England B team on one occasion and was selected as a member of the provisional England party for the 1954 World Cup. Unfortunately, he never made the final selection, but to be named as one of England's 40 best players gave the Burnley boy enormous satisfaction. He had played with some of the all-time greats in English football including Raich Carter, Len Shackleton, Neil Franklin, Stanley Matthews and Tom Finney and worked with such coaching giants as Bill Nicholson, Ted Drake, Walter Winterbottom, Matt Busby and the Italian, Enzio Bearzot, with whom he became close friends. He enjoyed a modest playing career, but specks of the angel dust that showered down on these wonderful names, landed on the shoulders of the bright young coach.

Ron Greenwood had received the perfect football education and his arrival at Upton Park in May 1961 could not have been better timed. The inspirational Lancastrian was the right man, for the right job, at the right club. On arrival at his new club Greenwood decided to retain the Hammers' experienced backroom staff. Chief scout, Wally St Pier, and the coaching team of Albert Walker, Ernie Gregory and youth team coach Jimmy Barrett had a wealth of experience between them and knew the club inside out. With Eddie Chapman and Pauline Moss in the office, Greenwood could settle in and focus solely on his first team duties. Young Lyall – eager to learn as much about coaching as he could – was captivated by his new manager's style and admitted that he owed everything he knew about football from the man who was soon to became his mentor and great friend.

EX Magazine editor Tony McDonald spent several hours with Lyall in his Suffolk farmhouse in preparation for his excellent book, West Ham United: the Managers. In the course of the interview Lyall discussed in depth the relationship he enjoyed with the man he called the Master:

'Every time I watched Ron at work, he was unbelievable to me. He went beyond clever. He had such an insight and foresight into the game – he was revered by other top coaches.'

Greenwood showed his protégé that he had a ruthless streak when decided to offload club skipper, Phil Woosnam. The new manager thought the Welsh international 'smothered' the younger players and robbed them of their individuality. He might have also thought Woosnam had too much power at the club and was unhealthily close to West Ham's so-called property manager, Jack Turner. The latter had increasing influence over the senior players and acted as their eyes and ears. Goodness knows what Greenwood would have thought of today's seedy bunch of players' agents. Both Woosnam and Turner soon left the club.

The new manager also made an immediate impression on former Hammers' winger, Harry Redknapp:

'Ron was on another level to anyone else I've ever seen. If he was coaching today, he'd still be the best, because I still haven't seen anyone else to compare with him.'

This is rare praise from the former manager of Bournemouth, Portsmouth, Southampton and Tottenham. Of course, Redknapp also spent seven years as the Hammers' manager and remembers Greenwood's keen interest in the development of the club's young players:

'He took a big interest in us kids. In 1963 I remember Ron bundling six of us into his car and driving us to Wembley to watch the European Cup final between Benfica and AC Milan. He remains the most knowledgeable man I have ever met in the game.'

One of Greenwood greatest achievements at West Ham was to turn a bunch of local young boys and a few senior professionals into a successful team with a European reputation for playing eye-catching, attacking football. The new manager was an internation-alist, heavily influenced by continental coaches like Bearzot, Rinus Michels and Helmut Schoen. He would return from watching Ajax or the Brazilians enthusing about new training methods and playing styles as John Lyall explained:

'Ron would go to games – internationals and matches in other parts of Europe – and he'd come back and say to me: "I saw a player do such and such a move and I think we can introduce it." And we would go out and work on it.'

Later Greenwood invited his youth team coach along on his European excursions, as Lyall remembered:

'Ron and I regularly boarded a plane after our home games to go and see Ajax play on a Sunday. He'd say to me, "We think it's an English game, but it's not – it's a European and World game and we've got to learn to compete with them."'

Greenwood's prophetic words were not lost on Lyall and the young coach was only too aware he was experiencing the football lesson of a lifetime. For his part Greenwood quickly recognised Lyall as a kindred spirit, bright and intelligent enough to accept his advice and guidance.

Lyall quickly realised that Greenwood was an excellent communicator, able to get new, often complex ideas across to his players. Martin Peters summed up Greenwood's approach to bringing new ideas to the side:

'What Ron Greenwood taught me was locked in my brain for the next 20 years.'

Johnny Sissons, a young player who flourished under Greenwood's tutelage, recently reflected:

'I'd align us to the way Arsenal play when they're at their free-flowing best. We played a lot of one-touch football – it was second nature to us and something we practised off the walls in the roller skating rink at Forest Gate. It was all triangles and intelligent off the ball running.'

West Ham legend Billy Bonds endorsed Peters' views:

'He was a great coach who was years ahead of his time… he was always planting little seeds in your mind, and using simple little terms like, 'always be on the half-turn', and, 'If the space isn't in front of you it's behind you'.'

Greenwood set about his new job with his customary zeal and enthusiasm. One of his first tasks was to transform Geoff Hurst from a lumbering half-back to one of the most feared and respected goalscorers in world football. It was a master-stroke as Hurst recognised:

'Ron was the single most influential figure of my career. He opened the door to modern football for me.'

In his early days at West Ham Greenwood trusted his youngsters and worked tirelessly to improve the skills and tactical awareness of more experienced players like Ken Brown and John Bond. He was fortunate in that he inherited a highly talented crop of local lads, including Moore, Hurst, Peters, Sissons and Ronnie Boyce. But he was astute enough to know he needed some experience to support his youthful team. In came Peter Brabrook, Jim Standen, and the hugely influential, Johnny Byrne.

The near-post cross, bending the ball with the outside of the foot, body shaping, angles and triangles, and training on your toes were all innovations introduced by Greenwood to the unsuspecting players and fans of West Ham United. These technical improvements were to radically change the fortunes of this homely, if under-achieving, football club. An exciting new era had begun at the Boleyn. The new manager's arrival had a tremendous influence on young John Lyall, who despite the sad ending to his injury-ravaged career was encouraged to believe he had a future in the game he loved so much. The careers of the two coaching connoisseurs were to be inextricably linked during the course of the next 20 years. It was to become a partnership made in football heaven.

Most of what John Lyall came to know about football he learnt from Ron Greenwood. The new West Ham manager taught his youth team coach something that shaped Lyall's career and his whole outlook on life; the importance of high standards. Greenwood was often referred to by his players as the 'Reverend Ron' because they never heard him swear and knew he attended church regularly. Professional footballers are simple souls.

Former professional cricketer Neil Burns, now director of London County Cricket and the founder of the Greenwood/Lyall Legacy Fund, is a passionate Hammers' fan and said recently:

'Greenwood and Lyall inspired other people with their enthusiasm and their deep love for their fellow man and the game of football.'

Burns is referring to the way the two men instilled in their players a sense of decency in their dealings with other people, whether they were fans, their family, or the people who clean the dressing rooms at the training ground. Greenwood and Lyall were both caring men, in today's parlance, who believed players should work hard, act honestly and be courteous at all times. He would have been horrified by the inflated sense of entitlement that exists with many Premier League players today, who evidently believe that being interviewed after a big match is at most an infringement of their right to privacy, and at the least, an irritating nuisance.

As Burns remembers, Lyall learned to absorb quality of information and was constantly curious, things he so admired in the man who became known as the 'professor of football'. Lyall ate heartily from Greenwood's table from the beginning, as he started out on a career which in many ways mirrored that of his mentor and close friend.

The Academy takes shape

The West Ham players were far from strangers to their new manager. As England coach at U23 and Youth level, Greenwood had worked with a young Moore and taught several West Ham players on FA coaching courses. He quickly gained the respect of his new squad, who were aware that Greenwood had coached many of England's outstanding youngsters like Jimmy Greaves, Peter

Dobing, Jimmy Armfield, George Eastham and Bobby Charlton.

The fans looked forward to Greenwood's first game with keen anticipation. In April 1961, the Hammers were too close to the relegation zone for comfort and the home match against Manchester City had become critical. In the absence of a manager, club captain Phil Woosnam had run the side for a few games. Greenwood allowed the Welshman to pick the team for the City match, enabling him to observe the players in action, prior to making his first selection. The game ended in a draw and confirmed Greenwood's first impressions of his new team. Firstly, they were disorganised defensively – something any West Ham fan could have told him. Secondly, and encouragingly, his new players were tremendously talented.

The following week was a crucial one for Greenwood. His new team had a rearranged fixture against Burnley on the Tuesday, followed by Cardiff City away on the Saturday – two games in which he could make an early impression and get the passionate West Ham fans on his side. Greenwood realised the importance of these two games. He wrote in his autobiography, Yours Sincerely:

'The following week was important ... We had ... Burnley on the Tuesday, Phil Woosnam was to play for Wales against Spain in a vital World Cup qualifying game at Ninian Park 24 hours later, and the following Saturday we were to play Cardiff. We decided to stay in Manchester on Tuesday night, travel down to Porthcawl on Wednesday morning, watch the international and then stay on for the weekend game.'

The trip gave Greenwood an early opportunity to bond with his players and the opportunity to communicate some of his ideas. Early in the week, physiotherapist Bill Jenkins had given Greenwood an insight into the thinking of some of his new players. Full-back, John Bond had pronounced himself unfit for the Burnley game, but insisted he still wanted to make the trip and would be available to play in Cardiff on the following Saturday. Bond was a dominant character in the Upton Park dressing room and at this stage of his career he was effectively picking his own games. Keen to stamp his authority on the squad, Greenwood duly left Bond out at Turf Moor and called up the reserve left-back, young John Lyall, with 17-year old Ronnie Boyce coming in as replacement for the missing Woosnam.

In their Manchester hotel Greenwood took the opportunity to have a long discussion with his players. He acknowledged their ability, but wanted them to play with more flexibility and ditch their rigid man-to-man marking in favour of the more modern zonal system. It was a talk which young Lyall was to remember for many years. Greenwood decided to keep the same team for the Cardiff match following the Malcolm Musgrove inspired 2-2 draw at Burnley. Bill Jenkins had pronounced John Bond fit and the full-back expected to resume his usual place in defence. When the team to play Cardiff was announced Bond immediately complained to his manager, "Why am I not playing?" The new manager told his most senior player that Lyall had played well at Turf Moore and deserved to keep his place in the side. By making it clear to one of the West Ham 'old school' that he was the boss, Greenwood had stamped his authority on the club within weeks of being appointed. The Hammers drew the Cardiff game in which Lyall again performed creditably. John Bond, a popular character at Upton Park, quickly recovered from his sulk and later admitted Greenwood was right to leave him out of the Cardiff match.

Lyall kept his place for the final game of the season at home to Burnley. He had made a good impression on his new manager with three solid defensive performances. The Hammers had successfully escaped relegation and the fans were full of hope for the following season. Greenwood quickly got to grips with the cliques and personality clashes among the playing staff in an attempt to raise morale. He also dealt with a perennial problem at Upton Park over the years – the influence of a few undesirable outsiders at the club who enjoyed too close a relationship with some of the players. John Lyall was highly impressed by Greenwood and lapped up his manager's new ideas and innovations like a sponge.

Injuries take their toll

If 1960/61 was the happiest and most productive in John Lyall's short playing career, the following season was a cruel disappointment when the 22-year-old made just four appearances in the claret and blue of his beloved Hammers. The season began badly. Even such a positive character as Lyall would have been disheartened when Greenwood preferred Joe Kirkup to partner Bond for the first game of the season. However much he tried to hide it, the constant battle with injuries was beginning to affect the youngster:

'I'd had my first ligament operation at the age of 17 but it hadn't solved the problem... It got to the stage where I wasn't really concerned about the level of performance on the playing field; I was more concerned with finishing the 90 minutes.'

Clearly, this was an intolerable position for a young professional sportsman. He had his whole life ahead of him and his dreams of becoming a West Ham favourite lay in tatters. He was recently married, had a young son, a house in the country and was only too aware of his responsibilities to his new family. The season was a near disaster for Lyall. The only encouragement for the young full-back came in March and April and it was to be short-lived.

A combination of injuries and the good form of Joe Kirkup, kept Lyall out of the first team until the final weeks of the season. His first opportunity came on 3 March when an injury to Bond gave Lyall his chance. The Hammers were enjoying a successful season, despite losing 0-3 to Plymouth Argyle in the 1st Round of the FA Cup back in January. That Saturday they travelled to table-topping Burnley confident of a good result. The Lancashire side had other ideas, produced their best form of the season and thumped their visitors 6-0. The claret and blue clash was no contest. Greenwood's side were outfought, out-paced and out-played. Only Lawrie Leslie – Greenwood's first signing for West Ham, Ken Brown and Bobby Moore came out of the game with their reputations intact. Young Lyall was distraught, but may have been cheered up a little if he saw the match report which read:

'Full backs Lyall and Kirkup stuck to their jobs but were outrun by the two Burnley wingers.'

Uncharacteristically, Moore was very nearly sent-off in this match for allegedly pushing the referee to the ground, but the official accepted the great man's apology and the whole incident was forgotten. Despite their outstanding performance against the Hammers, Burnley could only end their season as runners-up to eventual champions, Ipswich Town.

Lyall lost his place after the Burnley thrashing, but returned to the side for the home match against relegation-threatened Cardiff City. How he must have relished the prospect of running out onto the Boleyn pitch in front of nearly 25,000 expectant fans. Lyall remained positive and believed his knees could stand up to a run of games and he never lost the belief in his own ability. His chance came against the Welsh side. The Cardiff match was notable for a number of reasons. Ron Greenwood made Bobby Moore captain in front of the watching Phil Woosnam, *Budgie* Byrne scored his first goal for the Hammers, six weeks after joining the club, and teenager Martin Peters made his debut. The Good Friday crowd witnessed a lively Hammers' performance which brought an emphatic 4-1 victory. Peters had a fine game and, despite his youth, showed the cool maturity which characterised his play over the years for West Ham, Tottenham and England. Alan Sealey and Tony Scott also played that day, while Bill Lansdowne proved an adequate replacement for the injured Ken Brown. Slowly, but surely, Greenwood was changing the team, giving youth a chance at the expense of some of the more established players.

Lyall kept his place for the following game against Arsenal at Upton Park as the home side chased a top six finish. Nearly 32,000 partisan fans packed into the Boleyn for the end of season derby match and the atmosphere was electric as the teams emerged from the players' tunnel. Greenwood had stayed loyal to his youngsters with Peters, Lansdowne, Scott and Lyall all retaining their place in the side. The match was to prove eventful for the Hammers' injury-prone left-back.

To the frustration of the home fans packed into the North Bank, Arsenal took an early lead, before Scott's equaliser brightened their mood. The match was no late season stroll as the teams tore into each other on the bumpy pitch. Then an injury to Lawrie Leslie changed the course of the game in the visitors' favour. The Hammers' 'keeper suffered a broken finger diving at the feet of the Gunners' speedy winger, Danny Clapton. Leslie was unable to continue and Lyall took over in goal for the remainder of the second half. The goalkeeper later returned to a hero's welcome, spending the rest of the match out on the left wing, being a total nuisance to the Gunners' rearguard.

Taking advantage of the temporary confusion in the West Ham defence, the visitors quickly went 3-1 ahead. But the Hammers were far from beaten. Inspired yet again by skipper Moore, who won his personal duel with the impressive George Eastham, the claret and blue shirts laid siege to the Gunners' goal before Jackie Dick nodded in a precise cross from Peters, who had taken over from Lyall at left-back. In the 85th minute the Boleyn faithful were in dreamland. Makeshift winger Leslie cunningly stepped over a pass from Scott, allowing Billy Lansdowne to slide in the equaliser. Greenwood's young team showed terrific spirit to gain a precious point in a pulsating encounter. After the match the manager revealed, "I should have brought in the youngsters earlier in the season."

This was little consolation for Lyall, but Greenwood delighted in the fact that the Hammers' future belonged to the young players, led by their immaculate captain, Bobby Moore, who was soon to be named in the England party for the 1962 World Cup in Chile. John Lyall was an integral part of Greenwood's plans, provided he stayed healthy and injury-free. It was a very big if indeed for the young full-back.

Lyall's fourth and final appearance of his injury-hit season was at Bolton Wanderers in late April. Following the courageous comeback by his young side against Arsenal, Greenwood made just one change for the next match – and that was enforced. He brought in 18-year-old Alan Dickie for his debut to replace the injured Leslie in the West Ham goal. Dickie was the third choice 'keeper behind Brian Rhodes and Leslie, but more than repaid his manager's faith in him, showing maturity beyond his years in a tough match at Burnden Park. The teenage 'keeper made two acrobatic saves in the first half to keep the Hammers in the match. At the other end of the pitch England 'keeper, Eddie Hopkinson applauded his opposite number's agility and composure. I was privileged to meet Alan Dickie while researching for this book and he clearly enjoyed the opportunity to look back on his days at Upton Park – a true gentleman.

After a bright start in the match against Bolton, Johnny Byrne faded as the home side began to control midfield. But the visitors looked to be holding on for a well-deserved draw when, with the stadium clock showing 90 minutes, Martin Peters lost the ball under pressure from Wynn Davies and the ball fell loose to winger, Doug Holden. Within a couple of seconds the ball was nestling in the back of Dickie's net, following a stunning 25-yard drive from the England man. Bolton had won a dreary encounter 90 seconds into injury time. The West Ham defence, superbly marshalled again by Moore, held firm for most of the match and John Lyall had another solid game at left-back.

Once again Greenwood was delighted with his young side. Without the experience of Musgrove, Brown and Bond they had held their own against some strong opposition. But Greenwood brought back Bond for the final game of the season in place of the frustrated Lyall. The Hammers beat Fulham convincingly at Upton Park with two goals apiece from Crawford and the prolific Dick. The centre-forward had another tremendous season, showing what a great goalscorer he had become. The Scottish international had been top scorer for three of the previous four years and scored an impressive 166 goals in 351 league and cup appearances for West Ham. His goals helped the Hammers to end the season in a respectable 8th position. The club's renaissance was underway.

John Dick was part of Ted Fenton's great side which was gradually being dismantled by Ron Greenwood. The new manager wanted his team to play football in the style of the Hungarians of the 1950s and Di Stefano's Real Madrid and believed Byrne was the nearest thing in the English game to the Argentine genius. Greenwood was fortunate to have inherited a brilliant crop of young players from Bill Robinson and Wally St Pier. Bobby Moore was always destined for great things and Ronnie Boyce was ready for an extended run in the side. Martin Peters was displaying the kind of maturity that led Sir Alf Ramsey to describe the great midfielder as 'ten years ahead of his time', and the young winger John Sissons was about to be unleashed on unsuspecting 1st Division full-backs. By the summer of 1962 the ambitious and determined Greenwood had assembled a squad ready to challenge for major trophies. But he knew only too well they remained raw and far from the finished article. The manager needed some experience to augment the youngsters' potential and enthusiasm, so the following season he brought in John Lyall's old adversary, Peter Brabrook from Chelsea and the Luton Town goalkeeper, Jim Standen.

During his first season at West Ham the new boss arranged a coaching week at Lilleshall for the whole squad. All the players attended, with the exception of Johnny Dick who stayed back in Essex to do some coaching with his local youth team. The club took over the national centre for the whole week – the first time a professional club had ever done this. The week was an opportunity for Greenwood to get his ideas across to the players and to develop team bonding. He was keen to impress upon his team just what coaching was all about. This was a revolutionary advance for an English coach. For Greenwood the week was a great success. He wrote in his autobiography that the innovative was,

'...one of the most exhilarating courses I can remember. Every day we worked morning, afternoon and evening. My plan was to give everybody a notion of what coaching was all about so that it would be easier for me to transmit my ideas.'

The players responded brilliantly, helped by Musgrove and Woosnam who were both fully qualified FA coaches. The week was no mid-season 'jolly'. On Friday afternoon the players sat a two-hour theory examination and a short paper on refereeing. The week was a tremendous experience for young players like Lyle who remembered it for many years to come.

Having established his authority on his new squad, Greenwood showed the fans he wasn't frightened to make important decisions. Following the arrival of Byrne, Brabrook and Standen, he allowed Woosnam to leave for Aston Villa, long-serving Malcolm Musgrove to Leyton Orient and the loyal John Dick to Brentford, where he enjoyed several successful years prior to a well-earned retirement.

The foundation for the triumphs of 1964 and 1965 were laid, not at Chadwell Heath or Upton Park, but thousands of miles away in America. In the summer of 1963 Greenwood took his young squad to the US to play in an international tournament featuring some of the world's best teams. John Sissons believed the trip was a fantastic experience for a young player:

'Although I was only 16-years-old and only really went along to America as kit boy, Ron brought me on at half-time against an Italian team. It was mind-blowing.'

Greenwood explained his reasons for the US trip:

'It could have taken two or three years at home to gain the experience we achieved on our American adventure. Every one of our ten games was a lesson in itself and our reward came in the form of increased confidence, understanding and team spirit.'

The Lilleshall coaching week and the American adventure were examples of Greenwood's far-sighted imagination and attention to detail. Both were to pay rich dividends as the expectation around Upton Park began to grow in intensity. John Lyall desperately wanted to be part of the new manager's plans. He enjoyed a run of four games in the first team at the end of 1961/62 in which he played well and impressed his manager. Lyall had every reason to look forward to the summer with renewed confidence, and of course, more treatment on his fragile knees.

The dream begins to fade

Lyall missed the first game of the following season – a 1-3 defeat at Villa Park, before being brought back for the next match at home to Wolves. In front of just over 30,000 disbelieving fans, the Hammers crashed to a humiliating defeat – not an auspicious occasion for the returning left-back. Stan Cullis' young side – average age just 20 – completely outplayed the Hammers who had centre-half, Ken Brown back in their side. Wolves had sent out a warning to the rest of the division by thrashing Manchester City 8-1 on the opening day of the season. They came to Upton Park full of confidence and thumped the Hammers by four goals to one. As Brian Moore wrote the following day:

'Wolves' golden hordes of youngsters blazed their message across Upton Park last night... that Cullis is back in business.'

By the time Musgrove scored a late consolation goal the orchestrated sound of slow hand-clapping reverberated around the ground and out across East London. The Hammers had made a disastrous start to the new season and their defence was a shambles. But Greenwood kept his nerve and retained Lyall for the visit of high-riding Tottenham on the following Saturday.

A crowd of 32,000 packed into Upton Park to see the super Spurs take on a Hammers side that were thrashed in the opening two games of the season and roundly booed off the pitch in their previous game. For Greenwood, things were about to get worse as Bill Nicholson's great side eased to a 6-1 away win, and Jimmy Greaves, fresh from his aborted trip to Italy, helped himself to two well-taken goals. The West Ham manager and his team received a football lesson that day. However, arch perfectionist Nicholson refused to be satisfied with his side's performance. Rubbing salt in the West Ham wound, he said after the game, "We were good in spasms, but not varied enough in the last 20 minutes."

There were a few boos for pay rebel Phil Woosnam, but generally the home crowd had been cowed into submission by their side's miserable start to the new campaign. After three matches the Hammers were rooted firmly at the bottom of the League table, conceding 13 goals in three games, with just three in reply.

Concerned about his shaky defence, Greenwood introduced full-back Jackie Burkett into the side, leaving Lyall as third choice left-back behind Burkett and Joe Kirkup. The young full-back had every reason to feel dejected as his knees continued to give him problems. He wrote in his autobiography:

'I spent... three seasons in and out of the reserves, in hospital or on the treatment table at Upton Park.'

The future for John Lyall at West Ham looked increasingly gloomy. But he was brought back into the side to play Manchester United at Old Trafford in late October. Inspired by Denis Law and Albert Quixall the Reds ran out 3-1 winners in a one-sided encounter. Ex-Hammer Noel Cantwell quietened Peter Brabrook, while at the other end of the field Bobby Moore, for once, lost his composure and the following day was awarded an embarrassing 4/10 for his uncharacteristic performance. Capping a miserable return, Lyall managed to help Denis Law's half-hit shot into his own net for the Red Devil's third goal. He wasn't to know at the time, but Lyall had just one more game to play in the claret and blue of West Ham's first team. Fortunately for Greenwood and his coaching staff, the Hammers rallied in the second half of their League season to finish in a respectable 12th place.

Cold war and cold feet

The 1962/63 season is best remembered by two events which threw a blanket of uncertainty over the country and sport in particular. October began promisingly and saw the release of the Beatles first single and Bob Dylan's debut album. In the autumn of '62 President John Kennedy announced to an excited world that the Americans were making plans to put a man on the moon. Then in mid-October, the mood suddenly changed. The Cuban Missile Crisis placed the world on the brink of nuclear war as Kennedy and Khrushchev vied with each other for global supremacy. I can remember taking the underground to Upton Park for a home match and not knowing whether we would return home – it was that scary. The memory remains vivid 50 years later. Fortunately, sense prevailed and the crisis was over within a couple of very harrowing weeks.

On 28 December temperatures plummeted and London was hit by a heavy snow-storm. From January to early March the whole of the country was covered in snow, temperatures were the lowest ever recorded with a heavy frost every morning from late December until 5 March. The 'Big Freeze' of 1963 brought chaos on the roads, trains stopped running and all major sports programme were cancelled and hastily rearranged. An indication of the severity of the weather was that West Ham played just one game in the weeks between 29 December and 2 March.

The weather improved with the approach of spring and professional sport resumed a near normal programme, much to the delight of the sports-loving British public. Hammers' fans had good reason to welcome the warmer weather. Thousands of them watched in delight as the club's junior team lifted the FA Youth Cup, beating the mighty Liverpool 6-5 on aggregate in the final. The victorious Hammers' side included crowd favourite John Charles and wingers John Sissons and Harry Redknapp. But one member of the playing staff was not in the mood to celebrate.

John Lyall's final first team appearance was against Blackburn Rovers at Upton Park on 4 May 1963. Greenwood chose to bring in three of his Youth Cup-winning heroes, Charles, Sissons and centre-forward, Martin Britt. Of the three, the 18-year-old Charles had the best game, benefitting from playing alongside Moore, who was back to his outstanding best. The Hammers lost 0-1 failing to cope with the dazzling skills of Lyall's old Rover's adversary, Bryan Douglas. On the day, Douglas proved the main difference between the teams. Lyall came out on top in a previous meeting with Douglas back in 1961, but this time the England man was too good for the Hammers' left-back, who to his credit, had been out of the first team for seven months. The troubled full-back had played just four games in the whole of 1962/63, all of which West Ham lost convincingly, and now, on his return, he struggled against his international opponent.

A shattered dream

Lyall lost the battle with his knees and his dream of a long career as a professional football was shattered. His knees hurt and he must have been concerned about the long-term damage he might be doing to them. But he was nothing if not courageous and refused to accept the inevitable, as he explained,

"I was good enough to do the job. I battled on...and didn't begin to feel disillusioned until my last season (1963/64). In the first game... I played in the reserves against Tottenham. I remember turning sharply and the knee immediately coming out of joint."

Yvonne remembers being at home with John when his dodgy knee popped out again. "Shall I call the doctor," enquired Yvonne?

"No, it's OK Von," he replied, "I'll pop it back myself." This typified his no nonsense approach to life. More treatment, more recovery time, even further operations failed to deter the young full-back. One last chance was all he needed. It came in a match in January 1964 against the Metropolitan Police at their delightful ground at Imber Court in Surrey. Encouraged by the watching Ron Greenwood, Lyall felt great going into the match. But as he recalled, things did not go to plan:

I played a ball with the outside of my foot and suddenly my knee popped out of joint again. It was a devastating moment for me. "It's no good," I thought, "I just can't do it anymore."

After the game Greenwood sat in the dressing room with his forlorn full-back and Lyall told him, "The knee's just no good. There's no point in going on."

One month short of his 24th birthday, Lyall finally accepted his career as a professional footballer was over. He had made just 35 League and Cup appearances for West Ham since his promising debut against Chelsea on 6 February 1960. It was some consolation that in his brief playing career he had the opportunity to play in West Ham's defence alongside a youthful Bobby Moore. The youngsters grew up together and were great friends. For Lyall, Moore was the perfect role model, a hard trainer, imperious, commanding, composed and a meticulous person both on and off the pitch. Lyall wrote in his autobiography,

'...the man I most enjoyed playing alongside was, without question, Bobby Moore. He was a dream to play with. He spoke to you every minute of the game... He had time to play your game as well as his own.'

In his autobiography Lyall offers a glimpse of Moore's character and hints at the secret of the Barking lad's incredible success:

'We had grown up together. When he first came to Upton Park he was a good player, but no more outstanding than some of the others. But he had a thirst for knowledge and he was a prodigious trainer.'

Moore would have been devastated by Lyall's enforced retirement. But in the way he conducted himself and in his attitude as a professional, the future England captain had taught his friend a lesson that he would never forget. The injury was diagnosed as a 'generally disarranged knee'. Today, with kneehole and reconstructive surgery, the ligament damage might have been repaired sufficiently for Lyall to have played a few more seasons. But on that cold January afternoon in Surrey his first thoughts were not about his injured knee, but about providing for Yvonne and Murray in the years to come.

Chapter 4
A true 'family' club

The Lyall's were a strong and resourceful young couple. Most young professionals would have been completely shattered at hearing the news that their career was over at such a young age. But Lyall showed great courage in the way he rebuilt his life. Such strength of character would stand him in good stead in his years as manager at West Ham and later Ipswich Town. For the moment he still had his office job at Upton Park.

Lyall recalls how early in his career, he missed a game due to his father's illness, only to find at the end of the week that Ted Fenton paid him the full wage of £38, instead of the expected £14. The gesture showed how much the club valued their unfortunate young full-back. Now in his hour of need, the club came to his rescue again, showing what an admirable club they were back in the 1960s. No longer part of the playing staff, Lyall was provided with what would now be called a 'portfolio' of jobs. He continued with his duties in the club offices, while undertaking some light coaching work.

Preparing the wages under the guiding hand of Mrs Moss wasn't going to be a problem for the grammar school educated Lyall. Being part of the club's coaching team presented more of a challenge. Even at an early age John had coached in a variety of youth and community settings. The general advice from the staff coaches was to 'do what we taught you in training' and adjust it to the level of the group. Lyall had been coached by Malcolm Allison, Ted Fenton and Ron Greenwood and observed others like Jimmy Barrett and Albert Walker working with the club's youngsters. All of these people were steeped in the West Ham way. There was no shortage of role models for a budding young coach. Even with this impressive background, the prospect of coaching the best East

London players of their generation must have given Lyall some moments of doubt and uncertainty. Ron Greenwood, never complacent, and aware that a young coach needed support, dispatched Lyall to Lilleshall to study for his FA coaching badges.

Lyall returned from Lilleshall with mixed feelings. He had high expectations of the FA's programme and was determined to succeed. So he was disappointed to return to Upton Park with just average marks. The conversation back at Ron Greenwood's office went something like this,

Greenwood: *"How did it go John?"*

Lyall: *"Fine, I enjoyed it, but..."*

Greenwood: *"I assume you got a distinction?"*

Lyall: *"Well no Ron, I got marked down for over-coaching."*

Greenwood was furious, immediately rang the FA and wrote a strong letter of complaint. Lyall's tutors told him that he stopped play too frequently and gave too much advice. There was no need, these are good players they continued, it isn't necessary to hold up play to remind players of small things like their body shape and positioning. Of course, this is how Lyall had been coached at West Ham where players were brought up on good habits and received detailed technical assistance. Attention to detail and a resolve to improve an individual's technical ability were fundamental principles of coaching at Upton Park. Once again, the West Ham manager was in the coaching vanguard and way ahead of his time. We don't know whether Greenwood got anywhere with his complaints to the FA – but he made his point. The whole incident was indicative of the gulf between the conservatism of the FA and Greenwood's pioneering methods which improved his team to such an extent that the Hammers threatened to steal the *Pride of London* away from White Hart Lane.

Patsy Holland and Tony Carr were members of the East London boys' side who beat Liverpool in the final of the English Schools Trophy in 1963. The two 16-year-olds signed professional forms for West Ham on the very same day, just weeks after their heroics with the East London schools' side. Holland, who attended George Green Grammar School, remembers evening coaching sessions run by John Lyall in a small gym near the Boleyn. At the start of his first session Lyall introduced himself to the nervous young winger, "Hello, I'm John Lyall and you are Patsy Holland." This personal greeting immediately relaxed Holland, who delayed signing apprenticeship forms until he completed his GCEs. The young winger was being pursued by Tottenham's Bill Nicholson at the time and Lyall's personal touch clinched the deal for Holland, one of the most promising East London footballers of his generation.

There were usually around 20 lively youngsters crowded into a tiny space on those winter evenings which presented Lyall with a real test of his coaching ability. It was in these sessions that Lyall devised a programme which focused on individual skills and teamwork. Following the Greenwood principles the sessions were varied, but always hard work. In those days West Ham ran A and B youth teams and it would have been part of Lyall's responsibility to train, coach and prepare the teams for their Saturday morning matches. As youth coach, Lyall worked alongside youth team managers, Bill Lansdowne and Jimmy Barrett. Ron Greenwood was now firmly established at the club and had transformed the club's coaching structure right down to the youth teams. Lyall was very much part of this structure which aimed to inspire everyone at the club into Greenwood's vision of the West Ham way. John Lyall could not have had a more inspirational environment in which to develop his coaching career.

When Sir Trevor Brooking arrived at Upton Park as a fresh-faced 14-year-old in the summer of 1965, he remembered Lyall as an office-boy and coach. Brooking had come to the attention of West Ham when he appeared for Ilford Schoolboys in their English Schools Shield quarter-final against Oxford. Both Chelsea and Tottenham were keen to sign the outrageously talented midfielder, but it was the persuasive Hammers' scout Wally St Pier who convinced Brooking and his parents that his future should be with his local club. Greenwood was at the Oxford match with St Pier and, richly enjoying young Brooking's performance, turned to his Chief Scout and demanded to know, "Why isn't the Ilford no. 4 playing for us?" The rest, as they say, is history.

Working every morning in the West Ham office, five afternoons at Stepney School and two evenings with the youth team, provided

Lyall with a rich and varied diet of football experience. He would have relished working with talented teenagers like Brooking and Pat Holland. Of course weekends without a game would be a constant reminder of what he had lost. But he was still able to provide for his young family and he remained positive – not being the type to dwell on a problem. Aware of Lyall's family responsibilities the club supplemented his modest wages in the off-season by working for a plastering firm in Rainham. If there is one word that sums up the young John Lyall it is resilient:

'If you have a setback in life, it's no good moping, you have to get up off your backside and go for it... I had a good education and I was brought up that way by my parents who told me never to feel sorry for myself.'

Yvonne Lyall tells a story which perfectly sums up her late husband's character:

'One day I came home from shopping and there was John, just after one of his many knee operations, dragging himself up and down the lawn with one leg heavily bandaged.'

This 'never say die' attitude saw Lyall through a difficult time. Accepting that his playing days were over, he turned his face fully to his new career. He knew he had the full support of good people around him,

'...I've always said that West Ham is its people and there were so many good ones around the club. I came from Ilford but I found the East End a very vibrant place, with lots of kind people who would do anything for you.'

His new career would begin for real on the West Ham bench at Wembley in the 1964 FA Cup Final. But in the meantime, there was work to do for everybody at Upton Park, including the chairman, the manager, the players, and last but not least, the fans.

The mood at the club was buoyant at this time, which would have helped young Lyall to adjust to his new role. In the 1963/64 season Ron Greenwood's new Hammers were getting good results and it felt an exciting time to be around Upton Park. But despite the optimism, Greenwood's team remained stubbornly in mid-table during the new manager's first few years at the club. Ultimately, the new boss was judged by the fans, not on his League record, but the quality of the football produced by his team of dazzling young players, particularly their brilliant performances in cup competitions. In the spring of '64 anticipation reached fever pitch as Greenwood's side confirmed their new-found assurance in two exciting cup runs. Wins against near neighbours Leyton Orient, Aston Villa and Swindon Town took the Hammers to the semi-final of the League Cup where they faced Leicester City over two legs. In the first match at Filbert Street two goals from Geoff Hurst and one from Alan Sealey could not prevent a 3-4 defeat. But hopes remained high for the second leg at Upton Park. Greenwood and his players felt confident they could overcome the one goal disadvantage. Unfortunately, the home supporters' dreams faded as Leicester ran out comfortable winners 2-0 on the night and 6-3 on aggregate. Greenwood was bitterly disappointed. He believed his team was heading in the right direction and had worked hard to get to a major final, only to badly underperform when it really mattered – a very familiar story for West Ham fans down to the present day. But the football gods looked down kindly on the Hammers that season and handed them a second chance of glory.

Pretty bubbles in the air

The Hammers' great FA Cup year of 1964 began in early January with a comfortable 3rd Round victory over Charlton Athletic in front of 34,000 excited fans at Upton Park. Goals from Hurst, Brabrook and Sissons settled the crowd and set up an away 4th Round tie against close neighbours, Leyton Orient of the 2nd Division. The O's had enjoyed their one and only season in the top tier of English football the previous year, but were now back in their more familiar surroundings. A 1-1 draw at Brisbane Road took the tie into a replay which the Hammers won 3-0, courtesy of two goals from Hurst and a third from Johnny Byrne. Goals from Byrne,

Sissons and Hurst brought wins against Swindon Town and Burnley in later rounds and set up a potentially classic semi-final at Hillsborough against mighty Manchester United.

The Hammers had lost 2-0 at home in the League on the Saturday prior to the semi-final and the pundits were quick to write off the East Londoners' Wembley hopes. A team that contained Best, Law and Charlton were bound to be red hot favourites to reach Wembley, but the West Ham players and their passionate supporters had other ideas. In torrential rain Bobby Moore led out his team for the Hammers' most important game since Ted Fenton's side took the club back to the top flight in 1958. The conditions were set firmly against these two skilful sides as the Hillsborough pitch quickly turned into a mud bath. Both teams began cautiously which seemed to suit the Hammers, who were happy to get through the first 45 minutes without conceding a goal.

The match remained a stalemate until the 75th minute when Ronnie Boyce attempted a speculative lob over David Gaskell. To the inside-forward's delight, the ball nestled into the back of the net sending the rain-drenched, claret and blue-clad fans into raptures as the sound of Bubbles echoed around Sheffield. Five minutes later the same fans were in Hammers' heaven when, following good work from teenager John Sissons, Boyce scored his second, glancing a Jack Burkett cross past Gaskell and into the net. With just 10 minutes left on the clock West Ham had a place at Wembley in their grasp.

Denis Law had other ideas. The Scottish international demonstrated all his courage and skill to climb above Jim Standen to put the Reds back in the game. But with just a few minutes left on the clock, the Hammers restored their two-goal lead. Moore ploughed through the mud leaving three red-shirted defenders in his wake, before sliding an accurate through pass to Hurst – something he had done thousands of times to his England colleague. The Hammers' no. 10 steadied himself before placing a right foot shot into the corner of the goal, just out of reach of the diving Gaskell. West Ham were back at Wembley for the first time since the famous *White Horse* final of 1923. Within a couple of years of succeeding Ted Fenton as manager, Ron Greenwood had accomplished something no other West Ham manager had achieved in over 40 years – a place in the FA Cup final at Wembley Stadium.

A future at Upton Park

If no longer part of the playing staff, the luckless Lyall remained at the heart of the exciting cup runs of 1963/64. Later Greenwood admitted using Lyall's injury to motivate his players. In his Wembley team talk he told Moore, Peters, Hurst, Brabrook, Byrne and the rest of the team just how fortunate they were to be playing in an FA Cup Final, while one of their former teammates had to accept his promising playing career was over. Lyall revealed later in his autobiography that Greenwood told his team,

'... that a trip to Wembley for the FA Cup Final would ensure a bumper testimonial match for me at the end of the season.'

Meanwhile the manager kept Lyall busy by sending him on trips to size up the FA Cup opposition. He appreciated the manager's gesture and enjoyed this, admittedly modest involvement in the FA Cup run. Following the win against Manchester United, Greenwood took Lyall to one side and explained that the team wanted him to organise the players' traditional FA Cup Final pool. Although the minimum wage had been abolished, professional footballers' pay remained at around £30 week throughout the '60s. The players' pool was an important way for the team to earn some extra money through promotions and newspaper coverage. Lyall jumped at the chance to be close to the players at this crucial time. He set up an office in the club's press room and went about his duties with his customary enthusiasm and attention to detail.

That same season West Ham generously granted Lyall a testimonial. The match was held on the Monday evening prior to the FA Cup Final against Preston. Greenwood raised a few eyebrows in the press and among the fans when he selected his Cup Final team to play against an all-star line-up that included Noel Cantwell, Johnny Dick, Malcolm Musgrove, Phil Woosnam and

Terry Venables. The Hammers won a good-natured contest 5-0 thanks to four goals from Geoff Hurst. A bumper crowd of 18,000 paid the princely sum of £3,590 in gate receipts and a further £207 through sales of the match programme. Lyall was genuinely touched by the occasion:

'Considering that my contribution as a player had not been very significant, the actions of the club and the fans that night underlined the strong sense of loyalty that existed at Upton Park.'

Lyall fully appreciated the gesture by Greenwood and the board. He was only too aware that he was facing unemployment at the end of the season and was grateful for the money. Lyall recalled later:

'I was full of gratitude, but the club avoided portraying that evening as something unusual. It was the West Ham way of doing things.'

Lyall was now 24-years-old and had been at the club since he left school. He knew no other life than football. But in those days West Ham looked after their own. He had worked in the office since the age of 15 and was familiar with most aspects of the club. Lyall was also popular with Pauline Moss, Eddie Chapman and the rest of the backroom staff. In addition to his administrative duties, Greenwood had offered his youth team coach a role in the run-up to the 1964 Cup Final. He seized the opportunity as the young full-back began to adjust to his new life. The manager was guiding his club into a new era and the next few years would bring West Ham to the notice of the world. The club was about to enter the most successful period in its long history. The cheeky East London upstarts were on their way to soccer glory and John Lyall was determined to play his part.

If 1964 was a defining year in the history of West Ham United, it was also the start of a coaching partnership that was to flourish over the next ten years. The Hammers' youth team manager, Tom Russell decided to take up a teaching appointment in Uganda. Russell's youth team won the FA Youth Cup in 1963 and the Chadwell Heath Academy was highly regarded throughout the professional game. Greenwood recognised the value of his youth set-up and was aware the club needed a man of the highest quality to replace Russell. He had the perfect replacement on his doorstep. Shortly before the FA Cup Final, Greenwood approached the now-retired full-back and offered him the youth team job. Both thrilled and shocked, Lyall accepted the promotion without hesitation: "I couldn't believe my good fortune."

Lyall's new coaching responsibilities and his work in the office with Eddie Chapman amounted to a full-time job. He was immensely grateful to the club and to Greenwood especially, as he later recalled, "Perhaps I wasn't going to be a great footballer, but at least I could support my family."

This new commitment was to transform Lyall's career and strengthen his partnership with Greenwood. He had the greatest respect for his boss and was eager to learn from the man he so admired,

'...I had struck a rapport with Ron. I admired him as a man and an outstanding coach, and most of what I have learned in football has come from him. His words of advice gave me a tremendous insight into coaching.'

John Lyall joined West Ham as a raw teenage striker. Ted Fenton had turned him into a resolute full-back with a real future in the game. He was awarded an England Youth cap and made a promising first team debut, before his fragile knees let him down for the last time. Taking his seat on the West Ham bench during the 1964 FA Cup Final Lyall could have been forgiven a few negative thoughts, but he was not one for looking back, as he recounts,

'...I could have been out there dogged, muscular, resolute, determined...It was a poignant day for me...my dream of becoming a great player was over. I wasn't sure what the future held in the long term but, whatever I did, I was determined to make a success of it.'

He could not have imagined how successful he would become.

At last – a return to Wembley

Back in the 1960s, Prime Minister, Harold Wilson tried to convince us that the drab and austere world of the '50s was a distant memory. According to Wilson, we had entered the age of 'the white heat of technology'. The new, glamorous world of professional football seemed to reflect Wilson's faith in the future and Bobby Moore's West Ham were leading the way.

Greenwood had every reason to be confident his team would win the FA Cup. He had put together a youthful side full of attacking intent and with an abundance of skill. His team had enjoyed an impressive cup run, although he would have been disappointed by their stubbornly low League position. Their young skipper Bobby Moore became the youngest-ever England captain and received the 1964 Footballer of the Year award. The fans loved the fact that Moore epitomised the Hammers' new glamorous image but remained a local boy at heart. The 1966 World Cup was still two years away and in May 1964 the Barking boy's fame still lay ahead of him.

23-year-old Moore had almost single-handedly steered his team to victory against Manchester United in that epic semi-final The Hammers would need an equally classy performance from their captain if they were to overcome a feisty Preston side. Following the triumph over their Manchester United in the semi-final, the Hammers found themselves in the unaccustomed position of being clear favourites for the final. The stage was well and truly set for the greatest day in the club's history since the *White Horse* Final of 1923.

The final gave Greenwood the opportunity to reflect on West Ham's recent performances. Had they made genuine progress since his appointment? How close were they to playing the kind of football he so passionately believed in? Here was an opportunity to convince himself, his team and the English football public that he was making a real difference. John Lyall was a low-ranking member of the claret and blue coaching think tank, but was unusually close to the manager for a junior member of staff. Greenwood had recognised the younger man's clear potential, but at this stage of Lyall's embryonic coaching career he would have been content to watch, listen and learn from the master. The Hammers' youth team coach turned out to be a consciousness learner and for Greenwood, a joy to teach.

The 1964 Cup Final featuring West Ham United and Preston North End was one of the most competitive in the history of the old competition, although the quality of the football on view was not always up to Greenwood's high standards. The Hammers' side that May afternoon contained 11 Englishman and eight of the side were either born or brought up within a few miles of Upton Park. Geoff Hurst was in Greenwood's team, but not the fast-emerging Martin Peters, left out for the more experienced Eddie Bovington. The exciting young winger, Harry Redknapp, did not make his debut until the following season. Always true to his attacking instincts, Ron Greenwood opted for young Sissons out on the left wing. With Ronnie *Ticker* Boyce, Brabrook and Byrne at the top of their game, this exciting West Ham team deserved to be favourites. Preston, of course, would have other ideas. Wembley was packed with over 90, 000 fans, mostly suited and looking well-turned out for the occasion. How times have changed in 45 years.

The 2nd Division Preston surprised their opponents by including the England Youth captain Howard Kendall in their side, at the expense of the experienced Ian Davidson. Kendall at 17-years and 345 days was the youngest player ever to appear in a Wembley Cup Final. The Lillywhites settled more quickly into the match and had the best of the early exchanges. The surprisingly assured Kendall was all over the pitch. Nobby Lawton and Alan Spavin were at the heart of Preston's best moves and helped their team gain control of midfield.

Greenwood set up his team in a 4-3-3 formation with Brabrook and Sissons wide down each touchline and Hurst alone up front. Enjoying the freedom handed to them by the opposition Preston quickly gained control of the match. Bovington, Byrne and Boyce were outnumbered and outplayed in midfield. From the kick-off Bobby Moore was content to play from a deep position, eyeing his lively opponents with some suspicion. The Hammers' skipper had every reason to be concerned. In the 10th minute Preston took an early lead. Kendall and Lawton exchanged passes in the centre of the pitch before releasing Alex Dawson to shoot from the edge of the area. The usually reliable Jim Standen fumbled the shot and outside-left Doug Holden was on the ball in a flash to put his side ahead. The hapless West Ham defence turned and stared at each other in disbelief.

Stunned by going behind so soon, the Hammers slowly began to find their feet. Shortly after Preston took the lead, Sissons raced down the left wing, played an exquisite one-two with Byrne before firing a low shot across the helpless Kelly in the Preston goal. It was a wonderful goal for the young winger, who earlier that season had played in the same England youth team as young Kendall.

One each after just 12 minutes! We were heading for a pulsating final. Crucially for the Londoners, late in the first half the mercurial Byrne began to assert his authority in midfield. A cult figure at the club, Byrne is generally regarded as one of the most skilful and influential Hammers of all time. Surprisingly for such a confident, even cocky, individual Byrne made a nervous start to the final, repeatedly giving the ball away at crucial moments. But slowly, the Hammers' no. 9 began to assert his authority. He went close to giving his side the lead before laying on a good chance for Hurst who, uncharacteristically, placed his header wide. Betraying his strong traditionalist instincts, TV commentator Kenneth Wolstenholme continually referred to Byrne as, 'the Hammers' deeply-lying centre-forward' and repeatedly questioned why 'Byrne needed to play all over the pitch'. For Greenwood, of course, *Budgie* was his very own Ferenc Puskas.

Despite a period of intense West Ham pressure midway through the first half, Preston were always in the game and began taking control again as half-time approached. The northerners also had two decent penalty appeals turned by referee Arthur Holland. With the West Ham fans looking forward to the interval and their Bovril and hotdogs, Preston took the lead for the second time. Hammers' 'keeper, Standen, and centre-half Ken Brown got into a terrible tangle trying to deal with a corner and burly centre-forward Alex Dawson was quick to take advantage, directing a downward header into the net. For the second time in the first half the favourites found themselves a goal behind.

The claret and blue section of the crowd were in shock. Unsure with the system, the players looked confused and continually gave the ball away. The worst culprits were the two full-backs, Bond and Burkett, who were being given a torrid time by the Preston wingers, Holden and Wilson. Hammers' fans could be forgiven for thinking that John Bond had received strict instructions before the game to hoof the ball upfield as far as possible in the general direction of Geoff Hurst. Each time Bond launched one of his missiles Preston regained possession. This was not the exciting West Ham philosophy of football Ron Greenwood had promised the fans. Bond's contribution would have looked more at home on Hackney Marshes than Wembley Stadium.

The West Ham fans had been unusually quiet throughout the first period as Preston took charge with their strong tackling and command of the midfield. It was not until the last few minutes of the half that we began to hear Bubbles ring out across Wembley Stadium, as the East End fans tried to rouse their floundering side. Given Preston's dominance, Greenwood would have been relieved to go in at half-time only 2-1 down.

The interval gave the manager an opportunity to make some tactical changes. As Bobby Moore said in his interview after the game,

'... we were playing too deep and being over-run in midfield – we had a chat about it at half-time, we were giving them too much space.'

In the second-half, with Moore playing a more advanced role and Byrne much closer to Hurst, the Hammers began to play. They were quicker to the ball, pressed the opposition higher up the pitch and took control. A rejuvenated Byrne was at the heart of their best moves. Moore began to dominate in his own imperious way – surging upfield and threading some delightful through balls to Hurst.

Early in the second period Byrne hit a venomous drive straight into a sensitive area of Tony Singleton's anatomy. Following treatment, the Preston centre-half recovered but was helpless to stop the Hammers' equaliser. Hurst levelled the scores with a header in circumstances which were oddly similar to his controversial goal in the World Cup Final two years later. Hurst's header hit the underside of the bar, rebounded from the back of Kelly's head and trickled over the line. Frustrating for Preston and not vintage Hurst, but his goal brought the scores level. Now West Ham went for the jugular and for the next 20 minutes played the best football of the match threatening to over-run the Preston defence.

Bovington, Sissons and Hurst all went close as the Hammers piled on the pressure. But, as is often the case in football, if a team fails to score when they are on top, they run out of ideas and let their hard-won advantage slip. Throughout the match Preston winger Dave Wilson ran at Jack Burkett, leaving him for dead several times. The watching John Lyall could be forgiven a rueful smile as he watched the West Ham full-backs struggling to come to terms with their clever opponents. Late in the game Wilson beat Burkett on two occasions, sending in accurate crosses towards the dangerous Dawson, both of which the Lillywhites centre-forward directed high over the bar.

The game looked to be heading for extra-time as both sets of players began to wilt. The previously influential Byrne now looked weary in the heavy conditions, while his midfield colleague Eddie Bovington was suffering from an attack of the notorious Wembley cramps. Despite showing clear signs of tiredness the Hammers surged forward in search of the winning goal, leaving huge gaps in their defence, which Preston failed to exploit. In what was becoming a titanic encounter, both sets of players hurled themselves at each other in the attempt to score the winning goal. In the 85th minute Kelly, the Preston 'keeper fell awkwardly and injured his back. Play was held up, but Kelly soon recovered, following liberal use of what the BBC commentator quaintly referred to as, 'embrocation'. At the end of 90 minutes the referee signalled two minutes injury-time.

As the seconds ticked by Preston looked the most likely side to lift the trophy, when, as every West Ham supporter knew he would, Bobby Moore intervened to turn the game. The skipper broke up another Preston attack and knocked a 30 yard ball to Hurst in the inside-left channel. Receiving Moore's accurate pass, the Hammers' no. 10 brilliantly turned Singleton and slipped the ball out to Brabrook, who was free out on the right wing.

In a flash the Hammers' winger whipped over a cross to the far post where, *Ticker* Boyce, repeating his semi-final heroics, arrived with perfect timing to nod the ball past Kelly and into the net. In the 92nd minute, on a churned up pitch, the inside-forward had run the length of the field to meet Brabrook's cross. Ronnie Boyce was a hugely popular figure at the Boleyn and it was appropriate that he scored the winner for his beloved Hammers. In truth Ticker had redeemed himself in the final seconds of the match. As he admitted in a post-match interview, he had been ineffective most of the afternoon. But the supporters loved Boycey and couldn't care less if he had had a quiet game. Their hero's goal had won the FA Cup for West Ham.

As Bobby Moore climbed the steps to the Royal Box to receive the FA Cup, Bubbles soared to a crescendo it hadn't reached in 100 years. In a lovely moment John Sissons took time out from his celebrations to commiserate with his England Youth captain, Howard Kendall. On the team's lap of honour we caught a glimpse of John Lyall, with his arm round Bobby Moore, congratulating his old friend on his triumph. The East Enders had won the FA Cup for the first time and were about to begin the most glorious chapter in their long history. Celebrations went on long into the night and the following morning in the pubs and streets of East London. The '60s were a good time to be a West Ham supporter.

Preston and their fans were inconsolable. They had dominated the match for long periods and lost in the cruellest manner – seconds before the final whistle. But they had played their part in one of the most dramatic matches in the history of the competition. That evening Ron Greenwood and his staff would have pondered why, after their commanding performance in the semi-final, did their team struggle to defeat a mid-table 2nd Division side in a Wembley final? There is a narrow margin between victory and defeat and Greenwood knew the result could have gone either way. That evening the West Ham manager slept with the FA Cup under his bed in his room at the Hilton Hotel. He knew his side had underperformed on the day, but had still managed to achieve a famous victory. West Ham had won the Cup against stubborn opposition and in so doing had qualified for Europe. The Greenwood adventure was underway and for once West Ham's bubbles didn't fade and die. But, perhaps oddly, the perfectionist Greenwood would have been concerned by the manner of his team's victory – even as his first trophy lay safely under his hotel bed. He knew there was still work to do.

In his autobiography, Greenwood provided us with an insight into his character. He revealed, *'when I led West Ham out in 1964, I felt no emotion at all. I was just doing my job.'*

This is an odd thing for a manager after to say as he looked back on one of the highlights of his career. It was this perceived emotional frigidity that eventually brought him into conflict with some of his players, not least the greatest of them all, Bobby Moore. But that was for future – for now Hammers supporters could enjoy the moment.

Back at the Office
The week following the historic FA Cup Final win over Preston, John Lyall returned to Upton Park and got on quietly with his new job as youth team manager, using every opportunity to watch and observe his boss in action. Unable to play or train John filled his week helping Mrs Moss with the wages, doing a bit of coaching at Stepney School and organising with the youth team. West Ham encouraged their apprentices to go into local schools in their spare time. Former club apprentice Tony Carr, now the distinguished director of the club's renowned Youth Academy, remembers that West Ham paid their young players £2 extra each afternoon to coach schoolboys. Brothers-in-law, Trevor Hartley and Bobby Howe enjoyed going into schools, Hartley recalled:

'Instead of playing golf in the afternoons, we'd coach in the schools. Ron also thought it was good for the young players to be learning how to talk to people, communicate and gain confidence.'

Howe added,

'...the people at Ashburton School in Whitechapel once contacted Ron and asked if any of his players would be interested in going back there to run the PE Department in the summer...so Trevor and I took over the whole show...teaching football, cricket and other games we invented. After Trevor went back to Holloway School, Clyde Best joined us at Ashburton.'

It is no coincidence that Carr, Hartley, Howe and Best all went on to enjoy successful coaching careers. It's difficult to imagine today's pampered Premier League footballers giving up their free time to coach local schoolchildren on a daily basis, but Greenwood believed the experience made his young players think about their football. When asked by one nervous apprentice what he should do with 30 lively 15-year-olds for an hour, Greenwood replied, "Teach them what we teach you here at the club – take them through the same routines and practices." Roger Cross, another successful coach from the Upton Park academy, trained a local Sunday side on Hackney Marshes and appreciated the experience it provided. Coaching in schools and local clubs made these young players think more deeply about the game. Greenwood also believed it was as important for the club's youngsters to develop as decent, well-mannered people who could communicate easily with others, as it was for them to become good footballers. Going into schools built self-confidence and self-assurance.

The keen and enthusiastic John Lyall certainly benefited from his coaching work in Stepney and reacted well to the responsibility. Gradually he began to recover from the mental scars that his career-ending knee injury must have left. Lyall, still only 24-years-old, impressed his employers with his commitment and hard work. He learned an immense amount about coaching from club trainer Bill Robinson and fully embraced the Cassetari café culture. In addition to Robinson, Lyall loved working alongside great clubmen like Eddie Bailey, Ernie Gregory, Albert Walker, Tony Carr, Jim Frith and Bill and Rob Jenkins. A bright young man, Lyall watched and listened. He began to appreciate the value of a football club's backroom staff. Deprived of his first love of playing, he threw himself into his work, aware that he was receiving a brilliant football education. Lyall was at Wembley with the coaching staff for the victory over Preston and was to take up a similar position the following season – this time for the final of the European Cup Winners' Cup. It would be difficult to imagine a better learning environment for a keen young coach.

European Night of Glory!
If the '64 FA Cup Final was a wonderful learning opportunity for Lyall, the Hammers' European campaign the following season was a coaching PhD. Ron Greenwood continued to hold Lyall in special regard and involved him in the European experience as much he could. Greenwood again sent Lyall to watch opponents and involved him in discussions about tactics and training. The manager knew that participation in a major European competition was an extraordinary educational experience for himself, his players and all his backroom staff.

In May 1965 West Ham United stood on the brink of creating history as the club prepared for the final of the European Cup Winners' Cup. The '60 were very early days for British teams in Europe, although Tottenham had won the Cup Winners' Cup in Rotterdam in 1963. This was a good time for English football, in addition to the Hammers' achievement, the national side had a good year and Liverpool came close to making their own European final. But expectations at Upton Park were not particularly high as the Hammers fans wondered quite what to make of their European adventure, but it was a cup competition and that, for West Ham, meant anything was possible.

The club had its best group of players for many years including Johnny Byrne, Ken Brown, Ronnie Boyce, John Sissons, Alan Sealey, Jim Standen, and of course, their three great World Cup heroes, Moore, Hurst and Peters. And at last their League form improved. Greenwood's men finished the 1964/65 season in an encouraging 9th place behind champions Manchester United.

Despite their FA Cup triumph and improved League form, the Hammers failed to capture the public imagination. As Ken Jones pointed out in his Mirror piece on the morning of the Cup Winners' Cup final, the club's achievements were largely ignored outside East London. They had been labelled as a talented team, lacking the character to dominate domestic competitions. But Jones maintained the Hammers' football was fashioned for European success and the side's temperament had been steeled by a tough campaign that season.

Jones wrote: 'I believe West Ham will win it... and convince the doubters of their greatness.'

The Cup Winners' Cup was second only to the European Cup in terms of prestige and this was the biggest club game that Wembley had hosted. The match was also significant for being the first time the BBC had shown a live broadcast of an English club playing in a European final. Here was the perfect opportunity for Greenwood and his talented team to show the world their poor performance against Preston the previous season was an aberration. In truth, that patchy performance was simply part of Greenwood's learning curve as a manager. He would have pondered endlessly on the effectiveness of his tactics for the '64 FA Cup Final. This time he was determined to get it right.

The 1965 Cup Winners' Cup final between West Ham United and TSV Munich 1860 is said to have been the greatest European club final of all time. Greenwood was confident his team would bring their A game to Wembley that evening. The Germans finished 3rd in the Bundesliga a few weeks before the match and were always going to present a real test. The claret and blue hordes in the great stadium were reassured by the sight of their captain, Bobby Moore, confident as ever, leading his team out alongside his manager. In front of a fiercely partisan crowd of 97,974, the Hammers were the first to settle, employing their quick passing style with a fluency and freedom that the Germans struggled to match. Moore's men began at a furious pace pinning the Germans back in their own half for long periods.

With just a few minutes on the clock John Sissons, infuriatingly for the home fans, missed a sitter from three yards, while 'keeper

Radenkovic, arguably the best goalkeeper of his generation, made brilliant saves from Brian Dear and Alan Sealey. The Hammers were at their irresistible best, although Munich had their moments in a breathtaking encounter. Both sides missed good chances in the first half, but at the interval the score remained stubbornly level at 0-0. As the players left the field for a well-earned break, all sides of the ground rose to their feet to applaud. Greenwood's half-time message to his players was short and simple – more of the same please.

The second-half began at the same blistering pace. You could not take your eyes of the action. Dear went close again, while Sissons was desperately unlucky to hit a post. The young winger was all over the pitch, one minute going past defenders down the left or linking up with Dear and Hurst down the middle. At the other end, Jim Standen needed to be alert as the Germans broke dangerously, Kruppers and Grosser both stretching the Hammers' 'keeper.

Gradually, the Londoner's more incisive passing began to take its toll, as Munich's defence struggled to resist their opponents penetrating attacks. In the 70th minute, just when both teams were considering the prospect of extra-time, the Hammers broke the stalemate. The persistent Ronnie Boyce threaded an inch perfect pass through the Munich defence to Sealey. Receiving the ball just inside the penalty area, the Hammers' no. 7 crashed a first-time shot past the Munich 'keeper high into the net. His spontaneous somersault perfectly expressed the sheer joy he felt scoring his side's first goal in a European final. The Hammers had taken the lead – could they hang on?

Two minutes later as the Hungarian referee called for the floodlights to be switched on, they answered the question. The Hammers were awarded a free-kick deep into the German half. In a move straight from the training ground, Hurst shaped to hit a shot, ran over the ball allowing Moore the space to cross into the German's penalty area. The Munich defence panicked and failed to deal with Moore's accurate centre. Sealey seized on the loose ball and drove it into the net from six yards out, sealing the match for his team. The noisy claret and blue section of the crowd began to relax as Bubbles resounded around Wembley for the second time in just over 12 months.

Ken Jones' judgement was vindicated. The victory earned the Hammers praise across Europe and took the club to a new level. In front of a record Wembley crowd and an estimated 30 million TV viewers worldwide, West Ham became only the second English club side to win a European trophy. Ron Greenwood was congratulated for the way his team approached the game and for the sheer quality of their football. This time the West Ham manager had got his tactics right and his team rose to the occasion brilliantly.

Alan *Sammy* Sealey was Greenwood's trump card that evening. A local lad from Canning Town, Sealey was not the most skilful member on the West Ham playing staff, but on that May evening he was the match winner. Throughout the final he was a danger to the German defence, while finding the energy to track back and help out Joe Kirkup whenever he could. Sammy was an unlikely hero. Aged just 23, his two-goals inside three minutes secured the trophy and put West Ham on the European map. 1965 brought mixed fortune for the young winger; apart from his historic Wembley brace he scored just three goals that season. Sammy got married shortly after the Wembley victory, with Bobby Moore as best man at his wedding. They were such good friends that the Moores even accompanied the newlyweds on their honeymoon. Everybody at the club, especially the fans, was delighted at Sealey's success in the most important game in the club's history.

But a summer that promised so much for the winger ended in tragedy when he broke a leg in a freak accident during an impromptu cricket match at the club's training ground. Like John Lyall, Bobby Moore and Geoff Hurst, Sealey was a decent club cricketer. He struggled to recover from the accident and missed the whole of the following season, in which West Ham reached the semi-finals of the Cup Winners Cup and final of the League Cup. He was to play just four more League games for the Hammers before moving to Plymouth Argyle and ending his playing days at non-League Romford. Alan Sealey died in 1996 at the tragically young age of 53. The club responded by staging an emotional minute's silence before an FA cup tie against Grimsby at Upton

Park and Alan's wife, Barbara was guest of honour at the club's 40th anniversary reunion held to commemorate the Hammers' great European victory of 1965.

If Sealey grabbed the headlines, two other players deserve a special mention for their contribution to the 1964/65 European campaign. Ronnie Boyce was West Ham through and through. A Plaistow boy, he made 342 appearances for the Hammers during the club's most successful seasons. Nicknamed *Ticker* because of his ability to keep things ticking over in midfield, Boyce allowed the likes of Peters, Byrne, Sissons, and later Trevor Brooking, the freedom to get forward and support the attack. Not a regular goalscorer, Hammers fans will never forget Boyce's winning goal in the FA Cup Final against Preston in 1964 and his two goals against Manchester United in the semi-final.

After joining the club as an apprentice in 1959, Boyce played his last game for the Hammers against Leicester City in 1972. He was a key member of the West Ham side in their glory years, and worked as coach under John Lyall in the Cup Final victories over Fulham in 1975 and Arsenal in 1980. Boyce was also assistant to former teammate Billy Bonds at Upton Park, before being appointed chief scout, a position he held until his retirement in 1995. Ronnie Boyce has a special place in the collective memory of Hammers' supporters and is a true Hammers legend – he certainly played a key part in the final against Munich, redeeming his disappointing Wembley performance the previous year.

Johnny *Budgie* Byrne missed out on the 1965 European Cup Winners' Cup after playing a crucial part in the previous rounds. Byrne was the team's metronome and set the tempo for his teammates. He was the pivot for the fast, free-flowing passing game encouraged by Ron Greenwood, and later John Lyall. Unlike Boyce and Sealey, Byrne was not a local lad, being born across the river in Surrey. He earned the nickname *Budgie* because of his non-stop chatter and bubbly personality.

So keen was Greenwood to sign Byrne, who had struck up a good understanding with Moore in the England Under-23 side, that he was prepared to throw Geoff Hurst in as makeweight for the Palace star forward. A few years later the whole of England had good reason to thank Crystal Palace for turning down the opportunity to sign the only player ever to score a hat-trick in a World Cup final. The faithful Hurst was given a specific brief to take the physical weight off Byrne's shoulders. Ironically, the move paid off for Hurst more than it did for Byrne. But the partnership did reap immediate benefits, turning West Ham from a moderate, if skilful side, to real contenders in all the major competitions, including Europe.

Byrne saved some of his best moments for the 1964 FA Cup Final in which his clever movement, subtle passing and delicate touches gave the Hammers the edge. His inch perfect return pass to John Sissons enabled the young winger to score the decisive goal, was a perfect example of his vision and quick thinking. Johnny Byrne had everything. Superb technique on a Brazilian scale, acute tactical awareness, and was a natural goalscorer. He enjoyed an extended run in the England side, but fell foul of Alf Ramsey's strict discipline. An England side containing Greaves, Moore and Johnny Byrne was always bound to push the boundaries a little.

Budgie Byrne played with a swagger and as a footballer he ranked up alongside the greats. It would be kind to say that the awful effects of his injury sustained playing for England shortened what should have been a glittering career. Sadly, that's only partly accurate, for as Greenwood believed, 'he was his own worst enemy,' but he remains a true West Ham hero and his play lit up Upton Park during the mid-1960s. Johnny Byrne died of a heart attack in South Africa in 1999 aged 61. For players like Byrne, Kirkup, Burkett, Sealey and Boyce, the Munich game was the undoubted highlight of their careers.

Greenwood would have been delighted by the way in which his team's magnificent performance against Munich was greeted by the press. Legendary sports journalist JL Manning wrote,

'... it was not only a European Cup for West Ham but the best football match I have seen at Wembley since the stadium opened 42 years ago.'

In an observation that would have delighted Greenwood,

Kenneth Wostenholme noted, 'West Ham put a lot of thought into their football'. The BBC commentator was referring to the team's quick use of the ball, and just as important, their constant movement off the ball. The Hammers' captain, about whom Wolstenholme perceptively observed in his commentary, 'this man lives for his football', remembered this moment in the club's history with typical understatement:

> *We benefited from the experience of the previous year and took part in what many people believe was one of the best matches ever played at the old stadium. There was a lot of good football and we played really well against a good side with a lot of good players. We felt lucky to get the chance of satisfaction at Wembley so soon after the FA Cup Final.'*

West Ham's victory over Munich was the highlight of Ron Greenwood's managerial career and he admitted his special debt to his captain with untypical clarity:

> *This was Bobby Moore's greatest game for West Ham. Technical perfection.'*

The normally reserved Hammers manager was clearly proud of his team's performance. "The match," he said, "exceeded my wildest hopes."

Why did the team that disappointed against Preston look so good the following year? For this observer the reasons for the improvement were clear. Firstly, the defence pressed the Germans higher up the field, allowing Moore to join Boyce and Peters at every opportunity. Secondly, Greenwood had set the team up differently from the Preston match. Wingers Sissons and Sealey were always in the game, coming deep or surging past their respective full-backs. In a master-stroke, which John Lyall was to repeat in the 1980 FA Cup Final, Greenwood asked Geoff Hurst to drop deep in the manner of the absent Johnnie Byrne? The ploy often left Dear upfield on his own but as Greenwood anticipated, Dear with his selfless running, was big and strong enough to handle the Munich defence on his own. The team played as a free-flowing unit. It was breathtaking football and the perfect illustration of the beautiful game in action. The 1965 European Cup Winners' Cup Final was the ultimate expression of the West Ham way in action, against which all future Hammers sides would be judged. John Lyall argued later, "The FA should show the video of the '65 Cup Winners' Cup final to coaches and everyone in football."

One of the major differences between the Preston and Munich performances was the performance of Martin Peters. Missing against Preston, the young midfielder was involved in most of his side's best moments and released goalscorer Sealey time and time again. Peters' Wembley display was a tribute to his increased maturity and the technical insight of the club's coaching staff. The principle feature of the elegant Peters' game was his ability to drift into the opponent's penalty area to score vital goals, as he did in the World Cup Final in 1966. Against Munich, Peters repeatedly opened up his body to receive forward passes from Boyce and Moore. The Hammers' no. 4 then allowed the ball to run ahead for him a few yards before taking a touch. This gave this most elegant of midfield players both time and space to look up and think about his options. Should he lay the ball off wide to Sealey, slide a pass through to Hurst or Dear or simply take it forward a few paces?

Both Greenwood and Lyall understood the need for players to think about angles. Lyall emphasised to his midfield players the need to 'get on the half-turn to receive the ball'. Brooking and Alan Devonshire later perfected this skill both for their club and for England. This kind of simple technical information was devastatingly effective at West Ham. In later years Trevor Brooking and the young Frank Lampard continued West Ham's tradition of producing goal-scoring midfield players in the manner of Martin Peters. John Lyall knew that Greenwood was not only interested in team tactics, but understood the importance of working on individual skills. It was another lesson he learnt from the master.

We should not underestimate the excitement generated by the joyous football on show that spring night back in the mid-'60s. The team's performance against the Germans suddenly made West Ham everybody's second favourite team. The Hammers' centre-half against Munich was the redoubtable Ken Brown. Years later he reflected eloquently on the match and what it meant for the players involved:

'It was an advert for the way the game should be played. There was no diving or feigning injury, players on both sides just got up and got on with the game.'

Brown also talked about the manager's psychological approach with his players:

'I was never good enough for Ron. I don't think he thought I could play. Perhaps this was Ron's way of geeing me up. I wanted to learn. Ted Fenton was the fitness man and gave us the basis but when Ron came in he had the ideas. People today should watch the Munich game – watch and learn about how the game should be played.'

Greenwood and his coaching staff were fortunate in that this group of players needed no special motivation. Individuals like Moore, Hurst, Peters and Brown felt a genuine pride in the quality of their football and a real joy in playing, as Wolstenholme alluded to in his comments on the Hammers' skipper. The European Cup Winners' Cup victory over Munich remains the greatest moment in the history of West Ham United. As Moore climbed the 39 steps at Wembley to collect his second trophy inside 12 months, he would not have believed that in the following season he would back up those steps to collect the greatest prize in football.

On that glorious May evening the claret and blue planets were in perfect alignment as the Hammers achieved their destiny and produced their greatest ever performance. On that wonderful spring evening in 1965, the watching John Lyall's coaching education took a huge leap forward. For the record, the West Ham team against Munich was: Standen, Kirkup, Brown, Moore (c), Burkett, Sealey, Peters, Boyce, Sissons, Dear and Hurst.

Chapter 5
Learning from the master

When the Cup Winners' Cup celebrations finally died down, Greenwood, his staff and the players returned to some resemblance of normality. John Lyall, with the experience of two Wembley finals under his belt, couldn't wait for the new season to begin. The club were so impressed by the hard work and enthusiasm of their youth team manager that, in 1967, they offered him the job on a full-time basis. Lyall spent the next few years learning his trade under the expert tutelage of Ron Greenwood. As Yvonne Lyall testifies, John idolised Greenwood, who could do no wrong in the young man's eyes:

'He worshipped Ron and hung on his every word.'

Shortly after his appointment as successor to Ted Fenton, Greenwood, sensing the Lyalls were concerned about their future following John's enforced retirement, quietly assured Yvonne, "don't worry, we will look after you." The new manager was as good as his word as he undertook the role of John's friend and mentor.

Lyall blossomed as a coach under Greenwood, contributing to his mentor's tactical ideas like the famous near-post cross, richly exploited by Geoff Hurst in the 1966 World Cup. Martin Peters' signature drifting role behind Hurst and Clyde Best, forged on the training ground at Chadwell Heath, brought the England midfield star a hatful of goals. Now a full-time member of Greenwood's coaching team, Lyall was now at the centre of the West Ham Academy. His determination to overcome the disappointment of a career-ending injury was a testament to his resolve and courage – a point not lost on his manager.

The club's 9th place finish in the 1st Division in their European-conquering season was stratospheric by West Ham standards. The following season they set about defending their European trophy, while Greenwood was determined to improve the club's mid-table mediocrity. The Hammers reached the semi-final of the European Cup Winners' Cup but fell to Borussia Dortmund 2-5 on aggregate. Greenwood's team also reached the semi-final of the old League Cup losing to West Bromwich Albion 3-5 over the two games. As to be expected there were setbacks. A serious injury to Johnny Byrne meant they lost a key player for nearly half of the season. The defence failed to reach the high standards they set against Munich TSV, conceding a worrying 83 goals in the 1st Division, the principle reason for their 12th place League finish. But it was always going to be difficult for Greenwood's side to live up to the fans' expectation, following two brilliantly successful years. Today's Hammers' fans can only dream of two semi-finals and a mid-table position in the same season.

The late '60s usually found West Ham hovering above relegation at the end of each season. There were some highlights. The Hammers scored 17 goals in a single week during November 1966, and at the end of that year were involved in a spectacular 5-5 draw with Chelsea at Stamford Bridge. In the same season Johnny Byrne was sold back to Crystal Palace and Ken Brown to Torquay United, as the manager began to dismantle the great side of 1964/65. The youngster who Greenwood earmarked as Byrne's replacement, Trevor Brooking, made his first team debut in 1967 in a 3-3 draw against Burnley. Interestingly, the scorers that day at Turf Moor were England's World Cup heroes, Hurst, Moore and Peters. In an attempt to further attempt to reinforce his squad, Greenwood acquired a new group of players, often with mixed results.

In came Billy Bonds from Charlton Athletic, John Cushley from Celtic, Bobby Ferguson from Kilmarnock and Alan Stephenson from Crystal Palace. Other players left the club. Dennis Burnett was sold to Millwall and the '65 Wembley hero, Alan Sealey left for Plymouth Argyle. An enduring feature of the late '60s at the Boleyn was Geoff Hurst's goal-scoring heroics, as the Hammers' no. 10 grew in stature every season. More disappointingly, the period continued to involve speculation regarding the manager's continuing feud with his great captain, Bobby Moore, who became the subject of increased transfer speculation at this time.

West Ham fans were only too aware that their most successful player and manager did not enjoy a happy relationship – Moore and Greenwood simply did not get on. The complicated relationship between the two men festered for years and they never enjoyed the close connection that John Lyall later had with his skipper, Billy Bonds. You cannot imagine Greenwood inviting Moore into his office on Friday afternoons to discuss the team and tactics for the following day's match, as Lyall did regularly with Bonds.

The frustration on Moore's part ran deep. He believed that Greenwood simply did not have the motivational skills and sheer determination necessary to be a successful as well as a principled manager. Greenwood's insensitivity often offended Moore. When asked if he was sorry to see the former England captain leave the club. Greenwood answered coldly, "I'm sorry when all players leave the club."

Moore's frustration lay in his belief that the Hammers had a terrific group of players at this time, most of who were born locally. This team was good enough to win the League Championship, argued the Upton Park legend. If Greenwood was prepared to sign one or two exceptional players to strengthen the side, we could push on to greater things. Oddly, Moore urged Greenwood to sign the aggressive, but limited Maurice Setters to bring some much-needed grit to the Hammers' fragile defence. Understandably, the manager thought he knew better.

Ironically, Moore believed that nobody had more knowledge about football than Greenwood and despite their deep differences they usually presented a united front. After all, Moore could not deny his manager's achievements in the FA Cup and in Europe. But the Hammers' considerable, if limited achievements and their purist reputation, were simply not enough for the ambitious England skipper. Moore wanted a 1st Division championship medal and he was unlikely to achieve his ambition with Greenwood's West Ham. Strangely, a further nine years slipped away following the FA Cup Winners' Cup triumph in 1965, before Moore finally left Upton Park.

These were years in which West Ham as a club began to lose its way. Greenwood's complex football brain failed to adjust his famed quick passing philosophy to meet the demands of the modern game's emphasis on hard tackling, uncompromising defence and direct tactics. This complex and decent man, a practising Christian, could not compromise, made poor signings and despised the thuggery and violence into which his beloved football descended in the 1970s, both on and off the field.

The highpoint of the late '60s at Upton Park was when the Hammers' finished the 1968/69 campaign in an encouraging 8th place in the 1st Division. The highlight of the season was the 8-0 win against Sunderland, with a rampant Hurst treating the Upton Park crowd to an astonishing six goals. But the following season ended in disappointment with early exits from both cup competitions and a lowly League position. As we reached the end of the decade – a truly outstanding ten years for West Ham supporters – there were signs that Ron Greenwood was beginning to question his ability to continue to get the best out of his players. Bringing an ageing and troubled Jimmy Greaves from Tottenham seemed to be the action of a desperate man, while the sale of Martin Peters in the opposite direction was a clear sign that something was not quite right at the Boleyn. Peters left following a protracted quarrel with Greenwood over his future at the club. His spat with one of the club's greatest ever players was a further sign of the manager's inability to deal with top international footballers – first Moore, now Peters.

The club had failed to progress following their Munich triumph in the way many expected and Moore and Peters, in their different ways, both criticised their manager's lack of ambition and poor man-management. It was a criticism that was to haunt Greenwood for the remainder of his time at the club. Peters's replacement, Peter Eustace, good player that he was, found the England man an extremely hard act to follow. Greenwood had better luck with Billy Bonds who proved an inspired signing. Bonds' partnership with the brilliant Brooking was to prove a key feature of the West Ham side of the late 1970s and '80s.

Beer, Blackpool and Brian London

In January 1971, Bobby Moore, Jimmy Greaves, Clyde Best and members of the club's coaching staff were seen enjoying themselves in a Blackpool night club on the eve of a tricky 3rd Round FA cuptie. The well-documented incident proved the writing on the wall for one of the most successful manager/captain relationships in the history of English club football. Much to the disgust of the travelling fans, the Hammers suffered a humiliating 4-0 defeat at Bloomfield Road the following day. It was not the club's finest hour.

In the aftermath of the Blackpool incident, Greenwood's side just managed to escape relegation, finishing a massive 30 points behind champions, Arsenal. It was one of the most depressing seasons in the club's long and distinguished history. Arnold Hills, the founder of the Thames Ironworks FC and his manager, Syd King would have been appalled by the events of 1970/71. It was time for everyone at the club to take a long hard look at themselves.

Greenwood shuffled his pack again. Another of the Wembley heroes, Johnny Sissons, left for Sheffield Wednesday and Jimmy Greaves' brief encounter with West Ham ended with little credit on either side. More promisingly, centre-half Tommy Taylor came in from neighbours Leyton Orient and one of Greenwood's best ever signings, Bryan *Pop* Robson arrived from Newcastle.

As Geoff Hurst's astonishing powers began to fade – the normally reliable Hurst scored just 14 goals in 39 appearances in 1970/71, and only eight the following season. Clyde Best proved a willing partner for Hurst but could not be expected to match the goal-scoring record of one of the greats of post-war football. Hurst was always going to be a hard act to follow and the Hammers scored a paltry 47 league goals in the 1971/72 season. Greenwood was a highly intelligent and a ruthlessly honest individual – he knew that something needed to be done to stop the slide. When he invited John Lyall to become his assistant manager in 1971 the appointment hardly registered as a seismic event at Upton Park. Neither the players nor the fans would have seen Lyall's promotion from youth team coach to assistant manager as anything other than a shift around of personnel. But Greenwood had prepared Lyall for this day and knew exactly what he was doing.

Into a new era
Ron Greenwood's difficulties with Moore and Peters did raise serious questions about Greenwood's management style. Ken Brown, for one, felt unappreciated by his manager,
'I don't remember receiving any praise from him, and I don't think he was particularly happy with me.'

An encouraging word, an arm around the shoulder in the manner of Harry Redknapp, would have helped Brown's confidence. We know that Bobby Moore respected Greenwood and his ideas, but at the same time felt his boss was distant and aloof. In a quote from his biography, Moore describes how he thought Greenwood mishandled one his best signings, *Pop* Robson:

'His best buy was Pop Robson... and he should never have let him go... he should have told him he was the greatest in the world... that's all Pop needed. A boost... You could never go to Ron for inspiration.'

The evidence against Greenwood began to mount in the years following their spectacular Wembley triumphs in the early '60s. Greenwood's ideas on man-management were built on the concept of mutual respect. He simply assumed that players would always do the right thing. He wrote:

'I was always 'Ron' to my players, rather than the 'Boss', because that was the kind of relationship I wanted. I did not want to force anything on them. Respect is not something a manager can demand or expect...'

What Greenwood saw as a mature and democratic philosophy of leadership, others saw as weakness. Johnny Byrne admitted players took advantage of their manager's refusal to 'crack the whip', either in training or after a match. Others, like the much-respected Ken Brown wanted a more physical approach to training – more fitness work. Brown admitted he often went for a long run after training because Greenwood's sessions focused on technique rather than building up fitness. Despite their differences, Brown, Moore, Peters and the rest of the players had absolute respect for their manager – this was the great irony at West Ham in the Greenwood era.

Greenwood's weaknesses as a manager stemmed from his naivety about professional footballers. He expected them to be self-motivated, as passionate about the game as he was, and have pride in their profession. The Hammers' boss encouraged his players to be independent young men who could hold their heads up in the local community. The Blackpool incident shattered his belief in professional footballers and deeply wounded this highly sensitive man. Despite the manager's obvious disappointment, Moore didn't see what all the fuss was about and was sickened by Greenwood's handling of the affair. Brian Dear was more contrite, as he revealed a few years after the event:

'I knew I'd let Ron down, more than myself, which, over the years, has hurt me quite a bit. He had nothing to do with me after that. I knew I'd never play for him again.'

The last straw for the proud manager was the sight of GREENWOOD OUT banners on the North Bank, following Moore's suspension after the Blackpool high jinks. His absence from the side coincided with three successive defeats and when the skipper returned for the home match against Derby County, he was named as substitute. Some of us will never forget the sight of the illustrious Moore, dignity intact, warming up on the touchline before replacing young Bobby Howe. But even the appearance of the Hammers' great no. 6 could not prevent his side going down to another humiliating defeat. A lonely and isolated Greenwood had both a hostile crowd and several of his key players turning against him. He needed to act, as Tony McDonald points out:

'The beleaguered Greenwood needed help, more reinforcements on and off the field, and he soon found them.'

One of Greenwood's faults was he trusted people too much – it was a laudable quality in a decent man, but one alien to the increasingly commercial world of professional football. In the fantasy football world of today's Premier League, a manager presides over a small troop of assistants – defence and attack coaches, goalkeeping coaches, translators, full-time sports' scientists and physiotherapists. Perhaps the most effective managerial duo in football was Clough and Taylor at Derby and Nottingham Forest, but previously Ron Greenwood had never seen the need for an assistant. But he was brave enough to change his mind. In 1971 Greenwood turned to John Lyall for help.

Perhaps Lyall's promotion should have come earlier as Alan Stephenson pointed out:

'I think he needed someone like John Lyall, who was coaching the youth team when I first went there, to work alongside him as his assistant, to provide a link between the manager and the players, earlier than he did.'

Here is a perfect summary of Lyall's new job description. For Stephenson, it was clear Greenwood needed help:

'I think that was the reason for the demise of West Ham at that... time. The talent was there... but it just needed to be co-ordinated better. We had three World Cup winners but those players needed help as well. At the end of the day, it's a team game.'

Did John Lyall possess the motivational and man-management skills to complement the technical acumen of the cerebral Greenwood? The West Ham manager certainly thought so. In a recent interview, Terry Venables suggested that Lyall had an advantage over other coaches of his generation. Venables argued that Lyall was able to turn misfortune to advantage by having the opportunity to work under one of the most profound and innovative thinkers in world football. Working under Greenwood for ten years, before he was appointed Assistant Manager in 1971, meant that Lyall was effectively ten years ahead of other coaches and managers of his age. Venables had great respect for Lyall as a coach and invited him to join his coaching team at Tottenham in 1989. Perhaps Lyall was fortunate to have enjoyed a long apprenticeship at the West Ham Academy, but he certainly made the most of his opportunity. Greenwood was no fool and knew he had promoted the right man.

John Lyall had been coaching at different levels since the age of 16. He had a sharp football brain and a tremendous thirst for knowledge. His gradual progression up the Upton Park coaching hierarchy was no accident; there is little doubt that he was being groomed for the top job. We can get a glimpse of what the manager was planning from Lyall's own observations on his promotion:

'Ron would send me to watch players and then surprise me a bit by asking how much I'd give for them in the transfer market, if they ever became available. He never put pressure on me. We would just chat about the game and he'd ask my opinion more and more.'

Lyall had a very traditional upbringing. His parents taught him independence, self-control and the need to treat people with respect. They were values that were nurtured by Greenwood and the West Ham family at this time, as Lyall remembers:

'Whenever I consulted Ron Greenwood or Eddie Chapman about a problem, they always had time for me. Time is the most important thing... if one of your people has a problem, you sit with them until you can work it out... you have to give it the time. That's what West Ham people did – they were always like that.'

Lyall was brought up in the old West Ham tradition and his elevation to Greenwood's number two was well-deserved and timely. Greenwood was a sensitive soul, in spite of his often lofty demeanour. He was singularly unsuited for the hard-headed, money-driven world into which the game was about to descend. Looking back on this time, Greenwood wrote,

'...I had become disenchanted with football. Partly this was of my own making...'

The promotion of Lyall was Greenwood's escape route, but he was protective of his legacy and determined to leave West Ham in the best possible hands. In the meantime there was work to do. The Hammers had narrowly escaped relegation in 1971, suffered the self-inflicted trauma of Blackpool, and had been dumped out of all cup competitions in the early rounds. For the faithful, the glorious years of the mid-'60s must have appeared a distant memory.

Lyall's first season in his new job brought some improvement. A lowly 14th League place was mitigated by reaching the semi-final of the League Cup, losing to Stoke City at Old Trafford in the most dramatic fashion in a second replay. One of the highlights of this epic encounter was Gordon Banks' magnificent reaction save from Geoff Hurst's well-struck penalty. Banks' save will live long in the memory of both Stoke and West Ham fans that were fortunate to witness that dramatic moment first hand. The tie was full of dramatic moments, including the sight of Bobby Moore in the West Ham goal. It was pure football theatre as the skipper donned the green jersey following an injury to Bobby Ferguson.

The team's League Cup heroics that season encouraged Greenwood and Lyall, but they were brought down to earth when they lost 4-2 to Huddersfield Town in the 5th Round of the FA Cup. Despite the disappointment of losing a League Cup semi-final, things began to improve at Upton Park under the new management team. Trevor Brooking had become a regular member of the side and taken over the metronome mantle from *Budgie* Byrne. *Pop* Robson and Clyde Best shared the goals, while John McDowell and Frank Lampard provided strong support for Brooking and Bonds. The new Hammers looked as well-balanced as the team of '65. With young players like Johnny Whippet Ayris and Ade Coker knocking on the first team door, the club and the fans could look forward to the '70s with hope, even expectation.

Further improvement came in 1972/73, despite the customary early cup exits to Hull City in the FA Cup and lowly Stockport County in the League Cup. Greenwood's team fared much better in the League ending the season in an encouraging 6th position behind champions Liverpool. It was the club's highest ever finish in the 1st Division. The year was notable for Bobby Moore winning his 100th England cap and the signing of Ted MacDougall from Manchester United. Out went Harry Redknapp to Bournemouth and the rather unlucky Peter Eustace back to Sheffield Wednesday. Forty-six points seems a meagre total for 6th place, but Greenwood would have been happy to end the season above Tottenham, Manchester United and Chelsea – those were the days!

The following year was marked by Moore's transfer to Fulham following a star-studded 642 League and Cup appearances in which, surprisingly, he scored 27 goals. These few words disguise what was a distressing, even traumatic episode in the club's history, with nobody coming out with much credit. The relationship between Greenwood and his captain became increasingly fraught. First Martin Peters, then the great Moore of the Hammers three World Cup heroes had left the club. On the positive side, Trevor Brooking was awarded his first England cap, while Mick McGiven, Bobby Gould and Graham Paddon, all of whom had a positive impact on the side's performance, arrived at Upton Park. Ted MacDougall left for Norwich City as Greenwood tried to breathe life into his team. Clyde Best and Bonds were the club's joint top scorers in 1973/74 with just 13 League and Cup goals each. How Greenwood must have pined for the exploits of the prolific Hurst and the predatory *Pop* Robson who returned to the north east.

All this coming and going had a negative effect on Greenwood's side as they flirted with relegation before ending the season in an extremely disappointing 18th place. By this stage Greenwood realised it was time to hand over the reins to a younger man, more in touch with the modern game. The match programme for the home game against Sheffield United announced to the fans that John Lyall had been promoted to the position of team manager, while Greenwood had decided to step back from his first team duties to take up the new post of, what would now be called Director of Football. Lyall's time had come. This was no cosy coronation. Greenwood had worked with his young apprentice for over ten years and knew Lyall inside out as he reminded us in his autobiography:

'The time came when I knew he was ready to take over. "You be team manager and I'll become general manager and deal with financial matters... size up players we want to buy..."'

All first team affairs – team selection, tactics and training were now Lyall's responsibility and his alone. Could the man who had spent his professional life in a protected, even cosy, relationship with his manager and the rest of the staff, step up to the huge task of leading a club in the top flight of English football? And with a club whose fans had unreasonably high expectations. Greenwood provided an insight into his relationship with his assistant manager:

'Our relationship was a very good one. John is a strong character with a Scottish background, stable, straight and single-minded. He has a nice, easy manner and I discovered very quickly that he was a person after my own heart. He wanted to know everything about the job but, more than that, he cared passionately about the club and the game.... he cared about people for their own sake.'

Stable, straight and single-minded, Lyall would need these laudable qualities in buckets if he was to make a success of his new role at the top of the club. Greenwood also knew that Lyall was a tougher character than himself and more equipped to deal with the new pressures surrounding professional football in the 1970s. The combination of a caring nature, a natural gift for dealing with people and a strong personality, meant that Lyall was going to manage the club in a very different way to his predecessor, while at the same time holding firmly to the principles of the West Ham way.

Passing on the baton: iron fist in a velvet glove
Greenwood knew his legacy would be safe in the hands of John Lyall. The latter's succession was a handing over of the orchestral baton to a different conductor, a change of key, rather than a

change of tune. When the older man informed the young pretender that he wanted him to take over, Lyall reacted with typical enthusiasm. Greenwood later wrote,

'... a man can stay in a job too long... I decided John Lyall should take over in 1974... in John the club had the perfect man to take over from me. When I suggested to John that he took over he reacted like a man who had just been told he had won the pools.'

Of course, Lyall was delighted. He had a family to support and his new job would provide some much-needed security and, as Tony McDonald has written, Lyall enjoyed a,

'... love affair with the club that became his life.'

It seems extraordinary today that the manager could decide on who was going to succeed him. In the modern game, perhaps only Alex Ferguson wields that level of authority. The manner of Lyall's appointment sheds some interesting light on the extent of the gaffer's influence back in the early 1970s.

One of the many footballing virtues of West Ham United over the years has been continuity. Syd King had been followed by Charlie Paynter who handed over to Ted Fenton. Outsider Greenwood was brought in from Arsenal and the promotion of John Lyall restored what appears a seamless order of succession. If having just four managers in 100 years gave the club a much envied sense of permanence, the ownership of West Ham followed similar lines.

The Cearns and Pratt families served on the board for generations and were at the heart of West Ham for nearly a century. The Pratt family made their money in construction and erected the steel and concrete stands at the Boleyn. Both Greenwood and Lyall had a good working relationship with Reg Pratt, although the latter had a more ambivalent relationship with his successor, Len Cearns, or Mr Len, as he was known around Upton Park. Most football clubs enjoyed continuity on their board up to the introduction of the Premier League in 1992. Local businessmen like the Cearns, Pratts and Bob Lord at Burnley saw themselves as guardians of their club's traditions and never considered ownership as a business, leverage opportunity, or worse, a vanity project.

Reg Pratt became chairman in 1950 and served the club for 26 years, leading the Hammers into the modern era. He handed over to Mr Len in 1979, a few years after Greenwood left the club. Reg Pratt, a timber merchant, lived in Wanstead close to the police station where John Lyall's father worked. West Ham's new manager liked his chairman as he tells us in his autobiography:

'He was a local JP and had a charming wife, Gwen, who always enquired about Yvonne and Murray. I liked Mr Pratt very much.'

During his reign as West Ham manager, Ron Greenwood was treated like a full board member and attended all meetings in their entirety. Most managers would have given their report and left the meeting, but Reg Pratt trusted his manager and the chairman's inclusive approach fostered a culture of trust within the club. A year or two before Lyall took over as manager Greenwood began to take his assistant manager with him to board meetings. This was a sure sign that Greenwood had made up his mind about his successor. For Lyall, attending board meetings in the oak-panelled Boleyn boardroom was an invaluable experience. He recalled:

'At that time I felt it was a privilege, and it was all part of the learning process. By the time I was manager and had to make a report and give my observations. I knew the routine.'

With such friends at board level, Lyall's coronation at Upton Park was a formality. But he discovered at the time of the Blackpool affair that Pratt was very much his own man. Greenwood wanted to sack the miscreants there and then, but Pratt refused his manager's request, although Bobby Moore was stripped of his captaincy. There is little doubt that both Greenwood and his chairman were seriously wounded by the Blackpool incident and as a result neither man was ever quite the same again. In that sense Lyall was charged with taking the club forward in a new direction – one that incorporated the brave new world of professional football.

In Greenwood's last season in charge the Hammers finished in the bottom six of the 1st Division. With the introduction of the new regime, the West Ham self-appointed director of football stayed away from the training ground and spent his time weighing up possible signings and watching opponents. He wanted the new manager to be free to set his own direction, develop his training schedules and tactics and impose his personal philosophy of football. Ernie Gregory, Albert Walker and Eddie Bailey remained active at the club, while Ronnie Boyce was making his way as a young coach. Lyall also enjoyed a close working relationship with two men he had grown up with; physiotherapist Rob Jenkins, son of the former club physio, Bill, and secretary, Eddie Chapman. The old traditions were safe with this group of claret and blue stalwarts. Greenwood gifted Lyall a weak squad at the foot of the 1st Division, but a wonderful legacy of pure football and success in the 1960s. With a strong and trusted staff team behind him, the new manager couldn't wait to test his ideas and emerging leadership skills.

Chapter 6
A change of mood

If the '60s were a time of peace and love at Upton Park – although Canning Town and Plaistow never did embrace the hippy dream with the enthusiasm of San Francisco and Los Angeles – the '70s in Britain were a different matter. The oil crisis, a three-day working week, the 1978 Winter of Discontent, and the election victory of Margaret Thatcher in '79 were highlights of, to paraphrase WH Auden, *a low and dishonest decade*. And, in this bruising period, there was football hooliganism.

The most significant sporting event of the decade was the 1972 Munich Olympic Games. Eight Palestinian terrorists broke into the Olympic village and held 11 Israeli athletes and officials hostage in their apartments. Showing no mercy the terrorists shot two athletes dead in the first few minutes of the attack. Following an 18 hour stand-off all the hostages were gunned down in a botched rescue attempt. Many of us listened to David Coleman's sympathetic commentary with rapt attention as the horrific events unfolded on our screens. Incredibly, and in the spirit of the show must go on, the Games continued, allowing Mark Spitz to win an astonishing seven gold medals in the Olympic pool.

In continual crisis throughout the decade, Britain was dubbed by America as *the sick man of Europe*. The introduction of colour TV momentarily took our minds off the country's problems, but with 30% inflation and rubbish piled high in the streets, the public mood was grim. It was not really improved by the success of punk music which blew away the indulgent and complacent aesthetic of the hippy culture. Punk music simply added to the sense of a conflict-ridden society, although David Bowie, Abba, Pan's People and Spanish holidays did their best to cheer people up. Ten years of terrible haircuts, stack-heels and skinheads suggest this was an era best-forgotten.

In the 1970s Brazil, West Germany and a Maradona-inspired Argentina all won the football World Cup. Liverpool dominated the English game, although Derby County and Nottingham Forest enjoyed strong supporting roles. But the '70s will go down in soccer history as a time of overt racism and hateful violence. In the winter of 1975, I was strolling along Green Street one Saturday afternoon on the way to watch the Hammers play Fulham when, just a few yards from the Boleyn, a group of young West Ham supporters jumped on a Fulham fan, knocked him to the ground and beat him mercilessly – just for wearing a black and white scarf. His girlfriend cried in vain for help. This was 2.00 pm on a sunny Saturday afternoon.

A match at the Den between Millwall and Ipswich in 1978 ended in a pitched battle involving both sets of supporters. Police horses and police dogs, baton charges, and pitch invasions were regular sights on most football grounds. West Ham fans were among the worst culprits, with the North Bank's ICF one of the most feared bands of thugs roaming the country on winter Saturday afternoons. Just to the extent to which the game had declined, the Daily Mirror even published a League of Violence and the Hammers' fans were always shamefully near the top. As the violence escalated, crowds began to drop away and many older fans stopped going to football completely. After all there were many other attractions. Shopping malls, garden centres and DIY, all proved more appealing than a Saturday afternoon spent worrying if you were going to make it home without serious injury. It has been said that the lack of older supporters at matches meant that the younger fans lacked a restraining presence. Whatever the reason, the violence continued.

The Hammers' fans were also among the most racist in the land. Odd and ironic when you consider the club had a commendable record of encouraging outstanding young black players with Ron Greenwood regularly including the Charles brothers, Clyde Best and Ade Coker in his teams. Racism and violence tore the heart from the sport. The appalling events at Heysel and Hillsborough led to the Taylor Report and its recommendations for all-seater stadiums, segregation and safer grounds. The setting up of the Premier League in 1992 and the explosion of new stadia around the country rid the game of violence, if not racism which persists in professional football to this day, as in most other areas of British society.

One of Ron Greenwood's stated reasons for becoming disillusioned with football in the mid-'70s was because his family had become the subject of abuse – for this decent and proud man that was the final straw. Greenwood had not forgotten being booed and vilified by the fickle North Bank crowd following the Blackpool incident in 1971. But he could take that in the knowledge he had done the right thing. He knew only too well that, like most football supporters, Hammers' fans have notoriously short memories. What he could not take was the abuse his children received at school. An attack on his family would have deeply affected this most decent of human beings.

Passing on the baton

Greenwood was also concerned at the direction in which the professional game was heading. The increasing popularity of the FA-sanctioned Route One approach added to his general air of dis-satisfaction. With the boss in this frame of mind it was time to hand-over. This was the background for John Lyall's first season as the new manager of West Ham United. Lyall provided the prized Hammers' tradition of stability and continuity, but he knew he had to make his own mark and establish his authority quickly. Football was changing fast.

Lyall's respect for Ron Greenwood was profound and his promotion wasn't going to spark a revolution at Upton Park. Any change was going to be incremental rather than revolutionary. Lyall was steeped in the West Ham way, but he was a strong character, as Greenwood admitted, and would make changes if necessary.

What could the Hammers' fans expect of John Lyall? He may have been tough, but he was not quick tempered. Lyall was cerebral in the manner of Greenwood and Sir Alf Ramsey. He wasn't given to incendiary outbursts, teacup throwing and never signed up for the 'hairdryer' school of management. Players were unlikely to be treated to a loud-mouth rant. That just wasn't his style. Lyall's approach was far more subtle and nuanced – his players just did not want to let him down.

Lyall cared about his players as people and thought deeply about his responsibilities to them as their manager and coach. His job, as he saw it, was to develop individuals by improving their technique, tactical awareness and motivation. If he could achieve a 10% improvement in every one of his players, his team would grow stronger as a result. David Brailsford, England cycling supremo and one of the world's most successful coaches described his own coaching philosophy:

'We have this saying. 'The aggregation of marginal gains'. We are striving for 1% gains in absolutely everything.'

If we excuse the jargon, this is very much in line with Lyall's approach to improving performance. It would require immense patience and attention to detail from everyone at the club. But, like Brailsford, Lyall knew it would make a difference. Lyall needed to educate his players, staff, board of directors, and crucially, the fans.

But winning wasn't everything for Lyall. As Neil Burns, former professional cricketer and East Ender himself, recently revealed, 'he allowed people to fail in a safe way'. Burns' perceptive observation relates to Lyall's desire to improve the performance of each player by encouraging them to experiment. He would continually ask his coaching staff, 'how can we do it better?' This is very much in the Greenwood tradition, but as Burns has said, 'John was in awe of Ron, but that didn't stop him taking the project forward.' As West Ham recognised, Lyall had the necessary leadership qualities to build a better club and he had the patience, as Burns puts it, 'to wait for the cement to dry.' He knew the club would give him time.

As we will see, player after player stepped forward to say how much they owe to Lyall and how much he improved them as footballers. West Ham fans had a new manager in the best traditions of the club. They could expect a more restrained style of leadership with a good deal more finesse in handling the players than his predecessor. Perhaps a more caring individual than Greenwood, Lyall's modus operandi was what we might call today, tough love. The new manager was certainly a popular appointment. From the start he had the support of his senior players as he remembered:

'Hurstie and Moore were brilliant. They were still... top... internationals, but they came to me and said, "Anything you want us to do, you only have to ask."'

This shining endorsement from two of the most famous footballers in the world must have given Lyall an enormous boost. They knew him well and acknowledged his strength of character. Lyall admitted he had a few disagreements with Greenwood:

'People didn't realise that we did disagree at times.'

Moore and Hurst would have respected Lyall's tougher stance with the players, after the more trusting and laissez-faire regime of his predecessor. With the club's elite players behind him, Lyall could get down to business confident that everyone at the club had his total support.

In 1975 he had an early opportunity to put some of his ideas into practice – and the fans would not be disappointed. In his first season Lyall brought in Billy Jennings from Watford, Keith Robson from Newcastle and Alan Taylor from Rochdale. Controversially, he allowed *Pop* Robson to return to the north east with Sunderland. With 248 goals from 502 league and cup appearances, Geoff Hurst was always going to be a hard act to follow and Bobby Gould, despite his undoubted virtues, was no Hurst. Would the combined talents of Jennings, Robson and Taylor provide the goals?

Frank Lampard, young Mervyn Day, Graham Paddon and Kevin Lock were comfortably settled into the team. With Pat Holland and Alan Curbishley almost ready to compete for a regular first team place, Lyall believed he had a strong enough squad to challenge on all fronts. The new manager also had a trump card, or rather two trump cards. If Greenwood basked in the brilliance of his three World Cup winners Moore, Hurst and Peters, Lyall had world-class performers of his own in crowd favourites Trevor Brooking and Billy Bonds. But the lack of a natural goalscorer would have worried Lyall – and it was to prove a persistent problem.

The new manager's first season began disappointingly with just two wins in the first eight games. September brought improvement with a 6-2 win at home against Leicester City, a 3-0 victory over Birmingham and a 5-3 thumping of Burnley. Lyall had found his goalscorer in Billy Jennings, while the defence had tightened up after a nervous start to the season. The improvement continued and the new Hammers reached the giddy heights of 5th place in the 1st Division. But, typically, the goals began to dry up and the Hammers fell away, ending the season in a modest 13th place, winning just one of the last nine League games. However, if the League form that season was typically disappointing to Hammers' fans, the FA Cup provided a wonderful distraction.

West Ham had not won a trophy since that glorious night at Wembley in 1965. The old cup habit was in danger of being consigned to ancient history. Could John Lyall restore the Hammers' brave cup fighting tradition? His first opportunity came in the 3rd Round of the FA Cup against Southampton at the Dell. Goals from Lampard and Gould saw his side safely through to a 4th Round home tie against Swindon Town, which they scraped through after a replay. Lyall included Patsy Holland against Swindon and the youngster impressed his new manager with two well-taken goals and a prodigious work-rate.

Holland scored again in the 2-1 4th Round home victory against QPR, handing his side a plum draw away to Arsenal in the next round. The Gunners were struggling in the League that season, but over 56,000 turned up at Highbury to watch Alan Taylor score twice and put Lyall's team through to the semi-finals. The lad from Rochdale was beginning to repay his transfer fee with interest.

Lyall's team had made it to the last four, but faced formidable semi-final opposition in Ipswich Town. At the end of the 1974/75 season the Tractor Boys finished 3rd in the 1st Division, just two points behind champions, Derby County and were going to be extremely tough opponents. An excited crowd of 58,000 arrived at Villa Park anticipating a classic encounter between these two attacking sides. But as is often the way after so much expectation, a disappointing 0-0 draw sent the teams to a replay at Stamford Bridge the following Wednesday evening. This time Lyall's team grasped their opportunity. Two more goals from Taylor gave the Hammers a 2-1 victory in a tense and hard fought match. John Lyall's new West Ham was going to Wembley.

In a stroke Lyall had restored the Hammers' old cup tradition thanks largely to one of his new signings, Alan Taylor. The new manager could hardly have wished for a better start to his new job and Hammers fans could begin to dream again of victory. They were back at Wembley with another chance of FA Cup glory. In an odd twist of fate that football throws up from time to time their Wembley opponents, as in 1964, were from the 2nd Division. West London neighbours, Fulham were enjoying their own Wembley dream having reached an FA Cup final for the first time in their history. To add to the rather bizarre nature of the 1975 final, in the Fulham side that day was none other than the god-like figure of Bobby Moore, great friend of the West Ham manager.

You just couldn't make it up! Sir Alex Ferguson once said, 'bloody football'.

The 1975 FA Cup Final: West Ham v Fulham

While West Ham and Fulham prepared for Wembley, the Vietnam War dragged on, the Watergate scandal threatened to bring down a President, the country was gripped by the Spaghetti House siege and the IRA blew up the London Hilton Hotel. In the capital the Moorgate tube disaster brought tragedy to many East London families. On a lighter note, Ali beat Frazier in the Thriller in Manila, Leeds lost to Bayern Munich in a controversial European Cup Final, and Brian Clough's Derby County won their second 1st Division Championship in four years. But in East End London there was a reason to party – the Hammers were back at Wembley

Stadium in an FA Cup Final.

In the '70s the old Wembley Stadium was well past its sell-by date – a sad, shabby and rundown apology of its former glorious self. But none of that mattered to a single one of the 100,000 people jammed into the old place that Saturday in 1975. Both West Ham and Fulham were real old-fashioned football clubs. The Hammers were famous for their passionate support, although the glamour of the '60s side was fading fast. Their opponents had a pretty riverside ground, but were in the shadow of their trendier neighbours, Chelsea. The club could claim some celebrity status through its chairman, comedian and *cheeky chappie*, Tommy Trinder. The club's star player of the 1950s and early '60s was England captain and Brylcreem boy, Johnny Haynes, one of England's most famous post-war footballers. Bobby Robson, Jimmy Hill and Bedford Jezzard were all former Craven Cottage alumni.

In their team on that special Saturday in 1975 the West Londoners boasted not one, but two former England captains in Alan Mullery and the Hammers' legend, Bobby Moore. Moore and Mullery were Fulham's trump cards. Mullery had been a magnificent player with Tottenham and England, while Moore, his incomparable buddy in the Fulham team, was the most decorated and successful player ever to wear the claret and blue of West Ham United. The 1966 image of Moore lifting the Jules Rimet Trophy remained fresh in the memory now the great man was back at Wembley, sadly for the last time as a player.

In the '70s neither West Ham nor Fulham attracted the media attention of outfits like Leeds, Liverpool, Manchester United and Arsenal, but as we shall see, both clubs had characters in abundance. The 1975 Cup Final was one for the football romantics.

The clubs' two managers, John Lyall and Alex Stock, were well respected coaches who stood for the highest ideals in football. Stock was of Ron Greenwood's generation while Lyall represented a younger group of managers keen for early success. Greenwood admitted the 1975 Cup Final belonged exclusively to the club's new manager, although the former boss did present an imposing figure on the West Ham bench. Stock, mercilessly parodied by Paul

Whitehouse in the Fast Show, and despite his team occupying a mid-table spot in the 2nd Division, maintained his standing as one of the game's best managers. He had worked at the Cottage with illustrious names such as Haynes, Hill, Robson and Tosh Chamberlain and his reputation was well-earned. Stock's team had played superbly well to reach the final and were going to be no pushover.

Despite the romantic overtones, in reality the 1975 Final was contested by two moderate sides. Fulham was a mediocre outfit despite its two former England captains, and the Hammers had won just 13 of their 42 League games in the top flight that season. But against all the odds the fickleness of the FA Cup had thrown together two teams who, despite their modest form, had fought like tigers to get to the final. With three games against Hull City and four against Forest on their way to Wembley, Fulham had earned their Cup Final place the hard way. Birmingham City fought hard to deny them glory at the semi-final stage, but Fulham prevailed 1-0 in a replay. Both teams could reasonably claim their name was on the FA Cup that year.

On the night before the match Bobby Moore, as befitted his status, had a room of his own at Fulham's hotel in leafy Hadley Wood. The night before the match he slept well and set about calming the nerves of his younger teammates. He told the Fulham youngsters that West Ham were firm favourites, so let them do the worrying. Moore's presence in the Fulham team was sure to give them an important psychological edge going into the game. The sight of their legendary former skipper in the tunnel was guaranteed to jangle a few Hammers' nerves. Patsy Holland tells a story about his former teammate. One day during a summer break Patsy popped into Upton Park to do some light training only to see Moore knocking a ball round the pitch with a friend.

"Hello Patsy boy," as Moore always called the young winger, *"this is my friend Carlos Alberto, do you want to join us?"* Holland hadn't recognised the famous Brazilian full-back. He was hardly expecting to see one of the world's greatest players having a kick-about at Upton Park that day – the incident was pure Bobby Moore.

The 34-year-old Moore made his own preparations before the

game, his shorts going on last as usual. Firing jokes at the West Ham players in the tunnel, he strode out to take the warm applause of the Wembley crowd. The ex-England captain played well, but could not prevent the goalkeeping blunders that cost Fulham the game. "Bloody goalkeepers," he said after the match. "And that bloody Taylor only kicked the ball twice." Later Moore must have looked at his loser's medal with a wry smile – he wasn't use to losing on these big occasions.

As is the custom, both sets of players appeared on the Wembley pitch an hour before kick-off clad in their expensive club suits, enjoying the moment and the attention of the media circus. One player decided to miss the opportunity to answer the usual tedious media questions like 'what's it like to be at Wembley?' Bobby Moore was nowhere to be seen. Where was the great man? Alan Mullery explained he was having a quiet kip in the dressing room and wanted to save all his energy for the match. Moore's face during the playing of the National Anthem was a picture.

The West Ham manager probably never gave more than a passing thought to his old friend as he proudly led out his team to the sound of John Lyall's claret and blue army ringing in his ears. With his smart blue suit and '70s hairstyle hair he looked every inch the modern football manager. Lyall looked nervous as he took his seat on the West Ham bench, but his nerves would have been calmed by the familiar faces around him. Ron Greenwood looked relaxed on his right, while Ronnie Boyce sat just behind puffing away on a cigarette.

The two captains presented their teams to the royal of the day, Prince Michael. This was 1975 and there were plenty of beards on display on both sides, none more impressive than the one sported by the piratical Hammers' captain, Billy Bonds. The formalities out of the way, referee Pat Partridge brought the two captains together to begin the real business of the day. As he introduced the captains, Partridge glanced down to check Alan Mullery's boots for tell-tale signs of sponsors' logos. Fulham had been in the High Court the day before defending their right to wear sponsored boots. The FA objected and all signs of commercialism were removed from the offending boots – Mullery's boots were a pure and logo-free black.

The game kicked off in bright sunlight and Mervyn Day, the 19-year-old Hammers' 'keeper got a welcome early touch of the ball. The presence of Moore lifted the Fulham side, as Billy Bonds predicted it would, and the West London team started briskly. The Cottagers settled quickly and dominated the first 15 minutes. A couple of powerful headers from Busby and Lacy went close for Fulham, before a vicious long-range Brooking drive grazed the Fulham crossbar. Mullery kept a tight grip on Brooking and the Hammers just couldn't get their star player on the ball. The Fulham skipper was well-supported in midfield by Slough and Conway, while Busby and Barrett were causing problems up front. The West Ham defence struggled to cope with the movement of their West London opponents. The Fulham players were first to everything and dominated possession. BBC match summariser, Alan Ball summed up the first 30 minutes, 'West Ham are under the cosh, they just can't get into the game.'

On the Hammers' bench Greenwood and Lyall looked on nervously. The trademark sight of Billy Bonds with his socks round his ankles as early as the 20th minute hinted at desperation. With the East Londoners running out of ideas a Fulham goal seemed inevitable. Alex Stock knew his team needed to score while they were on top. What is it with West Ham and FA Cup finals? They disappointed in defeat in 1923 and were woeful in 1964, although eventually overcoming a modest Preston team. Here in 1975, they were second best against another lowly 2nd Division side.

What was the problem? Mullery and Slough had the better of the West Ham midfield and outpassed Bonds, Brooking and Paddon. Graham Paddon was a good player for West Ham but was anonymous in the first half. Up front Jennings and Taylor failed to hold the ball up and looked lightweight against the burly Fulham defence. McDowell and Holland produced one or two moments down the right and Brooking flickered from time to time. Billy Bonds worked tirelessly to plug the gaps left by his teammates and for much of the first period looked a frustrated figure. For Lyall, half-time couldn't come soon enough.

As the players emerged from the tunnel for the second-half, Lyall was the last to take his seat and would have been encouraged by the sight of Brooking gliding through the midfield to lay on a half-chance for Alan Taylor. The Hammers' elegant inside-forward was seeing more of the ball, but lacked support. Suddenly, Moore freed Busby with a wonderful pass, only for the impressive Lock – the latest new Bobby Moore – to deny the Fulham centre-forward with a superbly timed tackle. Young Lock was proving one of the few West Ham successes, ably supported by the energetic Frank Lampard to his left.

Frustrated by their inability to score despite their superiority, the Cottagers began to tire and concede possession. Graham Paddon, woeful in the first half, grew in stature, raising the spirits of the noisy Hammers' fans with some characteristic surges down the left wing. Holland began to switch wings to good effect, but the game looked to be slipping away from both sides. Jennings and Taylor continued to frustrate the Hammers' fans. Robbed of the energy and presence of the injured Keith Robson, Lyall must have doubted the wisdom of leaving Bobby Gould on the bench. Jennings and Taylor's failure to retain possession and pass the ball was, according to Alan Ball, 'a real problem within the English game'. The likes of Geoff Hurst and Roger Hunt come along once in a generation.

Then midway through the second-half, with Fulham on top and the Hammers there for the taking, a goal came out of the blue and against the run of play. Patsy Holland broke down the left and knocked the ball invitingly across the Fulham goal. *Duchey's* cross fell to Jennings whose deflected shot landed at the feet of Alan Taylor who gleefully tucked the ball into the back of the net. The claret and blue section of the crowd went bananas, while the Fulham fans look on in stunned disbelief. On the West Ham bench, Lyall and Boyce lit another cigarette and began to relax a little.

The *Cottagers* had given everything, were easily the best team, but found themselves 1-0 down. Moore, Slough and Mullery did their best to lift their teammates, but they now looked a beaten side. Brooking was running the midfield and Paddon surged forward at every opportunity. With the Hammers on top for the first time in the match, four minutes later Taylor scored again. A lovely through ball from Holland released Paddon whose fierce shot was fumbled by Mellor. Taylor was the first to react and drove the ball high into the Fulham goal. There was no question that the distraught Mellor was at fault with both the goals. Back in the '70s goalkeepers preferred not to wear gloves and Mellor's muddy hands let him down on the two occasions that mattered. Shortly after Taylor's second goal, a silky run by Les Barrett nearly got Fulham back in the game, but, as he shaped to shoot, he was pulled down in full flight by McDowell. But it was too little, too late.

Despite Moore's courageous marshalling of his defence and Mullery's persistence, Fulham fell away in the final 20 minutes. The two former England captains knew Billy Bonds was feeling his injury and the Hammers defence were there for the taking. Fortunately, both man-of-the-match Kevin Lock and Frank Lampard were at their very best, energetically covering their teammates and winning tackle after tackle. Lyall had huge respect for Lampard and admired his sheer professionalism. When it really mattered the Hammers' left-back was a tower of strength. As the minutes passed the Cup was well and truly on its way to the Boleyn. Ultimately, this was a pretty routine win for the favourites and there was to be no dream happy ending for Bobby Moore, who slipped quietly away after the game, leaving his former teammates to their triumph.

At last Bond's team showed the fight and determination they lacked in the first- half and saw out the rest of the game without incident. A midfield containing Bonds, Brooking, Holland and Paddon should have dominated the game from start to finish, but they struggled to impose themselves on their West London neighbours. There was little of the West Ham trademark free-flowing football that reached its peak in the '65 European Cup Winners' Cup final. But the Hammers had won the FA Cup for the second time in their history and how the fans celebrated.

On the day two players stood out, and for very different reasons. Alan Taylor only joined the East London club from Rochdale in the autumn of 1974. The club willingly paid £40,000 for the youngster who quickly became known as *Sparrow* to his teammates. The 21-

year-old could not have imagined the fairy tale season that lay ahead. His wife gave birth to daughter, Carley, prior to one of the earlier rounds and fatherhood must have suited the West Ham no. 10. He scored two goals in the quarter-final against Arsenal and two more in the semi-final against Ipswich. *Sparrow's* two Wembley goals won the 1975 FA Cup for the Hammers for the first time in 11 years.

Taylor's career peaked in the 1974/75 season as he went from 4th Division zero to Hammers' Wembley hero in just a few short months. Here was the West Ham centre-forward for the next ten years. For the celebrating Hammers' fans, Taylor was Geoff Hurst and Johnnie Byrne rolled into one. Sadly, the Fulham final was to prove the highlight of Taylor's career as he lost the golden touch of that season and it never really returned. Sadly, his career never scaled the heights of '75, but the whippet-like forward will never be forgotten by the Hammers' supporters for his exploits in that Cup winning season. Lyall must have thought long and hard about playing Taylor ahead of the belligerent, if predictable, Bobby Gould. It was a risk, but on this occasion, as in many others, Lyall's judgement proved sound.

Patsy Holland tells a story which gives an insight into Lyall's relationship with his players. Lyall would be trying something different in training and Patsy kept getting it wrong. For the umpteenth time that morning he apologised to his boss, "I'm sorry boss, I'll get it right next time."

Lyall replied, "Pat, all you ever say is – I'm sorry." Lyall knew Patsy would take the criticism the right way and would keep coming back for more – other players might have objected. The 1975 Final was the highlight of *Duchy's* career, as Cup Finals often are for players with his qualities of selfless running, decisive tackling and diligent marking.

Billy Bonds was another hero of 1975 playing through the pain of a knee injury and the discomfort of his recurring groin strain. Up in the Royal Box he lifted the FA Cup in tribute to unsung heroes like Holland and Kevin Lock, but most of all to the thousands of fans celebrating below. The skipper and his manager knew they had a good side and were frustrated they had underperformed on the day. The Boleyn faithful were desperate for success and would have taken any performance so long as their team won. They understood that in most seasons the FA Cup provided their only realistic hope of success. The boys in claret and blue won and in doing so denied their greatest player a fairy tale ending to his stellar career – the fairy tale moment went to the *Sparrow* such is the romance and unpredictability of the FA Cup.

Lyall and Greenwood rose from the West Ham bench, shook hands and shared a tentative embrace. Lyall walked out onto the Wembley pitch and, one by one, congratulated every member of his side. Bonds led his team on the customary lap of honour and as they disappeared down the tunnel, hundreds of young Hammers' fans invaded the pitch. To the relief of the Wembley officials they were in good spirits and left quietly after a few minutes larking around.

Meanwhile West Ham's greatest ever player had his own thoughts on the game which reveal the nature of his ambivalent relationship with his former coaching staff. On Taylor's first goal, Bobby Moore ruefully reflected:

'All the West Ham bench are on their feet except Greenwood and Lyall. They hold a private brains trust into the incident. Greenwood with his eyes screwed up, Lyall chewing and smoking. That is West Ham's way.'

Moore knew that Lyall was the strongest voice on the Hammers' bench and heard him repeatedly urging his players on, "Come on Patsy, run. Trevor, run. Get hold of them Frank," shouted Lyall as his players began to wilt under sustained Fulham pressure. His words reached his players who slowly overcame their gutsy opponents.

1975 was not a vintage West Ham performance in the club's great traditions, but a win is a win. It was the FA Cup Final and the last to be won by a side comprised entirely of English players. Despite their Wembley triumph, Lyall knew he had much to think about during the summer of 1975. The new manager had won the FA Cup in his first season and the Hammers were back in Europe.

The victorious West Ham team at Wembley on 3 May 1975 was: Day, McDowell, Taylor T, Lock, Lampard, Bonds (c), Paddon, Brooking, Jennings, Taylor A and Holland.

Chapter 7
Managing expectations

Lyall later reflected on his team's Wembley triumph:
'I was soon to learn days like that are few in the life of a football manager.'

As he settled into the reality of being in the top job, the FA Cup victory receded into memory. But Lyall had won the Cup and could look forward to an extended honeymoon at the Boleyn. For many West Ham supporters Lyall's ascendancy to the top job raised some interesting questions. Would he change the team and its style of play? How strong was his commitment to the West Ham way? Could the Hammers improve their modest League record? The next few seasons would bring some answers. The new manager was determined to improve his side's League form and could look forward to testing his managerial ability in Europe much sooner that he could have imagined. It was a good time to be a Hammers' fan.

John Lyall would have consulted long and hard with his predecessor about how he should approach the '75 FA Cup Final. Greenwood's ideas on football were clear-cut and the team of the 1960s was built in his image. He set his team up with a zonal back four which included Moore as his libero. Boyce and Bovington guarded the midfield allowing deep-lying centre forward, Byrne the space to get forward in support of Hurst. The side was completed with two touchline-hugging wingers – Sissons on the left and either Redknapp or Sealey down the right. Later, of course, he brought in Peters for Bovington.

Lyall was never going to be a simple 'picker of teams' manager, to borrow a Walter Winterbottom phrase. He was an independent character and had definite ideas of his own. In the Fulham game the Hammers played with a different, more cautious shape. The

135

strong back four were still there with Kevin Lock in the sweeper role. The midfield changed to a line of four stretched across the pitch, with Brooking free to support Jennings and Taylor up front. Missing were the flying wingers beloved of West Ham fans. The system was a straight 4-4-2 adopted by Sir Alf Ramsey in winning the World Cup in 1996. Lyall's pragmatism would have disappointed some football romantics, but the new manager insisted he believed in the West Ham purist tradition. Young Johnny Ayris, the Whippet, was the natural replacement for Sissons and Redknapp, but he never really made the most of his undoubted talent, much to the disappointment of his manager and the fans in the old Chicken Run. A whiplash of a player, Ayris was a regular for the England Under-21 side, but made just 68 appearances for the Hammers, scoring a miserly two goals. When he lost his first team place Ayris moved to South Africa, but later returned to the UK where he finished his career with Wimbledon. Outstanding young wingers were few and far between at that time and losing Ayris was a big disappointment to Lyall.

For now, Lyall had his first trophy and discussions about whether he would continue the great tradition could wait. Some less-generous West Ham fans argued that '75 victory was Greenwood's achievement – it was his team. But Greenwood went out of his way to deny this:

'By the time we won the FA Cup in 1975... there was a different team – and it was John Lyall's team.'

Using ideas as my map

Perhaps Greenwood was being unduly modest, but I doubt it. Lyall's influence on the team had grown over the years as Greenwood gradually took a back seat. The younger man extended the Greenwood project by taking it a step further. Both men were inspirational coaches who worked hard to get their players to think imaginatively about the game. Neither men took notes during matches or used a blackboard to put across their message. Greenwood particularly would have been horrified at the thought of Pro-Zone technology beloved of most contemporary managers.

These two football scholars believed strongly that coaches should paint pictures for players and get them to imagine situations for themselves. Lyall explained:

'Ron never used a tactics board – a tactics board never won anything. We used the football. He used to say to us coaches, "All we have to do is paint pictures, because once the picture is finished, they (the players) will see it and they will like it."'

One of the ways in which Lyall built on Greenwood's ideas was by developing his own visual approach to coaching. I spoke to several players who worked under Lyall, including Sir Trevor Brooking, Pat Holland, Ray Stewart, Phil Parkes and David Cross at West Ham, and John Wark, Simon Milton and Chris Kiwomya at Ipswich. They all spoke about Lyall's ability to get them to visualise a particular move or piece of individual play he wanted them to adopt. This worked much better, Lyall argued, than simply drawing crude diagrams on a blackboard.

A good example is the way Lyall asked Geoff Pike to picture threading accurate midfield passes into the path of the advancing Brooking and Devonshire. If Pike succeeded, these two attacking midfield players were released to take the ball forward without breaking stride. In Greenwood's time he asked Ronnie Boyce to imagine the same pass, but to Martin Peters, rather than Brooking and Devonshire. A further example was the near-post cross – an old West Ham ploy, originally involving Moore and Hurst. The no. 10 was asked to imagine timing his run late, to connect with Moore's accurate and quickly taken cross or free-kick. We have seen this on countless occasions at Upton Park. Hurst's goals in the '66 World Cup against Argentina and West Germany were perfect examples of encouraging players' visual awareness.

By thinking about their game visually, rather than as abstract figures on a flipchart, Lyall got his players to internalise and memorise his ideas. Intelligent footballers like Brooking, Devonshire, Holland and Hurst, were quick to respond to Lyall's imaginative coaching and many of West Ham's trademark football became second nature to them. The characteristic West Ham way was actually made up of tiny fragments of play which, when woven together, produced the open, free-flowing football beloved of the

Upton Park faithful. Lyall wanted his teams to be flexible and to understand how, like a game of chess, the pieces fitted together. But the players had to be taught the essential principles and Lyall's visual method was, for 20 years, a brilliant success. It took a very special coach and hours on the Chadwell Heath training ground to reinforce visual awareness. That it succeeded is a great complement to Lyall as a coach, as Billy Bonds recognised:

'John told me things I'd never heard before and improved me 75% as a player. I had an engine, but he made me better – made me believe – what an England manager he would have made.'

Lyall wanted his players to feel they could try something different and not to worry about failing – this was part of the West Ham way. He released them to play. It was a question of getting the players to be creative, believe in themselves and be positive. More than anything he wanted his players to entertain. Danny Blanchflower said back in the 1960s that:

'Football is about glory, it is about doing things in style and with a flourish, about getting out and beating the lot, not wanting them to die of boredom.'

West Ham may not have 'beaten the lot', but under John Lyall they were blessed with a leader both the players and fans genuinely loved and respected.

Home alone

In the summer of '75 the new manager could look back on his emerging career with a degree of satisfaction. He had signed for Ted Fenton as a boy, suffered a career-ending injury at the age of 23, spent a few years as youth coach, assistant manager, and finally the top job. As a 1st Division boss, Lyall was earning decent money and the family were happy in the Essex countryside where they lived for 23 years. Yvonne had her friends, family, and her Fiat 500, while young Murray was settled in a good school in Chigwell.

Yvonne no longer had to address envelopes in the evenings to supplement the family income, which she needed to do early in their married life. And her husband no longer needed to fill the summer months working for a local plastering firm and could relax in the close season playing cricket out at Fairlop or fishing down in Abridge.

Of course, success is welcome, but often comes at a price. Yvonne tells an interesting story which illustrates the extent of the pressures on top football managers. She revealed recently:

'Throughout his managerial career John never told me what time he would be home from work.'

Yvonne understood the pressures of the job – if John gave her a time, they both knew something would come up to make him late. He would need to see a player, talk to the press or meet with the directors, as he usually did after matches. They both understood the responsibilities of the job. One senses, talking to Yvonne, that the life of a football manager's wife can be extremely lonely and John was acutely aware of this. Ron Greenwood actually missed his own daughter's wedding because of the 1964 FA Cup Final – he never got to give his daughter away. There was little point in Yvonne warning young Murray, "wait until your dad gets home," on the rare occasions he was naughty.

As Murray remembers, "I could wait a long time."

Yvonne's increasing sense of isolation was a real concern for her husband. It was the reason John promised to retire from the game early in order to spend more time with his family and to repay Yvonne for her stoical devotion.

In a perceptive remark, David Cross, who Lyall brought to the Boleyn in 1977, recently suggested that Greenwood and Lyall worked on 'educating the crowd.' The crux of Cross's argument was that the two managers taught a notoriously impatient North Bank to enjoy the team's football, confident that the results would come. When they didn't, the faithful could enjoy the brilliance of their team – be especially proud of their club because of its international reputation for high ideals. Cross was right. Greenwood and Lyall knew the fans were critical to the club's success, but needed to be taught patience – a virtue not associated with passionate football fans. Right up to the present day, the Hammers' supporters expect the Hammers to play football of the highest quality. Grinding out goal-less home draws to end the season in Premier League mid-table mediocrity is simply not tolerated.

In spite of being a caring and sympathetic manager, Lyall kept a respectful distance from his team, although the new manager did allow his players to call him by his first name. Of all the ex-Hammers I met in researching for this book, I never heard one refer to Lyall by anything other than John, although from time to time he was known affectionately as Elvis, due to his luxuriant 1950s' hairstyle. As a big Frank Sinatra fan, he would probably have resented the well-intended Elvis tag.

We know he was hard but fair and treated everyone at the club, not just with respect, but genuine affection. In a recent interview, Murray Lyall gave an illustration of his father's professional standards. He revealed that his dad had some real pet hates, including being late for training – players were fined; hands in pockets during training (staff and players); talking while he was talking – a definite no-no. The whole group would be punished for any transgression by having the footballs taken away and the session turned over to hard fitness work.

Lyall possessed authority and presence and was not to be trifled with, but his leadership was tempered by compassion. The postman and the lady who made the tea at Chadwell Heath were as important to him as any of his players. He reached out to people and taught his players to do the same. Greenwood's successor quickly earned both the respect and affection of everyone at West Ham. Of course, winning the FA Cup in only his second season in charge was a huge bonus.

One of Lyall's highest priorities when he took over from Greenwood was to bring some consistency to the club's shaky

League performances. But in the short term, the new manager, his players and the fans could look forward to the mouth-watering prospect of another European trophy campaign. But first it was time to get down to some hard work. One of the most important things Lyall did when he took over at Upton Park had little to do with tactical awareness or inspirational leadership. He simply got the players to relax by taking the tension and fear away. Unquestionably a brilliant coach, Greenwood was a tense character and the players often caught the bug. It was one of the reasons they frequently underperformed. Lyall was a more relaxed and rounded individual and the players immediately responded to his confident and inclusive leadership. He changed the mood at West Ham, both at the training ground and on match days. It remained to be seen if the welcome change of mood would improve results. The Upton Park faithful relished the prospect of the new season. European nights were back at Upton Park.

Lyall's European Adventure
The Hammers were in Europe for the second time in 11 years – their reward for scraping through against Fulham. Since that glorious night at Wembley against Munich in 1965, the club had reached the semi-final of the Football League Cup twice, were beaten finalists in the same competition, lost a European Cup Winners' Cup semi-final and won the FA Cup. Under Lyall, Greenwood's legacy appeared secure.

But the team of 1976 was a very different outfit from the successful, star-studded team of the 1960s. Moore, Hurst and Peters had gone, but in their place we had the great Trevor Brooking and the admirable Billy Bonds. Alongside these two legends were a collection of solid professionals, who on 5 May 1976 found themselves in the semi-final of a major European competition.

The Hammers were making progress but this could not be said about football more generally. Ugliness and violence continued to spill onto pitches in major stadiums and into streets around the grounds. Police dogs, baton charges and pitched battles between fans became commonplace. The results of aggressive fan behaviour were wire fences, strict segregation and huge police presences.

Sadly, West Ham fans were at the heart of the trouble. Football-related violence in the East End began way back in the 1960s with the establishment of The Mile End Mob, but during the 1970s the notorious ICF seriously upped the level of aggression whether towards their own supporters or rival fans.

West Ham's ICF became a model for others to copy. They were highly organised. In order to escape police attention they wore casual clothes on match days rather than the usual club colours. They travelled to away matches on regular trains, rather than on the cheap and more tightly policed football specials. These travel arrangements reminded us that hard-core fans were not always the stereotypical unemployed youth of popular imagination, but often city boys, skilled workers, and even teachers. Films like The Firm and Green Street celebrated the ICF and brought the sheer intensity of football violence to the nation's front rooms.

In addition to the appalling violence, one of the features of the 1970s was the loosening of the close bond that formally existed between players and supporters. The warmth and sense of community of the '60s faded as the players' wages soared and they became detached from the fans and their neighbourhoods. This process reached its ultimate conclusion in 1992 with the introduction of the Premier League and Sky TV. No longer could the fans expect to sit in the same local pub alongside their heroes, as they would have done in the days of Moore, Redknapp, Byrne and the others. That was the background to English football in the 1970s and despite the Hammers' welcome success on the field, the hooliganism and violence is impossible to ignore.

But even with the continual threat of violence at Upton Park at this time, games under the Boleyn floodlights remained special. The return leg of the semi-final against Frankfurt was one of the most exciting, nail-biting confrontations seen at the Boleyn in modern times. The atmosphere was electric and the crowd that night were worth at least one, maybe two extra players. The fans knew only too well that for a club like West Ham these occasions didn't come along very often.

The route to the final was surprisingly trouble-free, given the

Hammers' miserable League form. Lyall's side managed just one win in 21 matches between Boxing Day and the end of the season, leaving the manager and his players baffled and frustrated. But this was West Ham after all – the ultimate cup specialists. Their European charge saw them account for Reipas Lahden, Ararat Erevan, and after a fierce encounter, Den Haag. Now only Eintracht Frankfurt could stop them reaching the final.

Reaching the last four was a terrific achievement in itself, but the Upton Park faithful began to believe their team were good enough to reach their second European final in 11 years. This was a very exciting West Ham side. Trevor Brooking, Tommy Taylor, Patsy Holland and Frank Lampard were local boys and remained close to their roots. For most of the '76 European campaign the team consisted of 11 Englishmen, 12 if you include substitute Alan Taylor. So there was plenty to excite the East End of London.

On the night of 14 April, Eintracht Frankfurt arrived at the Boleyn to play the second leg of the 1976 European Cup Winners' Cup semi-final. Over 39,000 excited supporters crammed into the old ground that night. They ignored the torrential rain and raised the roof of the old stadium in support of their side. Never in the club's history could Bubbles be heard for so long and so loud. By the end of the match everyone in the ground was soaked to the skin, but what a night!

The Germans came to Upton Park with a slender one goal advantage after their 2-1 victory in Frankfurt. Graham Paddon gave the Hammers the lead in the first game with a spectacular and precious away goal, only for the home side to gain 1st leg advantage with goals from Neuberger and Kraus. But there was everything to play for in the second leg.

As the teams strode out onto the pitch they were greeted by a deafening roar which lasted throughout the night. The football matched the electric atmosphere as the Hammers rained down on the German goal in a desperate bid to level the scores. Lampard, driving forward from left-back, twice went close, while in the 15th minute Keith Robson had what looked like a perfectly good goal disallowed for a foul on the goalkeeper. For all the passion in the ground and all the efforts of the home side, the breakthrough wouldn't come. Half-time arrived with the aggregate score unchanged. The German one goal lead remained intact.

During the interval John Lyall urged his team to step up the attack on the German goal by moving the ball forward more quickly. He also reminded his players what they had achieved to get to this far in the competition – now one last push and they were in the final. With the crowd notching up the sound to previously unheard levels, the home team came out for the second half and battered the German defence. After a few minutes the Hammers achieved the breakthrough they desperately needed.

Lampard once again tore down the left wing, much to the delight of the Chicken Run, before sending a perfect cross into the path of the on-rushing Brooking. The midfielder, not known for his ability in the air, sent a looping header over the German 'keeper into the net, right in front of the ecstatic South Bank. With Paddon's away goal in the first leg the Hammers were effectively a goal ahead on aggregate.

Everyone in the ground that night knew that Eintracht would fight back. The players and supporters were aware that a one goal lead would probably not be enough against this German side. Mervyn Day had to be on his toes to keep out a shot from Wenzel and Coleman cleared off the line as Frankfurt began to stretch the Hammers' defence. Fortunately for the home side Billy Bonds was on inspirational form, while Paddon, Brooking and Holland worked tirelessly alongside their skipper in midfield. The Hammers were fighting to maintain their lead and were playing with real purpose and no little skill. Both Brooking and Holland moved forward to support Jennings and Robson at every opportunity. All this led to tremendously exciting, end-to-end football. Midway through the second half, Brooking, who was beginning to dominate the midfield despite the thick mud, slipped a peach of a ball through to Robson, whose poor first touch brought groans from the crowd. But the combative forward quickly recovered and curled a delightful 25 yard shot over Kunter in the Eintracht goal, at last destroying the fierce German resistance.

A few minutes later Day turned a ferocious shot from Grabowski over his crossbar before the inspirational Brooking brought everyone in the ground to their feet with a goal of his own. This time Paddon released his midfield partner who jinked past two defenders before calmly sliding the ball into the net. The Hammers had a 3-0 lead and surely a place in the final. Not quite. The Germans refused to admit defeat and scored a very late goal – but it was too little, too late and when the referee blew for full-time the home crowd celebrated in style – their team had made the final of the European Cup Winners' Cup for the second time in their history.

In conditions not suited to his close control and stylish play Brooking was at his brilliant best all evening. After the match he remarked:

'To score twice and set one up for 'Mad Robbo' in such a key match was fantastic. Eintracht were a very good side and it all got a bit gritty in the end.'

In a tribute to the supporters, goalscorer Robson commented:

'Our great crowd were worth a goal... we were elated to hear the final whistle. That was the greatest night of my life.'

That night Lyall's team played to their full potential. Brooking and his mate Billy Bonds needed to be at their absolute best and the rest of the team to be 100% committed in support. Skipper Bonds said about his friend's performance that night:

'Trevor played many fine games in his career but if I had to name just one as his best, it was that electric night. He was sheer brilliance. He mesmerised a good German side and scored two goals.'

For once, thanks to the crowd's noisy support, the performance matched the potential. Manager Lyall was delighted with his side's display, but must have been left wondering, given their performance on this famous night, how on earth they had failed to win a League game since the QPR home match on 24 January. But for now, they were in the European Cup Winners' Cup final. With such an impressive victory over a top European side, the fans could look forward to the final with real optimism. Lyall's leadership at this early stage in his managerial career earned him iconic status at Upton Park. The West Ham team against Frankfurt that evening was: Day, McDowell, Lampard, Taylor, Coleman, Holland, Brooking, Bonds (c), Paddon, Robson and Jennings.

Following their semi-final triumph, Lyall had three weeks to prepare his players for the final against the Belgian side, Anderlecht. If the semi-final win against Frankfurt was close to heroic, the Hammers' League form continued to disappoint. Goals from Robson and Brooking earned a hard-fought 2-2 draw at home to Aston Villa, but successive drubbings at the hands of Everton and Ipswich Town left the manager frustrated and concerned. The 4-0 defeat at Portman Road was particularly disappointing, coming as it did just two weeks before the European final. Could the manager lift his side's sagging morale and raise their confidence in just two weeks? We would soon know the answer.

Heysel here we come!
The 1976 European Cup Winners' Cup Final was mercifully free of violence and incident between the two sets of fans. The match was played at the Heysel Stadium in Brussels in front of a passionate but respectful crowd of 58,000. Anderlecht began with a definite advantage because Brussels was their home city. Billy Bonds likened his team's task to playing Liverpool at Anfield, but the opposition's home ground was not the Heysel, but a few minutes away in another part of town.

How frustrating it must have been for Irons supporters to see a team which included Brooking, Frank Lampard, Billy Bonds and Tommy Taylor struggle in the League. But their beloved Hammers were in their second European final in 11 seasons and, for now, that was all that mattered. If the fans were expectant, the players knew they would need to repeat their outstanding form against Frankfurt, if they were to stand a chance against Anderlecht.

West Ham's Belgian opponents were one of the best teams in

Europe. On the way to the final they had beaten Rapid Bucharest, Borac Banja Luka, Wrexham and Sachsenring. The Anderlecht team contained some illustrious names including Robbie Rensenbrink, Francois Van Der Elst (of which more later) and the wonderfully talented Arie Hann. This group of players was highly skilled and experienced in top European competitions. They played a typical possession game and had technically-gifted players who could pass and move at bewildering speed. The Hammers needed to be at their very best just to compete with the Belgians.

The Londoners started the game well and pressed Anderlecht back into their half. The opposition's defence had not conceded a goal at home throughout the competition and it would need a moment of real inspiration to break them down. In the 28th minute the Hammers found a way through and scored from an unlikely source. The vastly underrated Patsy Holland put his side ahead with a well-hit left foot shot that left the Belgian 'keeper helpless. The midfielder later revealed:

'I just hadn't been able to get into the game but then I gambled that I would get on to a Bonds' flick-on, and Bob's your uncle, I caught the ball perfectly with my rarely used left foot and put us ahead.'

Holland's goal gave the Hammers hope and belief. The Anderlecht players looked stunned and ran out of ideas for a spell. But, just when the Hammers looked to be heading for the interval a goal ahead, the ever dangerous Belgians equalised. In the dying minutes of the first half, Trevor Brooking crashed a shot against the bar. Anderlecht broke forward from the rebound. The ever-dependable Frank Lampard stopped the attack and in an attempt to slide the ball back to Mervyn Day, tripped and twisted his knee. Peter Ressel was on it in a flash. Punishing the full-back's error, Ressel slipped the ball to Robbie Rensenbrink who scored with ease.

Brooking said after the game,

'... we had been playing well. Then poor Frank Lampard caught his stud in the turf and injured himself trying to pass the ball back to

Mervyn Day and they got an equaliser.'

The goal proved to be the major turning point in the match.

Encouraged by their stroke of luck before the break, Anderlecht begun the second-half strongly and their fast-flowing football threatened to overwhelm the Hammers' defence. Then the inevitable happened and the Belgians took the lead with a well-taken goal by Van Der Elst. The talented Belgian later joined West Ham from New York Cosmos, and Frankie, as he became known at the club, had everything – pace, skill, and the ability to score goals. Sadly, he found it difficult to adjust to the physical demands of the English game, although he did score some memorable goals for the Hammers, including a hat-trick against Notts County. But Frankie was better suited to international football with its emphasis on passing, movement and individual skill, and continued to perform well for his country. He was very popular with the rest of the players at Upton Park and was one of the Hammers' better foreign signings.

Van der Elst, Rensenbrink and Arie Hann began to play scintillating football and totally dominated the game for the best part of 30 minutes, when out of nowhere, the East London side conjured up an equaliser. In the 69th minute, Brooking by now struggling with a groin injury, curled in a speculative low cross which Keith Robson got to first and turned the ball into the net with a neat, low header. Somehow the Hammers were back in the match.

But in this see-saw encounter of a match, the away fans hopes of a recovery soon perished in the night sky of that lovely city. Rensenbrink scored from the penalty spot in the 73rd minute, after being hauled down in the box by Holland. The winger was appalled by the decision:

'No, it wasn't a penalty because I got the ball before he went down ...Robbie just got up and didn't even appeal but somehow the referee gave it.'

It certainly wasn't an obvious penalty, but the Hammers were 3-2 down with only ten minutes remaining. There was to be no reprieve as Anderlecht continued to dominate play. The Belgians, in total control, waited patiently for their moment. It came in the 88th minute when Van Der Elst raced clear of the tiring Hammers' defence, and slipped the ball passed Day to seal a comfortable victory.

At the final whistle a distraught Keith Robson, not normally an emotional footballer, had to be dissuaded from refusing to accept his runners-up medal. He said at the time:

'I may have scored in the final but that defeat destroyed me. After beating Eintracht, we were probably a bit too confident. We had done so much to get there but we made too many mistakes and, in the end, we just gave it away.'

To be honest Anderlecht were a joy to watch in the second half and were far too good for the Hammers, who had two of their best players, Brooking and Lampard struggling with injuries. Skipper Bonds, honest to a fault, summed up the game:

'We could have no complaints; the better team on the night won.'

For the Hammers' skipper the Anderlecht match brought mixed emotions. He wrote in his autobiography:

'It should have been the high point of my life, leading the Hammers in a European Final.'

The reality for Bonds was very different. Shortly before the match, his wife's mother had been taken seriously ill and he considered pulling out of the match, but was persuaded to play by Lyn and his father-in-law. The team flew out on the Monday that week, but Bonds travelled out later on the Supporters' Club flight from Luton. In the circumstances Bonds played well in the final – did he ever have a bad game? But rather than attend the post-match reception he flew straight home and found his wife in tears – her mother had passed away during the night.

The fans were not aware of their captain's problems that night and the 1976 European Cup Final was largely an anti-climax for the Boleyn faithful. But they could return to England once again proud of their team's achievement in reaching a European final, the year after they had triumphed in the FA Cup. Their League position was a different story. But as Trevor Brooking reminded us:

'We may have only been a little East London club but right from the 1960s, Ron Greenwood – and then John Lyall – imposed a philosophy at West Ham that meant we could adapt to a European style and cope at a higher technical level.'

Most Hammers fans would agree that the team of the 1970s failed to live up to the standards set by Bobby Moore's victorious side. However, they did win the FA Cup in 1975 and had two decent runs in Europe, but the glory days were over. But West Ham being West Ham there were moments of triumph and disaster to come in the years ahead. In Bonds and Brooking, Lyall had two of the best players in England and with these two exceptional talents in the side anything was possible. The swashbuckling Hammers' captain with his beard and flowing hair was an inspiration and the fans loved him because of his total commitment to the club. Bonds played 793 games for the Hammers between 1967 and 1988 – a club record and unlikely to beaten. His greatest disappointment was not losing at Heysel or frustration at his team's poor League form, but in never having won a full England cap. He was selected for the national squad by Ron Greenwood three times only to be denied his opportunity through injury. The only time the Hammers' no. 4 pulled on an England shirt was as an unused substitute in a match against Italy. When you consider the second rate players selected by successive national managers during Bonds' career, it is nothing short of outrageous that he didn't win at least 50 caps. He will hate being labelled like this, but he surely must have been the best player never to win a full cap for his country. Disgraceful! Bonds is a god at Upton Park, the word legend doesn't quite do it. And we know from Bonds himself that John Lyall had a significant influence on his career and was responsible for his continued improvement as a footballer.

In 1987 Billy Bonds was awarded the MBE for his services to

football. It was the proudest day of his life, and no one deserved it more. He received hundreds of letters of congratulation, including one from Kenny Dalglish, who wrote fondly, 'Congratulations. Now you've got an MBE, isn't it time you packed it in?'

Bonds and Trevor Brooking were best friends and roommates and when they retired from the professional game they played together for an Essex Sunday morning side. The pair of them simply adored playing football. They would have felt bitter disappointment losing to Anderlecht, but their greatest moment playing for West Ham was still to come.

The team of 1976 enjoyed a wonderful European cup campaign, but with their best players struggling with injuries in the final, the match at the Heysel was a step too far for Bonds and his men. Lyall's team against Anderlecht was Day, Coleman, Bonds (c), Taylor T, Lampard, McDowell, Brooking, Paddon, Holland, Jennings and Robson. Alan Taylor was substitute.

With the European campaign over Lyall had time to reflect on only his second season as manager:

'Dominating everything that season were our adventures in Europe.'

It was his first taste of European football and a tremendous learning experience. Naturally, he sought the advice of his coaching team, Eddie Bailey, Bill Nicholson, Ronnie Boyce and Albert Walker, all of whom, as Murray Lyall points out, were instrumental to his success in the early years. Nicholson joined the Upton Park staff after leaving Tottenham and proved a huge help to the Hammers' fledgling manager. Lyall invited Nicholson on his scouting missions to Europe and the pair spent hours discussing players and tactics.

The Anderlecht final was a wonderful game of football and the cerebral Lyall would have taken some consolation from that. But his team had lost, and the reality of a disappointing League season would have troubled him. For the following season Lyall was intent on breaking the old West Ham habit of exciting cup runs accompanied by disappointing League form.

Chapter 8
Facing the Future

Managing a football club is a stressful and difficult job. Boards of director are notoriously capricious and unpredictable. Fans can be unforgiving and, at times of crisis, downright hostile. In the short time Lyall had been at the helm at Upton Park he had experienced the ups and downs that are an integral part of the job. But, the managerial emotional roller-coaster aside, life was generally good for the genial West Ham manager. The family were comfortably settled in Essex and John's promotion gave the Lyalls a degree of financial security for the first time in their married lives.

The relative prosperity came at a price. Lyall was one of the most hard-working managers in football. His day began at a pre-training staff briefing, before the real business of the day began. Meetings with players and his coaching team took up most of the afternoon and Lyall nearly always finished his day back at Upton Park where club business was always waiting. In addition to the daily schedule there were press conferences, youth team matches, reserve games and trips to size-up the opposition for the next game. If you throw in regular outings to see top European sides in action and snatched opportunities to have a look at potential new signings, we have the workload of two men. But Lyall was young and full of enthusiasm and loved his job. He was determined to arrest the club's decline and get West Ham back to the top flight.

With the aim of achieving more consistency the manager initiated some comings and goings at Upton Park. Centre-forward Clyde Best left the club in 1976 to take up a player/coach position in Tampa, Florida. Best was a wonderful, whole-hearted player for West Ham and was well-liked by the fans. Like Clive Charles, he developed into a successful coach in the US and eventually achieved the ultimate honour of being appointed chief coach of his native country, Bermuda. The following year Lyall sold Graham Paddon to Norwich and, in an attempt to rebuild his side, brought in centre-half Bill Green from Carlisle, Bryan Robson back from Sunderland, striker John Radford from Arsenal and, with exquisite judgement, fleet-footed Alan Devonshire from non-League Southall.

Despite the transfer activity the Hammers failed to build on the momentum they achieved at the tail-end of the previous season. With just one win in the first 12 games, Lyall's team started the new campaign in depressing fashion. The excitement of Europe seemed a distant memory as the Hammers sank to the bottom of the 1st Division. The team's appalling form brought Lyall his first crisis as a manager.

On 5 March 1977 Lyall took his team to Roker Park to play Sunderland. Both teams had accrued a meagre 19 points and were fighting for their survival in the top flight. Lyall was appalled with his side's performance on Wearside that night as his team capitulated 6-0 to a very average Sunderland team. As the Hammers manager said after the game:

'We were appalling. It was one of the worst performances in my career as manager.'

'Just like my dreams they fade and die.' The travelling fans were shocked and humiliated in front of the passionate Sunderland fans, but nobody felt the pain of such a defeat more than Lyall himself. One can only imagine the atmosphere on the journey back to London after the game. As the coach sped towards a service station, the Hammers' manager turned to his chairman, Reg Pratt and said with anger in his voice:

'We are going to pull into the next service station we come to, and I'm going to get all the players off the coach and they can find their own way home.'

Nobody hated losing more than Reg Pratt, but he turned to his manager and advised caution:

'Do you think no manager has ever lost 6-0 before, if you want to be a good manager you must learn to accept defeat. The secret is to rectify the mistakes the following week.'

Pratt's calm advice appeared to work. Lyall re-grouped his players and the following Saturday they beat Manchester City 1-0, thanks to a goal from *Pop* Robson – the little goal-scoring wizard had missed the Roker Park fiasco due to injury. The players clearly responded to their manager's harsh words and finished the season strongly. The Hammers remained unbeaten for the last seven games of the season, but still needed to defeat a strong Manchester United side in the final game to avoid relegation. The Reds had already reached the FA Cup final where they were due to face League champions, Liverpool. With Coppell, Greenhoff, Pearson and Hill in their side, the Hammers looked to be staring relegation in the face. This time Lyall's men were up to the challenge. Despite going down 1-0 in the first minute, the crowd cheered their favourites on to a magnificent 4-2 victory. Two more goals from Robson and one each from Lampard and Pike secured victory that brought a last gasp reprieve from the humiliation of relegation. Lyall's team had secured their place in the top flight with just 36 points.

The success of a football manager is always measured by the performance of his team – as is often said, football is a results business. Following his internal promotion in 1974, Lyall won the FA Cup and reached the final of a major European competition. But during this time his team had finished no higher than 13th in the 1st Division and were a whisker from being relegated in 1977. The West Ham board believed in their manager and were not given to hasty misjudgements under pressure. The players adored Lyall and desperately wanted to give him the results they believed his coaching deserved. But, another season flirting with relegation would test the resolve and patience of any chairman. Lyall's new signings needed to make a difference as he sought to find the right blend of attacking football and resolute defence.

A brief glimpse of glory in Europe and the reality of 1st Division struggle was the situation for Hammers' fans. But despite the constant battle with relegation, the fans loved John Lyall. Why? Because he was claret and blue through and through and understood what the fans wanted. Lyall's mixed record early in his managerial career raised the fundamental question; what makes an outstanding coach? Success is a necessary, but not a sufficient condition. Lyall was a partial success when he took over from Ron Greenwood, but then his team consistently underperformed in the league.

A good coach develops individual players and improves team performance. For a West Ham manager, he also needs his teams to play the right way. But good coaching can't be measured by any one criterion – it's a mysterious process. Lyall knew his job was to win football matches by playing attractive, attacking football. But, he believed passionately that his job also included a particular responsibility, the responsibility of leadership. This marks out John Lyall from other successful managers and why he was held in such high esteem. He believed in people and treated everyone he met as a human being, as an individual, not simply a pawn in the football manager's game. We can look to his ex-players to confirm his essential humanity.

When Mick McGiven arrived at Upton Park from Sunderland in 1974 he began a close working relationship with Lyall which lasted for over 20 years. The pair had known each other at youth level so the young Wearsider was delighted when Lyall offered to take him to Upton Park on loan. A succession of injuries prevented the midfielder from gaining a regular place in the Sunderland side, and he was frustrated to find himself on the bench during the Black Cats famous victory over Leeds United in the 1973 FA Cup Final. He was ready for a move and had very fond memories of arriving at West Ham:

"Everybody went out of their way to help," he remembers. "I recognised straight away that this was a coaching club – all the staff would go that extra mile to help the players. Ron Greenwood and John would get out a big bag of balls after training and we would work on different aspects of our game."

McGiven believes that Greenwood and Lyall's approach to training was light years ahead of the competition: "They were intelligent, good people and well-respected by all the players – they would always see everything through. Their training was meticulous. John had a notebook and logged everything, including injuries, players' strengths and weaknesses and so on. They were a special group of people."

Patsy Holland helps us to understand Lyall's popularity and why he was loved and respected by everyone in football, and the reasons why he was such a fine coach. When Holland joined West Ham from George Green Grammar School, he believed he had left one grammar school for another such was the intense learning culture at Chadwell Heath. Holland believed the coaches were interested in teaching players to think about the game. But there was a less cerebral side to the training – practice, practice, practice was how Holland described Lyall's coaching. All practices were unopposed as the coaching team sought to reinforce their painting pictures method, or visualisation, as it is now called. Lyall was a creative and flexible coach who changed his ideas to suit his players, much in the manner of Brian Clough.

When Tony Carr began working with the Hammers' youth teams, the manager would get the coaches together before training and plan the morning's work. Carr valued those early morning planning meetings where he learned the importance of making each session both interesting and purposeful.

As Holland says, "John's sessions were not just give it to Trevor and go," but thoughtful, confidence building master-classes. With his technical knowledge and ability to communicate, combined with a personal commitment to each and every one of his players, Lyall proved an inspirational coach. Players did not want to let him down. Duchy was particularly appreciative of his manager's teaching:

'John turned me from a headless chicken, playing playground football, into a professional footballer.'

Lyall had the support of the players, the fans and everyone at the club, but narrowly escaping relegation with a lowly 36 points wasn't part of the plan. Things at Upton Park needed to improve.

After the Lord Mayor's show
The Hammers' European campaign of 1975/76, with its magnificent matches against Den Haag, Frankfurt and Anderlecht raised the hopes and spirits of everyone at the Boleyn. The manager believed his team's performance at Upton Park against Eintracht Frankfurt was the best he had seen by a West Ham team, and Lyall had witnessed the heroics of Bobby Moore's Wembley heroes of 1965 at first hand. He worked hard to improve his own knowledge of the game. Lyall was an internationalist. He travelled widely in search of new ideas and became friends with the world's top managers. As a coach he developed a European mentality and would have been comfortable with modern managers like José Mourinho and Pepe Guardiolo. Thirty years ago Lyall's West Ham were playing with a zonal back four, a holding midfield player and a withdrawn centre-forward – a system they used to stunning effect in the 1980 FA Cup final against Arsenal. Today most teams are set up this way, including the great Barcelona side of Iniesta, Xavi and Messi.

The club's successful European campaigns of the mid-'70s had raised expectations at Upton Park. One or two new players meant there was a real possibility that the Hammers could become serious contenders for the 1st Division title in the years ahead, after all London neighbours Queen Parks Rangers finished runners-up in 1976.

In truth, Lyall's team of that time was better suited to the patient patterns of European football rather than the hurly-burly of the domestic game. Despite the satisfaction he must have felt at the marvellous football his team produced in Europe, the disappointment of the three seasons following their European exploits would have hurt Lyall deeply. The great expectations turned to misery when Lyall's men were relegated in 1978 with just 32 points. The new signings hadn't worked and John Radford for Keith Robson was never going to provide the necessary spark.

Heavy defeats against QPR and champions-elect Nottingham Forest meant early exits from both cup competitions; 1977/78 was clearly a year to forget at Upton Park.

Lyall wrote in his autobiography:

'Relegation was a terrible blow to the club, the players and my own pride... but I had to keep it in perspective.'

As a manager he was pragmatic enough to realise he needed to re-think his philosophy and rebuild his team if West Ham were to succeed in the English game. Apart from Alan Devonshire, Lyall's new signings made little impact. Lack of goals was a problem. *Pop* Robson top scored in both 1976/77 and 1977/78 with 14 and 11 League and cup goals respectively – a poor return for such a prolific scorer. Desperate for goals, Lyall quickly shipped out Radford and brought in Derek Hales from Derby County and, in a moment of inspiration, David Cross from West Bromwich. Although both strikers settled quickly, they arrived too late to make a real difference to the Hammers' season. In their Essential History Blows and Hogg wrote,

'...it seems inconceivable that a side containing the firepower of Cross, Hales and Robson, supported by the likes of Brooking and Devonshire in midfield and warriors like Bonds and Lampard in defence, should get relegated.'

Here was a team with top six pretensions. Instead they required a point to avoid relegation from their final game of the season at home to runners-up, Liverpool. They lost 2-0. West Ham had been in the top flight for 20, largely successful years. Their bright young manager, popular with everyone associated with the club, was forced to admit failure. Lyall was a proud man and would have accepted full responsibility, but his team, strong on paper, must shoulder most of the blame. But chairman Pratt failed to panic and Lyall was given a genuine vote of confidence. His job was secure – at least for the first season in the 2nd Division.

Somewhat perversely, local reporter Trevor Smith blamed Lyall's predecessor when he wrote:

'I accuse Ron Greenwood... the downward spiral path began the day the team won the 1975 FA Cup final. His failure since 1975 to sign the right players at the right time must surely be regarded as the biggest single factor in the circumstances which combined to result in relegation.'

The European influence on the club's football philosophy contributed to the team's fall from grace. The players had forgotten how to win matches. These were top class players with European experience who had forgotten how to get down and scrap for points in English football. Bobby Moore has some interesting and not entirely uncritical thoughts on the Hammers' commitment to their purist philosophy. He commented in his biography:

'Ron Greenwood and John Lyall shied away when you mentioned putting some stick about. The emphasis was on skill.'

Of course as a tackler, Moore was the most skilful in world football and looked on tackling as a great skill – something not shared it seems by Greenwood, and later Lyall. Moore warmed to his theme:

'You don't have to go around kicking people up in the air to be a good tackler. The art is to deny a forward space and force him to knock the ball away... One of the problems was that sometimes West Ham didn't do this as a whole. They were obsessed with creating space for themselves... and could not recover when moves broke down.'

In addition to a reluctance to compromise what Moore describes as, 'their delicate football,' the Hammers were often a sitting target for gritty Northern sides determined to put the effete, southern pansies firmly in their place. This was the challenge facing the West Ham manager – how to toughen up his side without losing the purity of their football so beloved of their fans. Greenwood and

Lyall had educated the fans to expect great football – but they also demanded success. With Billy Bonds they had acquired some grit, but it was not sufficient to save them from relegation. Now the exquisite skills of Trevor Brooking were to be employed in the backstreet of Oldham, Preston and Cardiff, rather than the splendid arenas of Old Trafford and Anfield.

Lyall was still a relatively novice manager and it would take him time to learn the job and understand what it takes to build a winning team for all occasions. The Hammers' popularity with players and fans alike was admirable, but being popular is no substitute for success, as he would was forced to admit. With his side in the 2nd Division, Lyall was only just beginning his long education in management and leadership.

The Hammers stay loyal to their beleaguered manager

That summer, Lyall took the family up to Norfolk for a week's fishing. He was a member of a local angling club as a boy and saw fishing as an antidote to the pressure of professional football. It was during the Norfolk trip that Lyall made the decision to start his first season in the 2nd Division with an unchanged team.

Loyalty is a forgotten value in today's world of grubby agents and celebrity, multi-millionaire footballers. But professional football in the 1970s was a very different business to the greedy, money-driven culture of the Premier League. Relegation at the end of 1977/78 was disappointing for West Ham, but not disastrous. The club was financially stable and the chairman stayed loyal to the man who had been with the club since he was 15-years-old and had a five-year contract. I doubt if any other possibility was even discussed by the board. Moreover, the club's top players showed loyalty to their manager and the fans by agreeing to stay and fight for promotion. There was interest from the top clubs for Bonds and Brooking, but neither showed any enthusiasm to leave Upton Park. Brooking was quick to nail his colours to the mast. He knocked on his manager's door at the end of the relegation season:

'Sorry to trouble you, John, but have you got a minute. I just want to let

you know that I want to stay at West Ham and help get the team back into the 1st Division. I don't want to leave.'

Brooking's gesture would have encouraged Lyall. Of course, this was in the days before agents did the players' thinking for them. Lyall revealed his thoughts about his club's brand of loyalty to Tony McDonald:

'You have to be loyal to your players, because it's a 'we' situation, and that's what I always loved about West Ham. The staff in the office and the commercial department, the stewards – there was no hierarchy, they were all part of it... the fans stuck by us... They appreciated what we were trying to do and that's why people like me stayed so long.'
Lyall continued:

'It's why... when people talk to me about West Ham now, I still... use the word 'we'... because it's our club and it still belongs to us.'

Those certainly were the days!

With Brooking, Bonds, *Pop* Robson, Alan Devonshire, David Cross, Paul Brush, Tommy Taylor and Pat Holland as the heart of his team, Lyall could view the prospect of promotion at the first attempt with confidence, even excitement as he wrestled with the challenge of winning games while playing West Ham's unique brand of football. It's a curse that has afflicted many managers at Upton Park since the golden era of Greenwood and Lyall.

Lyall's side got off to a solid start in their new habitat with good wins over Notts County and Newcastle United, before suffering successive defeats at the hands of Fulham and Burnley. A 3rd Round FA Cup loss to lowly Newport County and an exit from the League Cup at the same stage, brought embarrassment to the fans and a few sleepless nights for the manager. Consistent home form kept the Hammers in the chase for promotion until they fell away badly in the run-in as Brighton and Crystal Palace took the two promotion spots.

***Psycho* arrives in the big city**

The club would have been disappointed at failing to achieve promotion in their first season in the 2nd Division – but help was on the way and from the most unlikely source. Struggling to find the right balance for his side, Lyall sold Kevin Lock to Fulham and Bill Green to Peterborough. For the second time in two years the board refused to panic, and the top players once again demonstrated their loyalty to the club. Despite his clear frustration at failing to go back up first time round, Lyall would have been greatly encouraged by two things: the form and goals of David Cross and, most importantly, the signing of the great Phil Parkes from QPR, who Lyall brought in to replace the demoralised Mervyn Day. Cross and Parkes were fine acquisitions and were both key members of the glorious West Ham side of the '80s. Lyall also knew he had outstanding youngsters like Paul Allen and Tony Cottee knocking on the first team door, as he sought desperately to lift his players for a second promotion bid. The signings of Cross and Parkes throw some interesting light on John Lyall as a man, as well as a manager.

David Cross had scored seven times in the Hammers' last seven matches of the relegation season and his manager was confident the centre-forwards' goals would take the club back to the 1st Division. A decent tally of 17 the following season was a good effort, but in fairness, the Hammers' defensive problems cost them promotion, rather than any lack of goals from Cross and *Pop* Robson.

Initially, Cross was reluctant to leave the Midlands for what he feared were the bright lights of the capital – he needed some reassurance. I was fortunate to interview Cross as part of the research for this book. We sat in his large, rambling house in Lancashire while he talked about his career and his time at West Ham. Cross was generous with his time and talked eloquently and with great fondness about his years in the East End of London and the relationship he enjoyed with John Lyall. David – known affectionately as *Psycho* by the North Bank, who adored their no. 9 – began his career at Rochdale. Spells at Norwich and Coventry followed, before he finally settled at West Brom. The Baggies manager, Johnny Giles signed Cross three times during his career and clearly had a high regard for the bustling centre-forward. When Giles was sacked, his replacement, club legend Ronnie Allen, preferred Laurie Cunningham and Cyrille Regis as his first choice attacking partnership. At the age of 26 Cross understandably wanted first team football and when West Ham expressed interest he felt he had to listen, despite initial reservations.

The Cross transfer provides us with a glimpse of Lyall's emerging skill at gaining the trust of his players. Knowing that Cross was sceptical about a move to the capital, Lyall invited him down to his home in the quiet Essex countryside. John and Yvonne reassured the Lancastrian that Essex was a long way from the bright lights of London. West Ham players were much more likely to be seen in the local pubs of Stratford and Plaistow than hot-spots of the West End. Cross enjoyed his day with the Lyalls and was persuaded that leaving the Hawthorns for Upton Park would be good for his career. He duly signed for West Ham on 8 December 1977, his 27th birthday. It appears a little odd that Cross, who described himself as a 'horrible, nasty bloke on a Saturday afternoon,' should be so nervous about signing for a relatively big club like West Ham. After all, he was a young, single professional who was being courted by one of the most talented young managers in the country. The reason for his hesitancy lies in Cross's lack of faith in his own ability. He simply did not believe he could play. As he revealed on that day at his house in Bury, "I never thought I was any good."

David Cross was extremely proud to have the words professional footballer on his passport, but knew he needed to work hard on his game if he was to achieve his potential. The fear of London was the fear of being distracted and losing his sense of purpose. On his way to Essex to meet the Lyalls, Cross asked himself two questions. Firstly, will the move improve me as a player? Secondly, would I be better off financially? He was convinced on both counts.

Lyall gave the aggressive striker his first team debut in the 1-0 defeat against West Bromwich Albion on 17 January 1977. Despite this temporary setback Cross was on his way as the Hammers ran out 2-1 winners with goals from Hales and Brooking. was on his way as his apprehension and fragile confidence evaporated into the East End air. As the Hammers' new centre-forward admitted, his self-doubt drove him to be the great goalscorer he became. He had turned a potential weakness into his greatest strength. As coach Mick McGiven recently said of Cross:

'He came to West Ham as a raw, very physical player, when he left he could score goals, join in the play, and was very comfortable on the ball. And, of course, he never lost the physical side of his game. He could mix it with the best.'

Lyall worked hard on inspiring confidence in his new striker. But, as Cross remembers, "he also added things to my game." When his new signing arrived at Upton Park, Lyall introduced special coaching sessions for his strikers where he worked with *Pop* Robson, Stuart Pearson and Paul Goddard on ways to improve their partnership. For example, Cross became adept at dummying passes and crosses to give Robson an opening on goal. To encourage Cross and Robson to play more closely together, Lyall told them to imagine they had a 20 yard rope attached to each other's ankles – a further example of the manager's painting pictures method. These special afternoon sessions were exactly what Cross needed at this time of his career. Lyall continually reinforced the need for Cross to get into the penalty area at every opportunity because he knew that like most natural centre-forwards, Cross was an average player outside the box. Of his 222 goals only four were scored from beyond the 18-yard area. David Cross was a highly intelligent footballer and quickly realised Lyall's coaching would dramatically improve his game and of course, it did.

West Ham's new signing offers an interesting story which gives us an insight into Lyall's coaching technique. In one particular game, Cross was put through on goal with just the 'keeper to beat. Caught in two minds, the centre-forward lofted the ball over the crossbar when he could have either gone round the 'keeper, or gently clipped it over his falling body. In the next training session following Cross's glaring miss, Lyall made him practice one-on-ones for an hour, but crucially gave Cross precise technical advice. He told his no. 9:

'Imagine you are going to clip the ball on top of the net and let's practice that.'

I'm not sure David Cross ever missed a one-on-one again. With such individual technical help Cross's game improved beyond recognition. He knew he had to keep on the move, lose his marker and work closely with Robson and Goddard. As Cross said, "John instinctively understood just what I needed, he wasn't a bully, as some managers are, and transformed me from a decent centre-forward into a proven goalscorer."

There is no question that Lyall's coaching and leadership played a decisive role in the determined David Cross's success. However, the forward must take some of the credit. This hard-working and perceptive footballer was a manager's dream. Despite his lack of belief in his own ability, he was a highly intelligent footballer who quickly grasped his manager's intentions. He also put pressure on himself in a way that would be foreign to today's Premier League players. Cross always described himself as a goalscorer, rather than a striker or centre-forward. He had no time for the view that a striker is doing well as long as he is making chances for others. Scoring goals was his job and he wasn't happy if the goals didn't come. This brutally honest self-assessment led to a rare moment of tension between Cross and his manager before the 1980 FA Cup final against Arsenal – of which more later.

A memorable season

For the 1979/80 season Lyall brought in the experienced Stuart Pearson from Manchester United and, in a surprising clear-out, released John McDowell, Alan Taylor, *Pop* Robson, Tommy Taylor, Mervyn Day and Billy Jennings. Pancho Pearson, proud possessor of 15 England caps, signed for the Hammers in August. In the same month Lyall made one of the best signings of his managerial career when he persuaded Ray Stewart to move south from Dundee for a fee of £430,000. The Scottish defender was a teenager when he joined West Ham and went on to make over 400 League and cup appearances, famously scoring a total of 84 League and cup goals, most from the penalty spot. Lyall consulted both Alex Ferguson and Jock Stein about Stewart's potential and received ringing endorsements. Lyall and Eddie Bailey travelled up to Scotland to meet the young Scot and his tough talking manager, Jim McLean. The youngster knew little about West Ham, but felt happy with Lyall and Bailey and agreed to sign. Later, McLean said selling Stewart was the worst mistake of his managerial career.

The 19-year-old full-back travelled south and stayed at the Lyall's house for a few days where he immediately felt wanted and at home. Yvonne quickly took to the youngster and at the end of Stewart's stay told her husband:

'Ray tidies his room and makes his own bed. You will definitely be alright with this one.'

How right she was. Stewart tells an amusing story about his stay at the Lyall's house. The Perthshire lad had few clothes and the ones he did have were not exactly straight out of Carnaby Street. He remembers trying to hang his clothes up his clothes in the Lyall's house in Abridge, but all the wardrobes were chocked full of John's suits. Young Ray had no choice but to lay out his clothes on the bedroom floor.

Moving to the London area was a major culture shock for a young Scot from distant Perthshire. When Stewart eventually moved out of the Lyall's house, the club put him up in the Post House Hotel in Epping. Most mornings Eddie Bailey picked up the new Hammers' full-back at his hotel and drove him through Loughton and Romford and on to the urban vastness of East London. When Bailey hit the usual traffic jam at the Moby Dick pub in Romford, Stewart was shocked. "I had never seen traffic like it," he admitted. However, the youngster soon adjusted to life at his new club, bought some new clothes and quickly made friends with his new teammates.

Form the start Lyall and Stewart developed a good relationship.

The Scot remembers his manager being very supportive around the time of his wedding. He said recently, "the Lyalls became like a mum and dad to me while I was with West Ham." Young Ray also became a good friend of Murray Lyall and the pair enjoyed playing cricket together for Abridge CC during the close season.

Stewart was popular at West Ham and quickly made friends, including club photographer Steve Bacon and the young midfielder Paul Allen, who became his roommate on away trips. It was six or seven weeks before the young full-back was able to return home to see his friends and family in Dundee, by which time he had found excellent digs at Rose Cross's house in Barking. Rose's son Roger never quite fulfilled his early promise at West Ham, but enjoyed a successful coaching career when his playing days ended.

Stewart enjoyed the training at Chadwell Heath and offers an interesting insight into Lyall's coaching style. Shortly after he joined the club, young Ray approached his manager for advice on improving his passing technique. Lyall loved it when his players showed enthusiasm and sought him out for advice. One afternoon later that week, Lyall had Stewart bending balls around an imaginary defender for two hours before he had perfected the skill. "I must have hit 400 balls that afternoon," he remembers. If a player failed to show Stewart's level of enthusiasm, Lyall would ask one of the coaches to work with him, so Stewart was impressed that the manager gave him so much personal attention.

Lyall began to trust Stewart to the extent that he asked him to keep an eye on the teenage Paul Allen – to act as a kind of mentor to the young East Ender. After his initial shock, Stewart responded to the responsibility and trust his manager gave him. As he grew in confidence, Stewart made a decision which was to define his career. When the Hammers' regular penalty taker Geoff Pike left the club, Lyall turned and asked the players, "Who wants the job?"

Stewart looked around the silent dressing room for a brief moment, before putting his hand up. "I'll do it John," he told his grateful manager. The rest, as they say is history. Ray Stewart became one of the most successful penalty takers in post-war English football. His readiness to take over from Geoff Pike as the club's penalty taker also showed Stewart's leadership potential. He was no longer the rookie with a questionable fashion sense, but one of the most valuable members of Lyall's new team.

Despite his developing relationship with John Lyall, Stewart also experienced the tougher side of his manager's personality. The full-back got into trouble with Lyall when the Scot allowed Alvin Martin to take a penalty to complete an unlikely hat-trick for the Hammers' centre-half. Lyall was furious.

"It's your responsibility to take penalties, how dare you let other people take them for you?" Of course, it was the last time anyone else took a penalty while Ray Stewart was in the team.

When Stewart was selected to play for his country for the first time, he was allowed to renegotiate his contract at West Ham. This was in the days long before agents negotiated players' contracts. Stewart sat down with his manager and agreed a new deal. Lyall told his full-back from the start that, "West Ham doesn't give boot money – we're not that kind of club."

Tonka, as Stewart soon became known, soon signed his improved contract and the matter was settled amicably. As he said recently, "I trusted John with everything. I would have trusted him with my life." Lyall gave Stewart responsibility and the confidence he needed to become a great player. The hugely popular full-back would have won far more than his 10 Scottish caps but for the excellence of Danny McGrain and George Burley at that time.

Lyall's brother, Jim, has become close to Stewart over the years and speaks very highly of his friend. Jim remembers:

'Ray's parents were kind to me and my partner, they lived in the same village where I have my flat.'

Both John and Jim travelled up to show their support for Stewart when he was appointed manager of Stirling Albion. Jim gave Stewart a copy of the book, One Minute Manager to encourage the ex-Hammer in his new managerial career. But, with very little money and a tiny fan base, Stewart's chances of success as a manager in the lower divisions of Scottish football were remote. Currently out of football, the former Hammers' full-back keeps in touch with the game by acting as a club ambassador at Upton Park where he remains a popular figure. One has the impression that Ray Stewart still has much to offer the game he graced with such distinction.

A worthy successor to Ken Brown
With Stewart settled in his new club and Tony Cottee and Paul Allen waiting in the wings, Lyall had another Academy youngster ready for the first team in Tommy Taylor's replacement, Alvin Martin. The young defender made his debut in the relegation season and made 23 League and cup appearances the following year where his presence and determination impressed his manager. Lyall's trust in his young centre-half was rewarded when Martin made a total of 55 appearances in all competitions the following season. Martin, a Lancastrian, was claret and blue through and through. The youngster had the unenviable task of replacing the incomparable Billy Bonds as club captain. An honour he carried out with distinction, providing a much-needed stillness and competence at the heart of Lyall's defence. He was to become one of the greatest Hammers of all time.

With Stewart and Martin joining Bonds, Brooking and Lampard, Lyall was clearly building a team in his own image. These were strong characters and born leaders, and all were magnificent footballers. Here was the basis of a new West Ham side capable of competing with the best in the country. Lyall's task was to encourage them to play a type of football that would get them out of the 2nd Division without alienating their passionate fans brought up on Bobby Moore, Martin Peters and Geoff Hurst. This was Lyall's greatest test. In 1977, his great friend and mentor Ron Greenwood left Upton Park after 15 wonderful years to succeed Don Revie as the England manager. Greenwood proceeded to take the national side to the 1980 European Championships and the 1982 World Cup finals. John Lyall was now firmly on his own – the honeymoon was over. Bill Nicholson had returned to Spurs with Keith Burkinshaw after one season, but with the arrival of Eddie

Bailey, Lyall found the ideal replacement. But Lyall was clearly the gaffer and made a bold and determined attempt to rebuild the side that failed to achieve promotion in its first season following relegation. He wanted to add some experience to his team and to give them a more ruthless approach to winning football matches and with Brooking and Devonshire in his side he knew the fans would be happy and the West Ham way would not be compromised.

One of Lyall's priorities at West Ham was to improve the out-dated training facilities. Essentially, he believed the players needed an indoor facility where they could train and prepare for games out of the extreme winter weather. So a determined Lyall set out to raise the cash for a new gym at the Chadwell Heath training ground. Training outside in freezing conditions throughout the winter months was not ideal preparation for players expected to play a close passing, attacking style of football. Lyall was convinced the gym would make a difference:

'The atmosphere generated by playing in a confined area considerably enhanced the skills and technique of the players... the ball is never out of play, and the speed of the game encourages movement and sure touch.'

With Lyall leading the drive for the new facility, the club was awarded £140,000 from the Sports Council. Chairman, Reg Pratt committed the club to spending £250,000 on the project and the sparkling new gym was completed in the summer of 1979.

Expectation was high among the staff and players as the new season approached. But despite the new addition to the training ground, the Hammers began the 1979/80 League campaign in disappointing fashion. They lost their first two League games 1-0 and suffered a further six League defeats in the first half of the season. Their League form improved after Christmas with six wins in seven games before, once again, falling away at the sharp end of the season. But their cup form was a completely different story.

The result of Lyall's ruthless rebuilding was two magnificent cup runs which included wins against Aston Villa and Everton leading to another Wembley FA Cup final appearance. The North Bank fuelled to incendiary levels in the 1970s by lager and Sham '69, was in Hammers' heaven. But an end of season 7th place in the 2nd Division frustrated the fans and was a sign the rebuilt team was not quite the finished article.

The Hammers reached the quarter final of the League Cup in mid-December, but following a hard-fought 0-0 draw at Upton Park, Lyall's men lost tamely to a strong Nottingham Forest side which included Garry Birtles, John O'Hare, John Robertson and Martin O'Neil. In the previous round, a hard fought tie against Southend United, Lyall decided to give 17-year-old Paul Allen his debut. The manager trusted the youngster to deliver:

'I felt we needed a little more devil in the middle of the field. All I asked him to do was to hold his position in central midfield and win the ball for us. He was a revelation. He transformed us.'

The Hammers won the second replay against Southend 5-1, largely thanks to Paul Allen's mature display. Allen held the record number of England Youth caps and Lyall had every confidence in the teenager. Four days later the young midfielder made his League debut in the 2-1 home victory against Burnley and the manager kept him in the team for the rest of the season.

Not to be disheartened by the Forest defeat, the revitalised Hammers enjoyed an FA Cup run that will linger long in the memory. A Phil Parkes inspired victory in a replayed 3rd Round tie against Ron Atkinson's West Brom was followed by a regulation 3-2 win over East London neighbours, Orient. Goals from David Cross and Paul Allen brought a comfortable 5th Round victory at Upton Park over John Toshack's Swansea City. The following week fortune smiled on the Hammers in the quarter-final draw – Aston Villa at home. Over 36,000 fans squeezed into Upton Park to witness a fiercely competitive match won by the home side in the dying seconds. The Hammers, without the injured Billy Bonds, were awarded a 90th minute penalty and the ever-confident Ray Stewart strode up to take the kick and hammered it past the despairing Rimmer in the Villa goal. Second Division West Ham was in the FA Cup semi-final and the fans could begin to dream again of an end of season trip to Wembley.

With their faint promotion prospects evaporating into thin air, Lyall and his team were able to concentrate fully on the FA Cup. A crowd of 47,000 crowded into Villa Park to witness the semi-final against 1st Division Everton. The Hammers fans' collective heart sunk when Brian Kidd converted a penalty shortly before half-time. Kidd was sent off later in the game but not before Stuart Pearson equalised to send the tie into a replay. The match at Elland Road four days later was played at fever pitch pace. An injury to Alvin Martin meant Lyall had to re-jig his defence, bringing back the fit-again Bonds to partner Stewart at the heart of the defence, while Paul Brush replaced Stewart at full-back.

The score remained stubbornly at 0-0 at the end of 90 minutes, and the match went into extra-time. A wonderful Devonshire goal broke the deadlock within four minutes of the re-start. But with only seven minutes left on the clock Bob Latchford, for the first time in the tie, slipped the attentions of Bonds and Stewart and scored with a stunning strike. But the Hammers were not to be denied. The semi-final against Everton will be best remembered by West Ham fans for Frank Lampard's late winning goal, with of all things a diving header. His outrageous goal celebration of sprinting to the West Ham fans before dancing an improbable jig around the nearest corner flag remains vivid in the memory. What was he even doing in the opposition's six-yard box in the last minute of an FA Cup semi-final? It was just the West Ham way!

Despite his last minute heroics, Lampard would concede that the man-of-the-match that wonderful April evening was Alan Devonshire. The elegant midfielder dominated the match with some exquisite football and scored an unforgettable goal, beating what seemed like the whole Everton team, before sliding the ball past the helpless Everton 'keeper. The midfielder later admitted that it was his best-ever game. "As close as I ever came to perfection in my career," Devonshire later recalled.

The Hammers were back at Wembley for the second time in five years.

Chapter 9
In Claret and Blue Dreamland

After five years in the job, Lyall's Hammers won the FA Cup in his first full season, suffered relegation and watched his team languish in the 2nd Division for two years. He transformed the club's training facilities and playing staff, before leading his team back to Wembley in glorious style in 1980. Lyall's roller-coaster early years as West Ham manager tested the patience of the fans, but they were fans who were well-used to this kind of white-knuckle ride.

The 1980s was the decade of Michael Jackson, Madonna and Margaret Thatcher. In May 1980 when John Lyall led his West Ham team back to Wembley Margaret Thatcher had been Prime Minister for just 12 months. Thatcher's divisive government led the country into war against Argentina and masterminded a vicious attack on the British miners, culminating in the violent scenes at Orgreave in 1984. Throughout the '80s violence and hooliganism continued to blight English football. Upton Park on match days was a dangerous place with pitched battles at local underground stations, dozens of police dogs shepherding fans to and from the ground, and barbed-wire fences separating rival supporters. The North Bank's ICF continued to glory in violence, bullying and intimidation. The Taylor Report and the glamour of the Premier League were 10 years away. But some things never change as Liverpool won the 1st Division Championship again in 1980, finishing just two points ahead of bitter rivals, Manchester United.

None of this mattered much to the 100,000 people who flocked to Wembley Stadium on that sunny Saturday in early May. For West Ham fans, beating Arsenal in an FA Cup final at Wembley is about as good as it gets. The Hammers had won the FA Cup in 1964 and 1975, but the 1980 final was special and remains a revered memory in the collective consciousness of the East London club. For those fortunate to be at the old stadium that day, the memory is simply unforgettable.

Wembley opponents Arsenal reached the final after four exhausting, bone crunching matches against mighty Liverpool. Most neutrals wanted an Arsenal/Liverpool final that year, and were disappointed when the two 1st Division rivals were drawn against each other in the semi-final.

The 1980 final was the 99th to be played at Wembley Stadium. The Hammers had reached the final on three occasions, while their illustrious North London neighbours had contested the previous two finals and were a formidable 1st Division side. Although most Hammers' supporters accepted their team were underdogs, skipper Billy Bonds had other ideas:

'We didn't really go into the game thinking we were underdogs because, although we were a second division side, we had a lot of very good players in the team. If you look at that team a lot of them became legends at the club.'

Bonds had a point – you could reel off the names – Trevor Brooking, Phil Parkes, Frank Lampard Snr, Alvin Martin, Alan Devonshire and, of course, Bonds himself. What was this team doing in the Second Division anyway, the fans continued to ask themselves?

The Hammers had beaten Charlton Athletic 4-1 in a League match the week before the final, showing some of their best form of the season. The 32-year old Bonds had every reason to be confident. He was a highly experienced player and captained the victorious 1975 FA Cup side. More or less recovered from his long-standing injury and disciplinary problems, Bonds was fit for the final and raring to go. But despite the skipper's belief in his team, the North London side were everybody's clear favourites on the day. Like many other Hammers' fans I arrived at the stadium early and, full of expectation I joined the supporters of both teams heading up Wembley Way. The area around the entrance to the stadium was a sea of claret and blue, and the noise from those already inside the ground added to the mounting tension.

The build-up to the game passed in a flash before the teams, Arsenal in yellow and the Hammers in white, emerged from the tunnel led by their respective managers, John Lyall and Terry Neil. Before the kick-off the two captains, Bonds and Pat Rice, presented their teams to the Duke and Duchess of Kent, while Bubbles rang round the ground drowning all attempts by the Gunners' fans to make themselves heard. At that moment, seconds before 3 o'clock, the atmosphere in the ground was electric.

Then something odd happened. A portly figure, with half a dozen cameras slung round his neck, wandered onto the pitch and took his place by the side of the goal at the West Ham end. To the utter confusion of the opposition fans, the claret and blue hordes began chanting at the top of their voices 'There is only one Stevie Bacon, one Stevie Bacon.'

One Stevie Bacon? What did all this mean?

The Hammers fans were paying their own tribute to the Stratford Express's legendary cameraman, Steve Bacon. Bacon is loved and respected at Upton Park and the fans' tribute was a genuine gesture of appreciation to one of their own. John Lyall made Bacon the official club photographer after the Arsenal game and the two men enjoyed a long and fruitful friendship. It was a moving moment on an emotional day.

The week before the big day the Hammers had trained as normal. Lyall was keen not to break the players' usual routine and stuck to the traditional Tuesday day off. On the Friday night before the final the staff and players stayed in the familiar surroundings of the Hendon Hall Hotel. David Cross was one of the players who appreciated the familiarity of the team's preparation for the big match. Cross was in the Norwich City side that reached the League Cup final a few years earlier and believed manager Ron Saunders over-prepared his players with a two night stay at the sumptuous Selsdon Park Hotel. The West Ham forward argued that this high-profile preparation was one of the reasons Norwich performed so poorly on the day.

Someone once said that, 'the only risk is not taking a risk.' Lyall was certainly not going into this game without making life as difficult as possible for the opposition. If the Hammers' preparation was low-key, Lyall's tactics were far from familiar and shook their opponents to the core. He knew the Gunners were the stronger side so he decided to take a gamble – what was there to lose? He wrote in his autobiography:

'I felt we needed to come up with something a little different, something that would confuse them and perhaps disturb their defensive organisation.'

Lyall decided to play David Cross as a lone striker and Stuart Pearson in a withdrawn position just ahead of the midfield – what today would be called playing in the hole. Lyall would have remembered *Budgie* Byrne playing the deep-lying centre-forward to such great effect back in the 1964 final. For this master-stroke to work Lyall had to trust both Cross and Pearson. No manager knew his players better than John Lyall:

'You couldn't have experimented with such a tactical move in a Wembley final with lesser players than Pearson and Cross.'

Lyall knew this was a sensitive tactical change and might be resisted by Cross who had 'goalscorer' written through him like a stick of rock. Following the manager's short analysis of the Arsenal players Lyall took his two forwards to one side, as Cross recalls:

John took Pancho and me into a shower room just before the final and told us he was going to play 4-5-1 rather than the usual 4-4-2.'

Pearson was being asked to drop off, while Cross was expected to occupy both Young and O'Leary, the two Arsenal centre-backs. Lyall knew Cross would not be happy and needed some reassurance. He told his centre-forward:

'I don't want to deprive you of the opportunity to score, and you will have the support of five midfield players.'

Cross played selflessly that day and did a magnificent job of hustling and chasing Young and O'Leary, but his failure to score bothered him for years afterwards. As the players assembled in the tunnel before the kick-off Cross turned to his close friend and said, "Pancho, you knew about John's plan all along, didn't you?"

Pearson smiled in acknowledgement and replied, "John thought you would worry about it if he told you during the week."

Lyall knew he had sacrificed Cross for the greater good of the team. The Gunners' centre-backs were formidable defenders and would give the Hammers' centre-forward a tough 90 minutes. As he walked up the tunnel and out onto the Wembley pitch to greet the roar of the crowd, Cross took a minute to attune himself to his new role. It would not be an easy game for the Hammers' centre-forward.

For Lyall the plan worked like a dream. The Gunners' defence were in two minds. They were unsure whether to come out and mark Pearson or leave him space to play. If they pressed, Lyall had instructed his midfield to play more directly to Cross higher up the field. Trevor Brooking reflecting on the game recently, remembers:

'The Arsenal defenders were arguing among themselves as to who should pick up Pearson who had his best game for the club.'

As Brooking has said:

'John had prepared us well. With Pearson as a fifth man in midfield we more than matched them. But you have to give Crossy credit for the way he went about his job.'

The game opened in predictable fashion with Arsenal having the majority of possession. Brady was pulling the strings in midfield, sending a stream of passes out to Sunderland and Rix on the flanks. But the Hammers had a plan and refused to grant the great Irishman the freedom of Wembley. We know Lyall had thought very carefully about his team's tactics for the match. His gamble with a deep-lying centre-forward was matched by a risky decision to play young midfielder Paul Allen ahead of the experienced

Holland. The Hammers' regular right side midfielder was devastated. It's every professional footballer's dream to play in a Wembley final and Holland was forced to sit this one out. He had played with distinction in '75 and had been a key member of the side for years. In fairness to Lyall, Holland did have injury problems that season, but insisted he was completely match fit. It took this popular and dedicated player some time to recover from the disappointment of being left out of the side.

Lyall detailed Allen, the youngest player to appear in an FA Cup final at 17 years and 256 days, to stick close to Brady and stop him dictating the play. The teenager and the tenacious Geoff Pike, fought tirelessly to disrupt the usually smooth Arsenal passing game. By stifling the opposition's best players, the hard-working pair gave the Hammers' more creative midfielders, Devonshire and Brooking, every opportunity to counter-attack.

With the Gunners' defence in a state of confusion and Allen snapping at Brady's heels, the Hammers' began to get into the game. And then a claret and blue miracle occurred. In the 12th minute, Devonshire broke free on the left wing and delivered a measured cross into the Gunner's penalty area. David Cross was the first to the ball and his half-hit shot was parried by Pat Jennings. The ball rebounded awkwardly for Stuart Pearson who scuffed his shot across the goalmouth. Waiting was the Hammers' England star Trevor Brooking, who stooped and steered a header through a helpless Gunners' defence and into the net.

Yes, Brooking had scored with a header in the Cup Final against Arsenal – and West Ham were 1-0 ahead. Needless to say, the Irons' fans went wild and, not for the last time that May afternoon, Wembley resounded to joyous choruses of Bubbles. How Brooking must have relished that moment. In the days before the match Notts Forest manager Brian Clough singled out Brooking for criticism. He rudely alleged the classy midfielder 'floated like a butterfly and stung like one.' The outspoken Clough accused the East London club of being more interested in the glamour of a Wembley than in being promoted back to the top flight, not that it was any of old Big Mouth's business. To be fair to Clough he later apologised to Brooking for his scandalous remarks.

Having taken an early lead, could the East Enders retain it? The Gunners dominated the last 30 minutes of the first half, but Lyall's defence held firm, with Bonds, Martin and 'keeper Parkes outstanding. The best efforts of Sunderland, Stapleton and Rix foundered on the rock of the claret and blue defence. The East Londoners reached half-time with their lead intact.

During the interval the West Ham fans speculated nervously about what might happen in the second period. Over the years they had become hardened to disappointment. But from the evidence of the first 45 minutes, the East Londoners were entitled to believe that this time their dreams wouldn't fade and die.

The second half continued the pattern of the first, but with one encouraging exception. As Pearson, Devonshire and Brooking grew in confidence they started running at the Arsenal defence. The Hammers rearguard took heart in their teammates attacking intentions as they withstood everything the tireless Brady could throw at them. With minutes to go the claret and blue end of the ground began to prepare for victory. As the tension mounted Lyall's men came close to scoring a second goal which would have put the 1980 Cup Final beyond doubt.

The spritely young Allen skipped through the Gunners' defence and with only Pat Jennings to beat was cynically and cruelly brought down behind by an appalling Willie Young tackle. The Arsenal centre-half remained on the field and only received a yellow card – the professional foul rule had not yet been introduced. But justice was well and truly done when the referee blew for time minutes later and the jubilant Hammers fans could celebrate at last.

Billy Bonds received the FA Cup from the Duke of York, turned to his left and lifted the trophy high and joyously to the victorious legions of West Ham fans below. For once the Hammers fortunes failed to find a hiding place and the East End was about to enjoy its momentary place in the sun.

As the Hammers' fans made their way back down Wembley Way a spontaneous outburst of singing broke out and continued onto the station platform and on the trains heading east. One by one we sang our tribute to the West Ham legends of the past, pride of place given to the saintly Bobby Moore. What a day!

On the Sunday the sun continued to shine for the victory procession which began in Stratford Broadway, just across the road from Mooros pub. The police estimated over 200,000 people lined the East End streets that day to show their appreciation and join in the fun. The team's open-top bus took over two hours to cover the short journey to its destination, East Ham Town Hall. Trevor Brooking expressed his own feelings about the team's reception that Sunday:

'The old East End did know how to celebrate and people came out of hospitals and babies were held up crying their eyes out. The atmosphere was fantastic on that Sunday because winning a match like that against Arsenal was something that the East End wanted to celebrate. It is something I will always remember.'

Billy Bonds later said he couldn't remember much about the celebrations, apart from putting Ernie Gregory and physio Rob Jenkins to bed early because they had both drunk too much Champagne – straight out of the FA Cup itself. Neither Gregory nor Jenkins were drinkers, but West Ham had won the cup, so why not?

With typical generosity, Bonds attributed the victory to his manager, John Lyall:

'John got his tactics spot on. He brought Stuart Pearson back into midfield and left David Cross up front and played five across the middle with Geoff Pike chasing everything down.'

Brooking echoed his captain's tribute, recognising the manager's tactical triumph:

'John said the game plan was to get the ball and then pass it well. West Ham sides have always been brought up to pass the ball and John had taken up Ron Greenwood's mantle and had the same coaching

philosophy and the one that got us back into the top level the following season.'

Billy Bonds, Trevor Brooking, Frank Lampard, Alan Devonshire, Alvin Martin and Phil Parkes were wonderful West Ham players who would be included in most fans' all-time West Ham X1. Geoff Pike, Ray Stewart and Paul Allen pushed them close. Brooking revealed recently that, 'the 1980 defence was the best I have ever played with.' Praise indeed!

A few hours after the final Lyall asked his opposite number, Terry Neil,

"... why didn't you change things when you saw the way we were playing?"
Neil replied, rather complacently, "...we thought we were always going to win. It was just a matter of time."

On that wonderful day for West Ham supporters, Lyall had out thought Neil and Don Howe, two of the most respected coaches in the game. Victory over Arsenal helped to further Lyall's growing reputation as a top coach – if he could only get West Ham out of the 2nd Division. But for now the West Ham way was safe in the hands of their unassuming manager.

Later that weekend, Lyall took the FA Cup back to his parent's house. His dad had suffered four heart attacks and was in poor health. James Lyall died at Wanstead in 1977 at the age of 77, after collapsing in his barber's chair. John's mother, Catherine passed away 15 years later in 1992. How proud they must have been of their son whose passion for football they encouraged all those years ago. In turn John was always extremely grateful for the support, encouragement and love he received from his parents. The winning West Ham manager had come a long way from those childhood years playing football in the parks around his Ilford home and kicking a ball against Peter Lorenzo's back wall. Following his career-ending knee injury in the late '50s Lyall had risen from office boy and youth coach to lead West Ham to their second FA Cup victory in five years.

For the record, the West Ham team on the victorious day was: Parkes, Stewart, Lampard, Bonds (c), Martin, Devonshire, Allen, Pearson, Cross, Brooking and Pike. Sub: Brush.

Chapter 10
Back to the top flight

Since that wonderful Wembley day in the sun in 1980 West Ham have failed to win a single trophy and the club has been troubled by problems on and off the pitch. The '80s and '90s brought a much-improved stadium at the expense of massive debt, bond schemes and a squandering of the club's best young talent for a generation. Joe Cole, Frank Lampard Jnr, Rio Ferdinand, Michael Carrick and Glen Johnson should have provided the core of one of the great West Ham's sides, but were all allowed to leave within the space of a couple of seasons.

Managerial incompetence and boardroom farces beyond the imagination of John Cleese severely damaged the reputation of a once proud club. Only the fans have remained constant in their loyalty and unwavering support – on that Saturday in May 1980 they thoroughly deserved their day in the sun as did their inspirational manager.

With Phil Parkes in goal, Bonds, Martin, Lampard and Stewart in defence, the craft of Brooking and Devonshire in midfield, topped off with the goals of David Cross, Lyall had assembled a team that should have been good enough to be challenging for the 1st Division. Instead, despite their magnificent cup form, West Ham ended 1979/80 in a disappointing 7th place in the 2nd Division well behind champions Leicester City. Lyall's team did finish their League programme strongly, but 14 defeats over the season was no more than mid-table mediocrity. Cross was the top-scorer with just 12 goals, while Stewart was the only other player to make double figures. The defence conceded nearly 50 goals and continued to give the manager cause for concern.

It was a constant cause of frustration for Lyall that his team failed to achieve promotion to the 1st Division. He knew he was close to having an outstanding West Ham side and went to the board and asked for their support. Just a few days into the new season Lyall returned to QPR, where he had signed Phil Parkes, and paid £800,000 for 20-year-old striker, Paul Goddard. Lyall knew that Stuart Pearson was troubled by injury and coming to the end of a distinguished career. The side needed a fully functioning partner for David Cross. He found it in Paul Goddard. The diminutive forward quickly became a crowd favourite and announced his arrival at Upton Park with two goals in the 4-0 defeat of Notts County at the end of August. The new season was up and running and the fans would have relished the prospect of European nights returning to Upton Park – the reward for beating Arsenal at Wembley.

What a season it turned out to be, as Lyall's team at last transferred their stunning cup form to the day-to-day business of winning the 2nd Division championship. After a hesitant start the Hammers took the division by storm, winning an impressive 16 home League games in succession between August and March. The away form was equally impressive, losing just three just games away from fortress Upton Park. The Hammers were crowned champions as early as 11 April following a 5-0 thrashing of Grimsby, in which David Cross scored four goals. That season the Hammers' centre-forward was in the form of his life and was at times unstoppable. Cross repaid the club every penny of his transfer fee and every minute of time his manager spent working on his game. Under Lyall's sympathetic guidance the Lancastrian continued to improve to the point where his manager could say he was the complete English centre-forward.

Cross and Goddard scored 56 goals between them that season. The pair's goalscoring feats were instrumental in the Hammers amassing a post-war record of 66 points. Their outstanding performance was even more impressive when we remember the Hammers played 19 cup matches that year and came very close to achieving a remarkable League and cup double. West Ham had its strongest squad for many years with winger Jimmy Neighbour settled into his second season in claret and blue, and stalwart Patsy

Holland making a total of 35 League and cup appearances. For the first time in his five years as manager Lyall enjoyed a few selection problems.

Lyall's cup runs over – almost

An early exit at the hands of Wrexham in the 3rd round of the FA Cup was probably a blessing in disguise, although the defeat revived memories of former frailties in the minds of the West Ham faithful. Exciting runs in the League Cup and European Cup Winners' Cup were tremendous fun for the fans and brought the club within a whisker of another European triumph. Sadly the opportunity for foreign travel failed to broaden the mind of some of the more violent members of the North Bank.

The League Cup campaign began in late August with a 6-0 aggregate victory over Burnley and was followed with wins over Charlton, Barnsley and, deliciously, Tottenham. A 3-2 aggregate win over Coventry in the semi-final took the Hammers back to Wembley for the third time in 12 months, if we include the Charity Shield curtain-raiser. By one of football's odd coincidences, the final of the League Cup brought the Hammers up against their Charity Shield opponents, Liverpool. John Lyall, a realist by instinct, knew full well the extent of the challenge that faced his team. Nobody outside East London gave the Hammers the faintest chance of victory. The powerful Liverpool machine was a football juggernaut that rode roughshod over English football in the 1970s and '80s. This was a real David and Goliath clash.

The 1981 League Cup Final

On 14 March, 1981 West Ham were 10 points clear at the top of the 2nd Division and heading back to the top flight. John Lyall's men were enjoying a wonderful season. Less than a year after defeating Arsenal in the FA Cup Final they returned to Wembley, this time for the final of the Football League Cup. The West Ham players would have relished the thought of another tilt at one of the best sides in the Europe.

The Hammers' Wembley opponents were English and European Champions, and if the Merseysiders needed any motivation, the League Cup remained the only trophy the Merseysiders had failed to win. The Liverpool side for the final included such famous Anfield names as Kenny Dalglish, Alan Hansen, Graeme Souness, Ray Kennedy, Sammy Lee and Terry McDermott. They had a substitute that day in Jimmy Case who would have walked into any other 1st Division side. The only star missing from the Reds line-up on the big day was the great goalscorer, Ian Rush who missed the game through injury.

The Hammers' side at Wembley was the same as the one against Arsenal in the 1980 final with two exceptions. Jimmy Neighbour came in for Paul Allen, while Paul Goddard replaced Stuart Pearson who dropped to the bench. John Lyall picked a very attacking side and they were confident they could test the famous Anfield defence. It was a sparkling West Ham line-up that today's supporters can only dream about, with ten Englishmen and one Scot making up the team. One man almost spoilt the day. Match referee, Clive Thomas managed to upset the Hammers' players, fans and management with his controversial handling of the game.

A crowd of 100,000 people piled into the old stadium to witness the north versus south clash. As this was the League Cup, tickets were evenly distributed between both sets of fans and Wembley was full of true football supporters. A real people's final.

The pitch was wet and slippery and creative players like Devonshire, Brooking and Dalglish were denied any time on the ball as the defences dominated the game. The football was scrappy, with defenders of both sides diving into mistimed tackles. An early Sammy Lee shot was ruled off-side and Parkes saved comfortably from Dalglish. At the other end the Hammers had little opportunity to stretch the Liverpool defence, although in a rare attack Goddard struck his volley just over Clemence's cross-bar. Alan Kennedy was lucky to stay on the pitch after a nasty foul on winger Neighbour, but the Hammers refused to be intimidated by the Merseysiders and slowly began to find their feet as Brooking, Devonshire and Pike took control of midfield. Just on half-time Frank Lampard joined the attack and thumped one of his typical efforts just past Clemence's far post. The England 'keeper was making his 32nd appearance at Wembley and his experience was

186

proving vital to his side.

The first-half remained goal-less with the teams cancelling each other out. But the Hammers were still very much in the game and their fans could look forward to the second half with real belief.

To be brutally honest, the second half produced little of note apart from more bone crunching tackles. On one occasion Goddard broke free from Hansen, but Clemence was out quickly to smother the shot. Right on 90 minutes Billy Bonds stormed forward, only to direct his header wide of the Reds' goal. Bonds later admitted that the first 90 minutes produced very little to get the fans excited:

'All that really mattered came in the last few seconds of extra-time.'

Perhaps the players sensed the tense atmosphere in the ground. The capacity crowd were expecting better football with so many great players on the pitch, but the defences kept a stranglehold on the match. Surprisingly on such a big pitch Dalglish, Devonshire and Brooking struggled to produce the kind of football the crowd were expecting – the result was a war of attrition. But for West Ham, a win remained possible until very late in the game.

As Bonds reminded us, the game came alive in extra time. Alan Devonshire just failed to convert a Neighbour cross, before Case, on for the tiring Heighway, smashed a drive against the bar. A few minutes later, and for the first time in the match, Cross found some space but his header was acrobatically tipped over the bar by Clemence. Much to the displeasure of the Irons' supporters Stuart Pearson was brought on for Goddard for the final 15 minutes, presumably to tighten up the midfield. With just three minutes left on the clock the game suddenly exploded into life in the worst possible way for the Londoners.

Alan Kennedy thundered a 20-yard shot into the West Ham wall laying out Sammy Lee in the process. The Hammers raced out in a unit as they had done a thousand times on the training ground. Kennedy smacked the rebound into the net over the stricken Lee lying prostrate by the penalty spot. Parkes was helpless to intervene. The Hammers well-drilled defence were relieved when the linesman raised his flag for off-side, but to the astonishment of everyone in the ground, including the Liverpool supporters, Thomas over-ruled his linesman and allowed the goal to stand. The Cockney element of the crowd joined their manager in vehement protest – but the Hammers, for all their protests, were 1-0 down and heading for defeat.

The tension on the pitch threatened to overspill into violence, with Stewart gaining revenge on Kennedy for his first half challenge on young Neighbour. The full-back chased Kennedy half the length of the field, but referee Thomas let Stewart off with a caution. The 100,000 people in the stadium that day knew exactly why the Scot was allowed to stay on the field. West Ham poured forward in a desperate effort to equalise, Devonshire tricked his way gracefully past two Liverpool defenders before being cynically fouled. The furious Stewart hammered the free kick at Clemence, who showed his class and calmly tipped the ball over the bar. With their supporters urging them forward, the Londoners were doing everything they could to get back into the game.

The Hammers were not to be denied. Jimmy Neighbour drove the resultant corner high into the Liverpool penalty area and onto the head of Alvin *Stretch* Martin who powered a header past the helpless Clemence. As the Hammers supporters rose to their feet in anticipation of a goal, McDermott, standing on the line, deflected the ball over the bar with his hand. No goal, but a certain penalty.

You could have heard a pin drop in the ground as regular penalty-taker Stewart stepped up to take the kick. The Hammers fans were confident their man would score, he always did. After a quick reassuring word from skipper Bonds, Stewart ran up with 100,000 people holding their breath and coolly placed a precise kick past Clemence for the equaliser. Stewart later recalled:

'I knew the pressure was on. And the ball seemed to bounce 15,000 times before it reached the net but I knew it was in from the moment it left my foot. It was a dream come true.'

The match was over, but not before John Lyall was booked following an angry spat with referee Thomas. The West Ham manager was still furious with the Welshman for allowing

Kennedy's goal. But nothing could spoil the day for the Hammers' supporters. The after-match formalities were a little bizarre as both teams climbed up to the Royal Box before embarking on the traditional lap of honour.

For the Lyall's men justice was done. It was also gratifying that Jimmy Neighbour played his part in the equalising goal. My young brother went to school with Jimmy in Chingford and although he played for Tottenham early in his career, the West Ham supporters claimed him for themselves. West Ham paid £150,000 for the winger and he was an immediate hit with the fans. Jimbo scored the winner in the semi-final against Coventry in 1981 to put his side back at Wembley, and Billy Bonds knew his value to the team. He said of the winger:

"Little Jimbo was always among the most popular men among teammates."

Neighbour later joined Bournemouth on a loan spell, eventually ending his playing career in America.

The winger returned to Upton Park as youth team trainer and coached Enfield Town when the north London club won the FA Trophy in 1988. To the delight of local youngsters and their dads, he opened a sports shop in Station Road, Chingford, close to his family and friends. Jimmy Neighbour died tragically of a heart attack at his home in Woodford on 11 April 2009, aged 58. He was a hugely popular figure in the Chingford area and in the world of football more generally. He is sorely missed by everyone who knew him.

April Fool's Day
The much-anticipated League Cup final replay was held at Villa Park on 1 April. Liverpool brought back Phil Thompson for Irwin, Ian Rush for Heighway, while Jimmy Case replaced the injured Graham Souness. These changes probably strengthened, rather than weakened the Merseysiders. The Hammers were unchanged.

Despite his problems in the first match Clive Thomas was again the referee. This did not trouble the Hammers' skipper, as Bonds later explained:

'I considered him a good ref, largely because you knew where you were with him.'

Bonds agreed that Thomas had made a mistake at Wembley, but realised his team needed to put the controversy behind them. They certainly started the match with a positive attitude and no thought of refereeing issues.

The Hammers took the lead when Paul Goddard scored with a well-taken header. But on this occasion Liverpool were too strong for the East Londoners and won comfortably with goals by Alan Hansen and Kenny Dalglish. It was no disgrace for the Hammers to lose a League Cup final replay to the English and European champions, and they had the consolation of winning promotion back to the top flight.

Paul Goddard would have been consoled by his goal. The Hammers' goalscorer in the replay was nicknamed *Sarge* by his teammates because of his involvement with the Boys' Brigade and his obvious leadership qualities. Lyall knew he had made a very good signing with Goddard and £800,000 was a reasonable price for a player of his ability. *Sarge* made 213 appearances for West Ham and scored 71 goals, a decent return for this popular player. He also managed five goals for the England Under-23 side and scored in his only full international, against Iceland in 1982. Goddard left the Hammers for Newcastle United but returned briefly to Upton Park as Assistant Manager. He finally left the club after Alan Pardew's appointment as manager.

In truth, Goddard's goal hardly mattered. Despite their Wembley heroics and their early lead, the Hammers were well-beaten in the replay. Professional footballers hate losing cup finals and some of the side had experienced defeat at the hands of Anderlecht in the European Cup Winners' Cup. As Billy Bonds said, "All you can do is try and show dignity in defeat – while the winners are rushing about celebrating."

John Lyall escaped punishment for his outburst against Clive

Thomas when he was exonerated by the FA. The manager had a busy summer ahead preparing his team for their forthcoming season in Division 1. Despite the defeat against Liverpool, the Hammers could look forward to the next few seasons with growing confidence. They won the 2nd Division Championship in 1981 with a record number of points, reached the final of the Football League Cup, and the last eight of the Cup Winners' Cup. Lyall had put together a group of players whom he trusted to take the club forward. As Paul Goddard later remembered:

'It was a wonderful team and some of the football we played was out of this world.'

The West Ham team for the replay against Liverpool was; Parkes, Stewart, Lampard, Bonds (c), Martin, Devonshire, Neighbour, Goddard, Cross, Brooking and Pike. Sub: Pearson.

'Night of havoc'
West Ham's much-anticipated return to Europe after a five year absence was a disaster for the club and for English football. The 1st Round opponents were Real Madrid nursery club, Castilla. The Hammers went in front in the first leg through David Cross, but a technically accomplished Spanish side took them apart in the second half and ran out 3-1 winners. The match was played in the famous Bernabeu Stadium and should have been a fantastic football occasion for everyone concerned. However, as Lyall remembered:

'We lost 3-1 – but the match was not all we lost.'

The appalling behaviour of West Ham supporters on that balmy Madrid evening severely damaged the reputation of the East London club. Around 40,000 people gathered in the Bernabeu to witness the first leg, including several hundred excited West Ham fans. Suddenly, Lyall became aware of a disturbance in the crowd when, 'a long troop of policemen, two abreast, marched across the face of the dug-out.'

Running battles broke out on the terraces, but the Spanish police presence calmed the situation, although the rest of the game was played out in a tense atmosphere. Lyall firmly believed the disturbance affected his team and was a contributory factor to their low-key performance. But the real trouble began as the fans began to leave the stadium and continued in the surrounding streets, as Lyall himself explains, "One West Ham supporter was hit by a coach and later died in hospital, a sad and tragic accident."

This appalling incident was an accident, but added to the chaotic and threatening mood among both sets of supporters after the game. Lyall was both angry and disturbed by the events in Madrid and appalled by the behaviour of some of the Hammers' fans. In the heat of the moment he called for three-year jail sentences for those involved. But he knew this was not just a West Ham problem. Hooliganism and violence had become a growing concern in towns and cities across the UK and throughout Europe. That tough character, Jack Charlton, was reduced to tears following a riot by Sheffield Wednesday fans at Oldham. Lyall had his own firm views on football hooliganism,

'...it was definitely a symptom of the times. The game reflects the daily life of the country... it is not confined to football terraces. It happens in pubs, clubs, dance halls, discos and on the streets of some of our quietest country Towns.'

This liberal view on a massive social problem is an indication of Lyall's quiet intelligence and was not reflected in the glaring newspaper headlines at the time. Lyall was right. In the early 1980s, England was a divided country. Race riots had disfigured our cities and destroyed communities and within a few years violent clashes erupted in northern cities as the miners fought to protect their livelihoods and communities. When the smoke cleared that evening in Madrid we learned that 20 people were injured, two fans had been arrested and five detained in custody.

Brian Blowers, the club's commercial manager at the time, remained in Madrid after the game to work with the police and attempt to establish the facts of the situation. There is no question that the trouble was the work of a small minority of the travelling fans. UEFA pointed the finger of guilt firmly at the Londoners. West Ham were fined £7,700 and ordered to play the 2nd leg at least 300 kilometres from Upton Park.

The club decided to appeal against UEFA's decision and meanwhile arranged to play the 2nd leg at Roker Park. At the end of September, Lyall, Blowers and board members, Jack Petchey and Brian Cearns flew to Zurich for the hearing. The West Ham contingent had prepared exhaustive reports and impressed the EUFA officials. As a result the fine was quashed and the club were allowed to play the 2nd leg against Castilla behind closed doors at Upton Park. Lyall needed to draw on all his experience and man management skills in order to prepare his players for the 2nd leg. He organised two full-scale practice matches at Chadwell Heath and instructed the reserve players to tackle as their lives depended on it. The phantom match was played in front of officials and media people and with none of the white hot atmosphere usually associated with European nights at the Boleyn. A David Cross hat-trick and goals from Pike and Goddard gave the Hammers a comfortable 5-1 victory on the night. Lyall could be proud of his players and in the way he had prepared them for this difficult occasion. But in all the legal wrangling over the fate of the tie, it is to be hoped neither club forgot the sad loss of a young life at a football match.

The 2nd Round brought an impressive victory over Romanian side, Poli Timisoara and with it a 3rd round clash against the crack Soviet outfit, Dynamo Tbilisi. Perhaps suffering the after effects of the League Cup final, the Hammers were roundly beaten 4-1 at home in the 1st leg. Showing their true colours, the West Ham crowd gave the Russians a standing ovation at the final whistle, applauding the technical quality and breathtaking forward play of the Dynamo players. It had been a long time since Lyall's side had been beaten so comprehensively.

The Hammers recovered some pride in the 2nd leg in front of 80,000 partisan fans in the snow-bound Lenin Stadium. A Stuart Pearson goal brought the Londoners a hard-fought 1-0 victory against the eventual winners of the competition. As a result of the Russian mid-season break, Lyall and Eddie Bailey were unable to watch their opponents before the tie, but gave no excuses and saluted the quality of what Lyall described as 'one of the finest European sides I've ever seen.'

Losing to such a wonderful team was no disgrace. The real loser in West Ham's last European Cup Winners' campaign in living memory was football itself and it took many years before the game recovered its self-respect, both at Upton Park and in grounds up and down the country. For the West Ham manager it was an experience he would rather have avoided, but he handled it with the dignity and sensitivity we had come to expect.

Pleasing Mr Len

Lyall admitted that the 1980 FA Cup Final victory was a tremendous personal boost. He had signed a new five-year contract in 1975, but knew his reputation had taken a knock following relegation. However, despite the cup success his position remained vulnerable. When Lyall succeeded Ron Greenwood as West Ham manager he remained on his previous salary of £4,000 a year, but following the 1975 FA Cup win Len Cearns increased this to £15,000. His team was showing good League form and the club's youngsters had just won the 1981 FA Youth Cup, with a side that included Tony Cottee and Alan Dickens. He entered his contract discussions in confident mood and a position of some strength. After all, not many managers have begun and ended their contract with FA Cup Final wins.

The West Ham manager had the complete trust of his board. He joined the club as a teenager, progressed up the coaching ladder before winning the FA Cup twice as manager. It seemed an almost unassailable record – but the doubts remained about relegation from the top flight and failure to achieve an immediate return. What happened next was not what he was expecting. Lyall regarded the hour before kick-off in the players' dressing room as absolutely sacrosanct and out-of-bounds for board members, as he explained:

'What I had to do in the hour before the kick-off was ensure that they

(the players) were going to channel all their physical and mental powers into the match ahead. I didn't appreciate disturbances...'

Imagine Lyall's horror when a few minutes before a home match against local rivals, Orient, chairman Cearns entered the tense atmosphere of the Upton Park home dressing room and enquired calmly, "I'm sorry to trouble you, John, but if you get a moment before the match do you think you could nip upstairs to the boardroom."

The manager gave his chairman short shrift, replying curtly, "I'm sorry, Mr Len, I've got a job to do. If I get the chance I'll pop in after the match."

Other managers may have been less polite, but gentleman that he was, Lyall felt he had been a little rude to his loyal chairman. He was also curious. Having prepared his players for the Orient match to his satisfaction, he nipped up to the boardroom in the final minutes before kick-off. Mr Len thanked John for making the time and said on behalf of the assembled board, "John...it's been a marvellous season already, and we felt we would like to show our appreciation now..."

The chairman presented his manager with a solid-gold watch, inscribed on the back, 'West Ham Utd FC. Well done John. March 1980.'

Lyall was speechless and mumbled something like, "Mr Len, I'm sorry, I was busy downstairs...I didn't realise."

After the 2-0 victory over Orient, Lyall travelled back to Abridge in good heart, desperate to show Yvonne his lovely new watch. But, of course, his wife was in on the secret and had even given the board her suggestions. That evening Lyall was understandably a very happy man, "It was the end of a perfect day for me."

With his board's enthusiastic and loyal support, Lyall's contract negotiations preceded without a hitch in the summer of 1981. With the best West Ham team for many years and a new five-year contract he could look forward to taking on the best teams in the English 1st Division. Lyall could concentrate on the job, safe in the knowledge his family were financially secure.

Happy days!

By August '81, Lyall believed he had assembled a group of players ready to cope with the demands of the 1st Division. His team had won the old 2nd Division at a canter, and enjoyed two successful cup runs the previous season. By the end of September his hopes were realised as the Hammers stood unbeaten at the top of the League. The fans must have had a collective nose-bleed as their team beat Tottenham, Sunderland and Stoke City in successive matches. In what must have been the highlight of the big man's career, the 4-0 victory at White Hart Lane was achieved courtesy of four goals from the ever-prolific David Cross. The Lancastrian's partnership with Goddard was running experienced 1st Division defences ragged. The Daily Express headline, bellowed:

'King Cross leaves Spurs in a shambles.'
Lyall was on top of the world as his team performed their version of the West Ham way. Billy Bonds and his boys were playing some of the best football seen at Upton Park since the glory days of the mid-'60s – all this without their talisman, Trevor Brooking, who missed the first seven games of the season through injury. The Express summed up the mood of the football public:
'West Ham is championing the kind of football everyone wants to see.'

Happy days! Lyall's team had restored the Hammers' reputation as every football fans' second favourite team. The manager's position was impregnable. He knew West Ham from top to bottom, took an interest in every aspect of the club, and was the undisputed leader of everybody from the tea ladies to the top stars. They all had nothing but respect and affection for Lyall. He kept faith with the same players in the season following promotion, bringing in 'keeper Tom McAlister from Swindon Town for the emigrating Bobby Ferguson.

Later in the season Lyall strengthened his squad with the addition of the Hammers' old adversary, Francois Van Der Elst who at the time was plying his trade with New York Cosmos. Van Der Elst had featured strongly for Anderlecht in the '76 European Cup Winners' Cup final and Lyall had long admired his silky skills. At the age of 26, the Belgian forward was a bargain at £400,000. Not for the last time Lyall showed great foresight in signing a top European forward. Today, of course, there are far more foreign players than English ones in the Premier League. The club also brought in Neil Orr, an Under-21 Scottish international defender, as cover for Martin and Bonds. Being a Scot himself, Lyall admired the character of players from north of the border and usually sought the advice of Alex Ferguson before signing players like Orr – he rarely got it wrong and liked to have one or two players from the country of his parents in his team.

A 9th place finish was highly satisfactory for the first season back in the top flight. Cross and Goddard continued to score goals and the defence was reasonably sound. But the highlight of the season remained the 4-0 thrashing of Spurs at White Hart Lane. It doesn't get much better than that for West Ham supporters. The tragedy of Madrid and the subsequent humiliation was now firmly consigned to the past, although the scars remained. Football violence was never far away at this fractious time and was to get worse over the next five years.

On a positive note, following the manager's ruthless clear-out of 1979 he was able to put together his own team. His young centre-half, Alvin Martin had been awarded his first England cap in the match against Brazil, and Parkes, Devonshire and Cross had all proved excellent additions to the squad, confirming John Lyall's superb judgement of players and their character. Parkes was a rock-solid, safe bet, but Cross and Devonshire were more of a gamble. Lyall quickly realised that these three outstanding footballers all possessed the desire and conviction to succeed at the highest level. But as new players joined the club, one of West Ham's most dependable players of the '70s, Patsy Holland, was forced to retire. Lyall had great affection for the Hammers' exciting winger. He later wrote:

'The one regret in this exciting and successful time was the serious injury to Patsy Holland.'

The long serving winger picked up a nasty injury in a match

against Notts County in January 1981. His knee ligaments were so badly damaged Holland never played for his beloved West Ham again. The Hammers' star loved playing football and found enforced retirement difficult to accept. He joined the coaching staff at Chadwell Heath and later enjoyed similar roles at Orient, QPR and Spurs, before returning to Brisbane Road as manager. Patsy is currently part of Arsene Wenger's coaching team at Arsenal. He continues to talk passionately about football and expresses strong ideas on the modern game. Holland was highly critical of the percentage game that dominated football in the 1970s and '80s. Brought up on the values of Greenwood and Lyall, the former Hammers midfield star has definite views on the merits of current coaching qualifications:

'They give away levels too easily. Level 2 is not really worth very much today – they should make it more difficult.'

Holland speaks passionately about football because, like his former manager, he cares about the beautiful game. He has a great affection for his time at Upton Park and believes the creative atmosphere Lyall fostered inspired him, Ronnie Boyce, Mick McGiven and others to become coaches themselves.

Early in his career, Holland felt that Ron Greenwood had no confidence in him, but Lyall had more patience and believed in the youngster. There were ten years between the two men, but Lyall became a father figure to the young winger. The winger appreciated his manager's commitment to improving his players and his ability to alter the team's style to fit particular individuals. Holland tells an amusing story which gives us an insight into the enormous enthusiasm of this under-rated footballer. He picked up an injury and looked likely to miss a Monday night game away to Charlton Athletic, in which he was desperate to play. Taking advantage of his eagerness, backroom boys Jack Walker and Jack Leslie, jokingly advised the young winger to immerse his injured ankle in sea water for a few hours: "An hour or two in the sea Duchy and you will be fine for the Charlton match," said Walker.

The gullible youngster headed straight down to Southend and strolled across the pebbly beach to the water's edge. After a few minutes up to his ankles in freezing cold water Patsy began to see the joke. But as he turned to go back to his car he promptly fell arse over 'ed into the murky estuary. After an uncomfortable drive home, the winger informed his manager he was fit to play. In on the joke, Lyall replied: "OK Patsy, but don't let me down."

Of course, *Dutchy* never let anyone down, least of all the man he respected most. Pat Holland is one of my favourite all-time West Ham players. Blessed with neither the silky skills of Brooking nor the deft, dancing footwork of Devonshire, Holland had other qualities and ones which earned him the respect of his teammates. When I was a young teacher in East London in the early 1980s, Holland came to our school to coach some of our best youngsters – they adored him, and he was always the most courteous of individuals and a tribute to his profession. Billy Bonds recognised *Dutchy's* qualities and had a captain's respect for his midfielder, he wrote in his autobiography,

'...Patsy was among the first I'd have wanted in any side of mine. He had far more ability than he was ever credited with. He could run all day.'

Holland could play as a tricky winger or box-to-box midfield player. He was respected by his teammates for his endless running and total commitment to the team. But he was never fully appreciated by the fans who failed to recognise his value to the side.

With his dreadful injury, Upton Park had lost a wonderful servant. Lyall and Holland had known each other since Patsy joined the club as a teenager in 1969, when Lyall was a youth team coach. The winger had the utmost respect for his manager, despite Lyall leaving him out of the side for the 1980 FA Cup Final. Holland made nearly 300 League and cup appearances for West Ham, scoring a total of 32 goals. He featured strongly in the 1975 FA Cup final and the Cup Winners' Cup final against Anderlecht in 1976. Blows and Hogg, in their Essential History, place Holland no. 17 in the list of top 50 all-time great Hammers – a sure indication of the Poplar boy's value to the club in its most successful period.

Two great signings
Along with Bonds, Brooking and Martin, the mainstays of Lyall's

great side of the early '80s were Parkes, Devonshire, and Cross. We have already mentioned Cross's arrival at Upton Park and how Lyall convinced the sceptical northerner to join West Ham. The capture of Parkes and Devonshire tell us much about Lyall's man-management style and what today would be called people skills. The transfers also provide interesting insights into the West Ham manager's powers of persuasion.

Alan Devonshire was one of the greatest players ever to play for West Ham. His sublime skills graced Upton Park for 14 years and, if not for a serious injury in 1984, he would surely have won more than eight international caps. Where to begin with the highlights of Devo's brilliant career; his terrific goal in the FA Cup semi-final against Everton in 1980 when he played, in his own estimation, the greatest game of his life; or, his delicate skills which set up Trevor Brooking's goal in the final against Arsenal. He was a wonderful sight in full flight and epitomised all that is good in the game of football.

Devonshire was actually signed by Ron Greenwood, but played out his time at the Boleyn under the caring guidance of John Lyall. It says a great deal about the judgement of the West Ham coaching staff that they recognised greatness in this lanky lad from Park Royal. Eddie Bailey received a tip-off about Devonshire from an old friend and went to have a look at the young mid-fielder, then playing for Southall in the Isthmian League. Bailey liked what he saw and urged Greenwood to sign him. Greenwood trusted Bailey's judgement and gave him the go-ahead. Alan Devonshire signed for West Ham in 1976 and made his first team debut against QPR on 27 October. He made a total of 446 League and cup appearances for the East Londoners, scoring 32 goals. He left Upton Park in 1990 to see out his career at Watford. For some fans, Devonshire was the best signing the Hammers ever made, not just for his contribution to Lyall's successful sides, but because his football represented everything that is special about the club. For £5,000, has there ever been such a bargain in the modern history of the game? Devonshire continued the tradition of ex-Hammers by coaching a succession of non-League clubs and is currently manager of the successful Conference club, Braintree Town.

With the signings of Devonshire and Cross and the emergence of the splendid Geoff Pike, Lyall's team was slowly taking shape. The industrious and skilful Pike – a fans' favourite – developed under the close guidance of Lyall, as he gratefully admits:

'John Lyall became a second father to me. He was a massive influence on my football career and my life in general. He wouldn't accept technical faults.'

Phil Parkes was 29-years-old when he joined West Ham. He had won his first and only England cap in 1974 and would have won more but for the brilliance of Peter Shilton and Ray Clemence. Parkes was a world-class 'keeper as Shilton acknowledged:

'West Ham have not gambled in paying that kind of money, they have invested.'

Lyall paid QPR £565,000 for Parkes, a world record for a goalkeeper at the time. But he was a special player and Lyall was more than happy to pay Rangers the asking price for the man who became the lynchpin of his superb side of the '80s.

Parkes, a Midlander, played non-League football before joining Walsall and later, Mansfield Town. QPR paid £13,000 for Parkes and he quickly became an integral member of the West London's 1st Division side. He immediately impressed the fans at Loftus Road and his good form was rewarded when Don Revie selected him for the England side. Despite his success the QPR 'keeper kept his feet firmly on the ground. On leaving school, he became a qualified carpenter and continued to work in the construction business throughout his football career.

The new Hammers' goalkeeper dropped a division to move across London, which no self-respecting player's agent would sanction in today's Premier League – it would be seen simply as career suicide. It says a great deal about John Lyall's powers of persuasion that Parkes was prepared to join a 2nd Division club. Of course, Parkes did not take the decision to drop a division lightly, but he knew QPR wanted to cash in on their most valuable asset. Chairman, Jim Gregory told Parkes that West Ham had made a silly offer and he had given them permission to speak to his goalkeeper. Gregory informed Parkes at the same time he intended to transfer-list him at the end of the season whether he signed for West Ham or not.

This modest and essentially straightforward footballer was placed in a genuine dilemma. He didn't want to leave, but if he didn't accept the West Ham offer, he would simply be put onto the open market at the end of the season. He was enjoying life at Loftus Road. He lived at Wokingham in Surrey and wasn't prepared to move his family across London. He was improving as a 'keeper and valued his Wednesday evenings of specialised coaching with the former Arsenal 'keeper, Bob Wilson. He may not have wanted to leave, but Lyall was determined to get his man.

Parkesy was a wonderful professional and outstanding talent, but he was not a great football follower. The Ranger's 'keeper had never heard of John Lyall before West Ham came in for him, but was immediately impressed by the way in which Lyall and Eddie Bailey conducted the negotiations. The West Ham pair travelled to Wokingham to meet Phil and his wife Lavonia, arriving in mid-afternoon. They explained their plans for the club in detail and the terms of his contract. Lavinia explained that they were settled and happy in the area and Phil would face a gruelling daily journey to reach Chadwell Heath by 10.00 am for training. Lyall had the answer:

'I'll tell you what... from now on we'll start training every day at 10.30 am.'

Phil and Lavinia asked if they could have a couple hours in private together to talk things over. Lyall and Bailey agreed and went into town for steak and chips, returning with a bottle of wine to close the deal. Parkes answered the door to the anxious West Ham pair with the welcome words, "I'll sign."

The visit to the Parkes' home in Wokingham was time well spent. The signing of the QPR 'keeper was crucial to Lyall's plans for the future. He was absolutely determined to get his man. Parkes settled in quickly at his new club and enjoyed the training, as he explains:

'At QPR, the warm-ups were always the same. With John they were always different – variations on a theme. John was always thinking. He was different to any manager I had known, including Dave Sexton.'

How did Parkes cope with the daunting daily journey across London? Alan Devonshire and later Paul Goddard, all lived south of the river and the three of them travelled together from Waterloo station to Barking, then on to Chadwell Heath. Billy Bonds or Tony Gale would pick up the trio at Barking Station and drive them the short journey to the training ground. Lyall kept his promise of delaying the start of training to 10.30 am where it stayed for the rest of the manager's time at the club.

Phil Parkes more than repaid Lyall's faith in him – he made 436 League and cup appearances, winning the coveted Hammer of the Year award in 1981. In his first season at Upton Park, the Hammers' new 'keeper kept an astonishing 22 clean sheets and helped his team to FA Cup victory at Wembley. Dropping down a division seemed an inspired move. Following his retirement at the age of 41, Parkes continued his interest in carpentry and built up a successful building business, while Phil and Lavinia still live in the family home in Wokingham. Parkes and Lyall became close friends, spending many hours on away trips happily discussing carpentry and the latest innovations in DIY, two things close to the West Ham manager's heart.

The Parkes story provides an insight into Lyall's methods in the transfer market. He would operate in total secrecy with only members of the Board in on the secret. On completion of a transfer he would share the exclusive with his closest friends in the press on a rota-type basis. The reporter would receive no payment from the club, but would have probably earned a bonus from his paper for the exclusive article. This was all part of the close bond he enjoyed with senior sports' writers. Son Murray throws some light on the maestro's transfer dealings:

'When a transfer was on, Lyall would literally drop everything else until the player was shown around the area and without undue haste, signed the deal, often in the early hours of the morning. Sleep would be the last thing on his mind.'

The early 1980s
Lyall's side took to the top flight like ducks to water, finishing no lower than 9th place in the first four years following promotion in 1981. The core of the squad remained, enhanced by Goddard, Van der Elst and Neil Orr. In front of over 33,000 happy Hammers, Tony Cottee scored on his first team debut in the 3-0 home victory against Tottenham on New Year's Day, 1983. He was the club's top scorer for the next two years. With a stable squad and young players like Cottee, Pike and Alan Dickens forcing their way into the first team, Lyall began to think realistically about winning the 1st Division title. But, just when the humiliation of relegation began to fade into the distant memory, Lyall lost two players who had been at heart of the club's success over the past few years – David Cross and Trevor Brooking.

Cross joined the Hammers in 1977 when he was 27-years-old. He had enjoyed the best five years of his career under Lyall, but at the age of 32 felt he wanted to return to his Lancashire roots. There was no shortage of clubs interested in signing the veteran striker, whose goalscoring record compared with the best in the 1st Division. He had done a fantastic job for West Ham and his manager had no intention of denying Cross his wish to move back home. Lyall said of his centre-forward:

'He was a player who gave me everything from the moment of his debut for us against his old club, West Brom in December 1977.'

At West Ham, Cross achieved his lifetime ambition of scoring 20 goals in a single season which he achieved in the promotion year of 1981. In fact, he scored an impressive 33 goals in all competitions that season. His record at Upton Park speaks for itself – 223 League and cup appearances in which he scored an impressive 99 goals. Cross needed to score twice in the Hammers' final match, away to Wolves on 15 May, 1982, to complete a personal tally of 100 goals.

Of course he scored, but his single strike left him one short of a century of goals in the claret and blue of West Ham. The Upton Park crowd loved him and I can still remember the North Bank chant as the players warmed up before homes matches 'Psycho, psycho, give us a wave.'

Of course he always obliged. The crowd gave this self-effacing character the confidence he lacked, encouraging him at every opportunity. "West Ham fans made the club," he later revealed. David Cross was a key member of a happy West Ham dressing room. If Brooking loved a game of cards, then Cross liked nothing better than to sit quietly completing The Telegraph crossword. His years at Upton Park were the best of his career, although he would have regretted narrowly missing out on an England cap.

Cross wanted to finish his career in the north-west and was pleased when Manchester City expressed an interest. West Ham wanted £600,000 for their striker, while City offered a derisory £50,000 for the man they wanted to replace Trevor Francis. The centre-forward did his homework on the Maine Road club and was happy to sign for them. In those days a tribunal made up of FA and PFA officials decided a fee when clubs failed to agree. Gordon Taylor remarked after the hearing: "We worked on the principle that if neither club was happy with the decision, we had done our job well."

They set the fee for David Cross at £135,000. Both clubs accepted the decision and Cross was on his way back to Lancashire. Cross talked interestingly about the way the two clubs conducted themselves at his tribunal. The Hammers were represented on the day by John Benson and John Lyall. Cross remembers:

"West Ham did everything right and with dignity."

The Manchester club attempted to influence the board's decision in their favour, while Cearns and his team behaved impeccably. Cross explained:

'City hadn't done any homework. West Ham had researched that Trevor Francis, who City sold for around £1 million, had the second best goal per game ratio over the past two seasons. The player with the best goal per game ratio over the same period was me. In effect, City was offering much less for me than they received for Francis when my stats looked better. That is the gist of what John Benson told me later.'

Cross remembers watching the West Ham contingent walk away from the hearing and, knowing he was staying with the City people, thought to himself

'What have I done? John was a fantastic bloke.'

Cristiano Ronaldo recently spoke about his relationship at Old Trafford with Sir Alex Ferguson, he said:

'He knows exactly the way I feel about him. If it were humanly possible I would like to have him always by my side. He has always been like a second father to me.'

You get the impression talking to Cross this is exactly how he feels about his former manager. He knew he wanted to return to the north, but he would have liked the circumstances to have been different.

Of course, being a great professional, Cross got on with his job of replacing Francis in the City forward line. Things worked out well for Crossie. He quickly settled back in the north and married a girl from the same village. The couple set up house in Bury where his wife is a lawyer in the town. They have three children who are all outstanding at sport. Robert played 2nd XI cricket for Derbyshire and Lancashire for many years and now scores his runs in the Lancashire League. Jennifer played netball in the Superleague and has featured in the Lancashire Women's set-up. Psychology graduate, Kathryn, the youngest, played cricket for Lancashire Women 1st XI at the tender age of 13, and progressed to the England Development squad. The talented youngster was also called up for the England women's tour of Australia in 2011.

Cross currently works for Blackburn Rovers where he prepares dossiers on Rovers' opponents. He made the right personal choice to leave West Ham and it was entirely his decision. But at the time he had some regrets, not least because he would no longer be working with the man he described as 'The best man I ever met in football.'

Lyall believed Paul Goddard, the young Tony Cottee and, in the short term, the Belgian, Van Der Elst, were perfect replacements for Cross. Cottee established his place in the side during the 1983/84 season when he ended the season top scorer with an impressive 19 League and cup goals. His four goals in the Hammers 10-0 thumping of Bury in the Milk Cup in October '83 confirmed Cottee's arrival as a top striker. The local youngster had the football world at his feet and looked like the natural successor to the great Geoff Hurst.

Life without Trevor

For the 1983/84 season Lyall brought in Steve Walford from Norwich City, Steve Whitton from Coventry and Paul Hilton from Bury, none of whom pulled up any trees at the Boleyn, while Francois Van Der Elst left after a short and more successful spell. The departure of the brilliant Belgian was a blow for Lyall, but nothing compared to the loss through retirement of Trevor Brooking. Rightly, Blows and Hogg place Brooking second only to the incomparable Bobby Moore in their list of all-time West Ham greats. The peerless midfielder entered Hammers' folklore when he scored the only goal of the match in the famous victory over Arsenal in the 1980 FA Cup final. He played some of the best football of his career during West Ham's European campaign in 1975/76 and in the club's path to the final of the League Cup in 1981. This quintessential one-club man joined the Hammers as an apprentice as far back as 1965, making his debut against Burnley in August 1967. Hammer-of-the-Year on five occasions, Brooking personified all that is good and special about West Ham.

With Bonds and Frank Lampard, Brooking was a cornerstone of Lyall's best teams at Upton Park. All three were hardworking, modest and level-headed characters and as Lyall said in his autobiography:

'Brooking, Bonds and Lampard had talent, but never felt the need to shout about it.'

Brooking was in Lyall's first youth group and he remembers the schoolboy inside-forward's development being worryingly slow. Such was Ron Greenwood's frustration with the youngster's progress that he considered selling him to Southampton for a modest £67,000. Fortunately, Greenwood resisted the Saint's advances. One of the problems was that, as a teenager, Brooking disliked the physical side of training, but never shirked a tackle and worked hard on this aspect of his game, as Lyall remembered:

'He had a competitive edge to his game that not too many people realised... it was his determination to succeed that eventually made him such a great player.'

Soon the Barking boy's talent shone through. Lyall believed Brooking's great strength was as an improviser:

'Many players have one particular skill they call upon repeatedly in given situations. Trevor had two or three for most situations.'

His exquisite touch, awareness and, his ability to play the ball as late as possible were the qualities that made Brooking such a wonderful player. Time after time at Upton Park you would see West Ham's no. 10 receive the ball on the left of midfield, allow it to run past his body, ghost to the touchline and deliver a late and tempting cross into the path of David Cross, *Pop* Robson or Stuart Pearson.

It is difficult to imagine, but Brooking did have an aggressive side to him as Lyall confirms:

'Sometimes I'd say to Billy Bonds or Geoff Pike in training – get after him and show him who's boss.'

But Brooking was no pushover and held them off. At the end of the session Bonds turned to his manager and said, "Sorry John, we couldn't get near him." Most defenders in the 1st Division couldn't get near the Hammers' midfield genius. Some of the most brilliant football seen at Upton Park involved glorious interchanges between Brooking and the almost equally gifted, Alan Devonshire. Between them they would cut usually competent defences to shreds. It was a breath-taking sight and evidence of what was special about West Ham's football.

There is little doubt that John Lyall played a significant role in Brooking's development. Body shaping, quarter turns, having the confidence to allow the ball to run past your body, were all trademark Lyall coaching ideas. Similarly, encouraging more defensive midfield players like Ronnie Boyce and Geoff Pike to knock the ball forward quickly into the path of the on-running Brooking and Devonshire were all classic West Ham ploys.

Brooking has some interesting ideas on Lyall's coaching methods and how they improved him as a player. I met Sir Trevor at the FA headquarters at Wembley Stadium the day Fabio Capello resigned as England manager, and Harry Redknapp was cleared of tax evasion charges. The media circus had arrived at Wembley and I was fully expecting a call from the FA postponing the meeting. But the call never arrived and the interview went ahead. Brooking was open and welcoming and gave me his undivided attention – a courtesy which would have been applauded by his former manager. The FA Director of Football since 2004 gave me over an hour of his time, while Capello faced his employers down the corridor. I had prepared some questions, but didn't need them, as Brooking talked fondly and at length about John Lyall and with great conviction about his own ideas on the modern game.

Under Lyall the players always enjoyed training. It was varied and based around their next opponents. They played keep-ball for hours on end to improve their movement and passing skills. When it came to the match everyone knew what was expected of them. Brooking believed the players were confident in their manager, clearly focused, well-balanced and happy with the shape of the team. As he said:

'Lyall was very good at being a leader. He was aggressive as a player and this was reflected in his character. On the other hand he was sensitive when he left players out and explained his decisions, unlike

Ron Greenwood who simply pinned his team to the notice board every Friday without explanation.'

Lyall was also not afraid to consult his senior players about the potential of new signings, as he did before giving Alan Devonshire his debut. Brooking paints a picture of a content and committed group of players who trusted their manager's instincts. In Pat Holland's words:

"We never stopped laughing. I have so many fond memories of that time."

How coaches work on getting their teams to play in a certain way can be mystifying to the uninitiated. Brooking has interesting thoughts on this and on Lyall's particular take on the West Ham way:

'We were encouraged to play through the three thirds of the pitch. All our players had enough quality to receive the ball under pressure. The 'keeper always threw it out and Bonzo and Martin were comfortable on the ball.'

When the defenders received the ball, it was important for them to play it through the midfield for Pike, Devonshire, or Brooking himself. The midfield needed to be available – normally Geoff Pike, or in earlier days, Ronnie Boyce. Brooking and Devonshire, a few yards further up the field would then find the right angles, allowing Pike to move the ball forward. Once on the ball, Brooking and Devonshire ran with it or looked for defence-splitting passes through to the forwards. If this wasn't an option then Holland would be available in a wide position.

Brooking pointed out that the players needed to be mentally strong and disciplined to play this type of game. Lyall knew this and was very good at building individual player's confidence as he did with Holland and Cross. In Parkes, Bonds, Martin and Lampard he had super footballers who loved being on the ball.

Pike was happy to be the link between defence and attack, and Brooking and Devonshire were the perfect creative influences the system needed. Cross, Goddard and Cottee did the rest.

One of Lyall's repeated messages to his players was 'don't lose it when you win it.' This sounds such a simple instruction, but to be good at it, players need the mental strength Brooking refers to, without it play either breaks down, or teams resort to the direct game beloved of England team managers over the years. West Ham was fortunate that, in Lyall they had a manager who trusted his players to play the right way. If they found it difficult he would spend hours on the training ground until they got it right. This kind of micro-management was something Lyall learned from Ron Greenwood and today most managers leave this to coaches who specialise in attack or defence.

Trevor Brooking certainly had the ball mastery his manager demanded of his players. His record speaks for itself. It was a joy to hear him reflect on his time as a player and listen to his memories of his former manager. Brooking's retirement left a huge gap at Upton Park, but Lyall was aware of his star player's intentions and had been making plans to replace the irreplaceable. Brooking's contribution to West Ham in those years was immense. Elegance, intelligence and sublime skill are all qualities we associate with this consummate footballer.

With 635 appearances, Brooking stands fourth in the club's all-time list. His 102 goals, which included the bullet header against the Gunners, place him eighth highest in the list of Hammers' goalscorers. Brooking enjoyed a long career, gaining 47 England caps between 1974 and 1982. The honours were showered on this immensely popular footballer. He was awarded an Honorary Doctorate from the University of Essex in 2001, and following his earlier CBE, he was knighted in 2004 for his services to sport. These bare facts are hugely impressive, but tell us little about the man, or the part he played in John Lyall's West Ham side of the late 1970s and early '80s.

We know about Brooking's intelligence and his reputation for high-mindedness, although he loved a game of cards on long European trips. But he was essentially a modest individual who was popular with his teammates and enjoyed a particularly close bond with the West Ham crowd. Who will forget the unexpected passion he displayed on the touchline when he stepped in for the stricken Glen Roeder as caretaker manager in 2002. With eight wins in 13 games, West Ham fans can only wonder what might have happened had Brooking taken the job on a permanent basis. But, like his close friend and room-mate, Billy Bonds, Brooking never took to management like Alan Curbishley and Harry Redknapp – it was never a career option. Brooking was, as the saying goes, the best manager West Ham never had. The Hammers' talisman was formally honoured by his former club when the Centenary Stand at Upton Park was renamed, the Sir Trevor Brooking Stand in 2009.

But Brooking's departure in 1984 was put into firm perspective by a telephone call that was to fundamentally change the relationship between Lyall and the club he had served for over 30 years. A 9th place League finish in the year of Brooking's retirement was a great encouragement to Lyall. His team was heading nicely in the right direction. Then a series of events threatened to derail his claret and blue dream.

Chapter 11
The QPR affair

One morning in June 1984, John Lyall's life took a dramatic turn. Thus far, apart from the bitter disappointment of ending his playing days at the age of 23, life had gone pretty much to plan. That morning Yvonne took a call at Abridge from their close friend, the journalist Denis Signy and John's life at West Ham changed forever. Lyall was always happy to speak to an old pal, but this was no ordinary social call. Signy was very close to Jim Gregory, chairman of Queen's Park Rangers, one of the most successful clubs of that period. Lyall knew that the QPR manager, Terry Venables, had recently accepted a fabulous offer to join Barcelona, but was shocked when Signy asked if he would be prepared to talk to Jim Gregory about the managerial vacancy at Loftus Road.

The Hammers had consolidated their position in Division 1. Their manager had gained experience in a promotion fight and in Europe, but was ambitious for West Ham to challenge the top clubs. He had no wish to leave Upton Park, but was aware there was just one year left on his contract. The call from Signy threw John and Yvonne into a state of shock. When they recovered, John felt he should listen to what Gregory had to say. Lyall told Signy that QPR should take the official route and formally approach West Ham. After a long discussion with his manager, the Hammers' chairman, Mr Len Cearns, reluctantly gave QPR permission to speak to Lyall.

Lyall had come to know and respect Jim Gregory through the transfers of Phil Parkes and Paul Goddard. He also knew that the longest-serving chairman in the Football League had rebuilt QPR from top to bottom and proved his ambition for the club by signing England midfield star, Tony Currie. Gregory had real ambition and wanted QPR to compete for honours with top clubs Liverpool, Everton and Nottingham Forest. What impressed Lyall most was how the QPR chairman had successfully managed the difficult job of rebuilding Loftus Road, while maintaining high playing standards – something that West Ham failed to do in the 1990s.

A meeting was arranged and John arrived at Gregory's house and the QPR chairman offered him the job on the spot. If he accepted the offer, John would be £200,000 a year better off and in the same pay bracket as top managers like Brian Clough and Ron Atkinson. Gregory made Lyall's decision even harder by offering a five-year contract, plus a new Jaguar. To show how much he wanted Lyall to join Rangers, the chairman threw in the house with a fishing lake that John always coveted. Gregory piled on the pressure. John could bring his own staff and have total freedom on all playing matters, including new signings. Lyall decided he would probably take Mick McGiven and Eddie Bailey, arguing that Tony Carr and Ronnie Boyce should stay and continue their work with West Ham.

Lyall was now in a real dilemma. Of course, he discussed the offer at length with Yvonne. He was very much aware that his wife and son had missed out on a normal family life and was anxious to make up for lost time. The QPR job would give the family financial security and allow John to retire in his 50s as he had promised his family he would. The family would be made for life. But West Ham had always treated him wonderfully and until Gregory's intervention, John had no thoughts of leaving the club he had served so loyally since the mid-1950s. But this time he let his head rule his heart and accepted QPR's generous offer. He was torn, but this time put his family first.

Having made his decision, Lyall informed the West Ham board. Then came the blow from which he never fully recovered. The West Ham board refused to let him go, insisting he stay at the Boleyn and serve out his contract. Later we learned that Cearns unreasonably demanded £150,000 compensation from QPR. John was devastated, but refused to be used as a commodity in an auction and eventually, with clenched teeth, turned down Gregory's generous offer and saw out his contract. Today, of course, get-out clauses are written into managers' contract, thus removing the moral obligations that troubled Lyall at this difficult time.

John Lyall had been at West Ham for 29 years and was the longest-serving manager in the 1st Division behind Lawrie McMenemy. Frustrated, QPR turned to Alan Mullery and when that didn't work out, appointed their coach Frank Sibley as caretaker manager. There were rumours for a while that John would go to White Hart Lane, before Spurs appointed Peter Shreeves. But finally, following some bitter wrangling with chairman Cearns, Lyall signed a four year contract in March 1989, due to expire in 1989. The QPR affair was closed, if not forgotten.

During this period of managerial uncertainty, the team's form suffered. Troubled by rumour and gossip, Billy Bonds approached his manager on behalf of his teammates:

"John, are you going to sign?" he asked. "The lads are constantly discussing it in the dressing room and I think it's affecting the way we play. They feel unsettled and unsure."

Lyall trusted Bonds and realised that there was a depth of feeling among the players and he had to make a decision:

"Tell them not to worry Bill, I'll sign."

Lyall believed he had a duty of care to his players, after all, "They've kept me employed here for five years." Once John's future had been settled things soon improved and the Hammers enjoyed a good run in the FA Cup, before losing in the 6th Round to a Whiteside-inspired Manchester United. But the team itself was in flux, weakened by the loss of Trevor Brooking and a serious knee injury to Alan Devonshire. The emergence of the elegant Alan Dickens and young Paul Allen partly compensated for the loss, but they would need time to adjust to the demands of 1st Division football. Despite his bitter disappointment over the QPR job, Lyall worked tirelessly to rebuild his new team.

However, something had fundamentally changed in his relationship with the board. He never forgot the way the club treated him over the QPR affair. Lyall gradually ostracised himself from the club's owners. He no longer spent time with board members after matches, preferring the company of his players and friends in the press. As Yvonne recently observed, distancing himself from the board didn't help John in 1989, when he needed help most. But he knew that the QPR offer was a lost opportunity.

Life goes on and Lyall got on with the job.

The Boys of '86

Football fans love to argue about who was their club's finest player or most successful team. West Ham supporters are no different and will talk for hours about their own favourites and which was the best Hammers' side of all time.

What criteria do we use to compare football teams? Sustained success, great football, top players, these are all necessary conditions. On these criteria we would have to place Bobby Moore's legendary team just above the Jimmy Ruffell, Len Goulden and Vic Watson team of the 1920s. Managers Syd King, Ted Fenton and Ron Greenwood were, in their different ways, all superb leaders. John Lyall's achievement was to hold West Ham together after Greenwood's promotion to the England job, while at the same time achieving success with two different teams over a 15 year period.

There are probably four candidates for the greatest line-up in the club's history. Syd King's wonderful side of the 1920s won promotion to the top flight and reached the FA Cup final. King's players included the great conjurer, Jimmy Ruffell, the incomparable Len Goulden and the legendary centre-forwards, Vic Watson and Syd Puddefoot. There is no doubt that the team of the '20s established the East London club's reputation for playing fast, attacking football. King's achievement was to lead his men from the Southern League to Wembley and the top flight of English football.

Ted Fenton's team of the late 1950s is probably the most underrated in the club's history. Captained by Noel Cantwell and with the likes of Andy Malcolm, Phil Woosnam, John Dick, Ernie

Gregory, Malcolm Allison and Malcolm Musgrove, this side had everything. In 1958 Fenton took the club back to the 1st Division after an absence of 26 years. It was individuals like Cantwell and Allison who pioneered West Ham's famous academy of football at Cassetari's café.

The most obvious choice for the Hammers' team of all time is unquestionably Ron Greenwood's side of the mid-'60s. Moore, Hurst and Peters led the club to both FA Cup and European glory in the space of two years. This highly decorated group of players became household names and gave West Ham its international reputation. Of course, John Lyall, as youth team coach and club administrator was at the heart of the success of this magnificent group of players.

The final candidate for the honour of being the best ever West Ham team is Lyall's Boys of '86. Their claim to fame rests on achieving the club's highest ever finish in the top flight. Lyall's side had genuine class and played some terrific football and in 1986 came within four points of winning the 1st Division title. Devonshire, Parkes, Ward, Cottee, Martin, Gale, Stewart and McAvennie were the heart of the side and would have been terrific players in any era. But the fact that the Boys of '86 were one season wonders, places them a little behind the other contenders. In fact, Lyall's side led by Bonds, which won the 1980 FA Cup and ran away with the 2nd Division championship, has a stronger case for being Lyall's best team, rather than Alvin Martin's men five years later. McDonald and Francis's grandiose claim that the Boys of '86 brand of football was the best ever seen at Upton Park is frankly preposterous.

One of the reasons why the Boys of '86 are remembered with such affection is that their exploits remain fresh in the memory and were Lyall's last group of players at the club. He rebuilt the fondly remembered Bonds, Brooking and Lampard side into one of the best West Ham sides of all time. John Lyall's Boys of '86 are the stuff of Hammers' legend, if a little over-hyped. But, as we shall see, like a shooting star, they burned brightly, before crashing into the ground in spectacular fashion. As the 1980s drew to a close, the Hammers' manager maintained his high professional standards, despite his problems with the board. Even with the QPR rumours, the Upton Park faithful adored him.

We have seen how the Hammers' boss had to face the late '80s without the great Trevor Brooking. Within a year of Brooking leaving the club, that wonderful club servant, Frank Lampard, also decided to retire. The Hammers' loyal defender made his last appearance for the club against Liverpool on 20 May, 1985. Born in East Ham, Lampard joined the club as an apprentice in 1964. He made 663 appearances for West Ham, following his first team debut against Manchester City on 18 November, 1967. A wonderful attacking full-back, Lampard was adored by the Chicken Run who cheered his rampaging runs to the echo. The highlight of Lampard's long career was probably the diving header he scored in the 1980 FA Cup semi-final against Everton. His two England caps – eight years apart – seem a paltry reward for such a talented defender. Lampard spent some time coaching at Upton Park in the mid-'80s under Billy Bonds, but left when his brother-in-law, Harry Redknapp joined the club. Lampard's son, Frank Jnr went on to achieve even greater things, but sadly not in the claret and blue of the club where he began his career.

They say things come in threes. No sooner had Lyall lost two of his most gifted and reliable players, than the club's long-serving skipper, Billy Bonds began to show signs of wear and tear. The old campaigner originally planned to retire around the same time as Brooking and Lampard, but stayed on to cover for the seriously injured, Alan Devonshire. Few clubs could afford to lose the services of three such committed, loyal and talented footballers around the same time. Lyall not only coped with their departure, but set about building one of the Hammers' strongest ever sides. He was still smarting a bit, but showed tremendous strength of character in accepting the challenge of creating a new West Ham team.

Lyall realised he needed a creative individual to operate in the area of the pitch that Brooking made his own, just behind his main strikers, Cottee and Goddard. The player he had in mind was St Mirren's Frank McAvennie. Lyall had watched the young striker several times and made up his mind. Just to be certain he contacted two old friends, Jim McLean at Dundee United, and Alex Ferguson at Aberdeen. The two Scots confirmed Lyall's instincts about McAvennie. Ferguson told Lyall the crowds loved him,

'...there was always a buzz when he had the ball at his feet.'

Lyall rang the St Mirren boss, Alex Miller, personally and the two men agreed a fee of £340,000. No agents and no interfering chairman – imagine!

Lyall arranged to meet McAvennie and Miller at the Toddington services on the M1 in the early hours of the morning. Along with a few tired looking lorry drivers, the mysterious group were the only people in the cavernous cafeteria. At 4.00 am, after endless cups of tea, it was agreed and Lyall had his man. The youngster signed in June 1985 and immediately impressed his manager in pre-season training. Lyall warmed to his new forward's enthusiasm and independent spirit and couldn't wait for the new season to begin. Once again, West Ham had done their homework.

Just when Lyall thought he had his final piece of team-building jigsaw in place, in the summer of 1985 young midfielder, Paul Allen decided he wanted a move. Local boy Allen was aware that both Liverpool and Tottenham had expressed an interest, which probably increased his to desire to get away. Allen eventually signed for Spurs for £400,000 and became the first of many young, ex-academy players to leave the club over the next 20 years. But again, Lyall was ready with a replacement. Eddie Bailey, so valuable to his manager, had watched young Mark Ward three times at Oldham Athletic the previous season and was impressed with his speed and tenacity. Lyall trusted Bailey's judgement and agreed to pay £200,000 for the little-known winger. It was a risky signing, but Ward fitted neatly into Lyall's reshaped side and proved a very popular signing.

The Hammers' manager now had his rebuilt team in place ready for the start of the 1985/86 season. Devonshire had fully recovered from his awful injury and played wide on the left. As planned, McAvennie played just behind Cottee and Goddard, with Dickens,

Parris and Ward joining Devonshire in midfield. The defence of Walford, Martin, Gale and Stewart was as strong as any in the division and with Phil Parkes in goal, Lyall was confident of a good season for the Hammers – it was to turn out one of the best in living memory.

Unfortunately, the season began disastrously when Paul Goddard dislocated a shoulder in the first game – a 1-0 defeat at the hands of Birmingham City. One of Lyall's key signings was seriously injured and out for the rest of the season. For the next match Lyall had little choice but to push McAvennie up alongside Cottee as a joint striker. The move was an instant success as the Scot scored twice, in front of a disappointing Upton Park crowd of just 15,500, in the 3-1 victory against West London neighbours QPR.

With one win in the first seven games, Lyall's plans looked in tatters. His main striker, Tony Cottee began the season poorly and was dropped for a few games as the team struggled to find form. But Lyall needn't have worried. The Cottee/McAvennie partnership prospered and the gates at Upton Park doubled as excitement mounted game by game. In the run up to Christmas Lyall's side went 18 games without defeat, which included a run of nine straight wins. The rejuvenated Hammers were back on track and suddenly found themselves genuine title challengers.

Pat Holland tells us that Lyall would change his training programme to fit the players. He was a flexible coach who could easily adapt to changing conditions. Holland reveals that in the early days of the Cottee and McAvennie partnership, Lyall banished cross-country runs and focused on more intensive work in the gym. Both the young strikers liked to run the channels, rather than have balls hit up to a big centre-forward like David Cross. Lyall's ability to provide bespoke training for different players paid huge dividends for Cottee and McAvennie, as a different method worked for Cross. It was yet another example of Lyall's imaginative philosophy of coaching.

Despite their glorious league form, the Hammers maintained their tradition for unexpected cup defeats. The Boys of '86 men were knocked out of the FA Cup by Sheffield Wednesday at the quarter final stage, while a 1-0 defeat at the hands of Manchester United in the 3rd Round of the Milk Cup was less of a shock. These temporary setbacks failed to halt Lyall's side from storming up the League. Thirteen wins in the second half of the season is not the sort of performance we have come to expect from the fair weather Hammers, who are expected to come down with the Christmas decorations. But this team was different. The tension mounted as, free of any cup obligations, Lyall prepared his players for the run-in. The Boleyn was at fever pitch as the fans began to dream the impossible dream.

The Hammers challengers for the 1st Division title were the two Merseyside giants, Everton and Liverpool. Lyall had the respect of the best managers in the game, including Kenny Dalglish in his first season as the Reds' manager, who certainly took the East Londoner's title challenge seriously. It is not widely known that as a teenager Dalglish had a week's trial at Upton Park, where he enjoyed the hospitality of the Greenwoods. Unfortunately, the young genius was homesick in East London and quickly headed back to his native Scotland.

With six successive wins in April, Lyall's lads had put themselves in serious contention. They needed to beat Newcastle at home on 21 April to rest third place from Manchester United. In front of an ecstatic Upton Park crowd, the Hammers walloped the Tynesiders 8-1, with skipper Alvin Martin scoring a highly unusual hat-trick. His three goals were scored against three different 'keepers, the third against England's star forward, the diminutive Peter Beardsley. The Geordies' injury problems aside, the Hammers served up a feast of football for the West Ham faithful, as Tony McDonald remembers,

'The Hammers caught their opponents by surprise with their superb, free-flowing one-touch and two-touch football played from the back to the front.'

This was classic West Ham way and their dazzling's displays took Lyall's team to within touching distance of the title. The climax of the season was almost unbearable. The League went into the final

Saturday with all three teams in contention. What a rollercoaster day it turned out to be for Hammers' fans. Lyall's team didn't disappoint with a comfortable 3-2 victory at the Hawthorns, thanks to goals from McAvennie, Cottee and Ray Stewart – from the penalty spot, of course. In the days before mobile phones, rumour spread like wildfire. The radio commentators reported that Liverpool was losing their last game of the season at Chelsea. The whole of Upton Park went crazy as it began to sink in that the Hammers could be League champions for the first time. The fans simply ached for results to go their way. At the final whistle the players quickly disappeared into the changing rooms, only to hear the news that Dalglish had scored a first half goal for the Reds, taking them to their eighth title in eleven seasons – the radio had got it wrong. The emotions in the ground did somersaults as the truth finally dawned. Lyall's men dragged themselves up to Goodison Park two days later for the final game of this amazing season. Not surprisingly, a deflated Hammers' side lost 3-1, as goals from Barcelona-bound Gary Lineker helped Everton claim the runners-up spot. The Hammers' bid for the biggest prize in English football was over.

No prizes for coming third
Perhaps the fans found some consolation in the way their team's performances were received, but I doubt it. Patrick Collins wrote:
'West Ham has proved that attractive football can also be effective football. They have grown into the most appealing side in England.'
Everybody associated with West Ham waited anxiously for the result of the FA Cup final between the two Merseyside teams, clinging to the hope of another year in Europe. Liverpool's victory over Everton gave them the League and cup double, but there was to be no place in Europe for any English team. EUFA banned English clubs from participation in all European competitions following the evening of 'death and destruction', as McDonald described it, during Liverpool's match with Juventus at the decrepit Heysel Stadium. The appalling events at Heysel set

English football back a generation. It is easy to blame Liverpool fans, but the truth is that English football was riven with violence and hooliganism as we have seen. And, West Ham fans were among the worst exponents, tough though that was for some fans to accept. One of the effects of the appalling behaviour seen at football grounds was that fans began to stay away. During the '80s the average attendance at Upton Park hovered disappointingly around 20,000.

The Bradford Fire disaster in May 1985, in which 65 people lost their lives, exposed the faultline running through English football in the most tragic manner. Most of the early football stadiums were constructed from a mix of materials, including steel, concrete and even mud. But wood was cheap and became the predominant material in most grounds. Nobody who witnessed the Bradford fire or watched it on TV will forget the harrowing sight. There is little doubt that the horrific events at Bradford led to a decrease in attendances across the country, as the British people fell out of love with their national sport.

Before the tragedy of Hillsborough four years after the Bradford fire, Upton Park remained one of the few grounds that resisted pitch fencing. The board did introduce CCTV cameras, disbanded the Irons Travel Club, and mounted a strong 'Keep the fences away from Upton Park' campaign. This was the gloomy backdrop of English football as the Hammers played out one of the best seasons in the club's history.

Despite all this appalling background noise, the players stuck to their task and Lyall was immensely proud of them. Not only had they come close to winning the League, they had performed with the style and verve football fans have come to expect from a West Ham side. Privately, Lyall had mixed emotions. His team had taken him to the brink of what all managers aspire to – the 1st Division championship. As he said later,

'...the football man's dream is the League Championship... it is a prize only a few have lifted. Most managers can spend a lifetime in the game and not get close. At least I got close.'

The Boys of '86 team were full of heroes and every single one of them, from Parkes right through the team, played their part in this memorable season. It is perhaps a little churlish to single out individual players for special praise or attention, but the goals of McAvennie and Cottee – 54 between them – were largely instrumental in helping Lyall's team accumulate a colossal 84 points that season. In Cottee's case his 26 goals in all competitions earned him the 1986 PFA Young Player of the Year award.

Frank McAvennie was one of the first celebrity footballers and, unfairly, was branded a playboy with a champagne lifestyle. Perhaps ill-advisedly, he appeared on the Terry Wogan show and was rarely out of the headlines at this time. Following George Best's example modern professionals were no longer satisfied, as Bobby Moore would have been, with a couple of pints at the Black Lion in Plaistow followed by a night out at the Ilford Palais. As the players' wages rose exponentially, so their attitudes and lifestyles changed. Modern managers like John Lyall had to cope with these changes. Despite his exotic lifestyle, McAvennie was the darling of the North Bank and popular with teammates and the coaching staff. It became clear to Lyall that the newspapers had got it wrong about the mercurial Scot:

'For me, he was an outstanding professional. He enjoyed the bright lights and spent a lot of his spare time with Arsenal's Charlie Nicholas. Like Charlie, Frank was much in demand as a celebrity, but he knew how to handle it.'

Lyall clearly enjoyed working with young Frank, who never missed a training session:

'He was an easy person to deal with, forthright and good natured.'

McAvennie was a great success in his first season, as was the player who joined the club at the same time, Mark Ward. The young winger was voted third in the 1986 PFA Young Player of the Year award behind Cottee and McAvennie. The youngster, at just 5' 6" tall and a mere 10 stone, had a terrific work rate, was very quick and a natural team man. The chirpy Liverpudlian was a lively presence in the Hammers' dressing room and was a winger in true West Ham tradition. Ward made 52 League and cup appearances in that golden year and adjusted comfortably with the transition from lowly Oldham to high-riding West Ham. His speciality, practised endlessly on the training ground, was a long angled ball hit with pace into the path of Cottee or McAvennie at the near post, the kind of pass perfected by England's Steven Gerrard in more recent times. Ward's incisive running and his accurate crosses brought a hatful of goals for his two forward partners in that wonderful season. For Lyall, the Liverpudlian was an inspired signing.

His move from Oldham to Upton Park proved a soccer culture shock to the young scouser, but he was a quick learner,

'...I was like a fish out of water. I found the pace, accuracy and precision of the passing unbelievable. The quality was something I'd not expected.'

Ward worked hard with Lyall and Ronnie Boyce on improving his game and he soon settled into the West Ham way of doing things. At the time he was within a whisker of gaining an England cap. It is regrettable that Ward left Upton Park when he did.

Mark Ward played 165 games for West Ham between 1985 and 1990, scoring a modest 12 goals, before he left Upton Park for Manchester City. Howard Kendall, City manager clearly believed that exchanging Ian Bishop and Trevor Morley for Ward, plus some cash, was good business. Later in his career, the little magician inspired Birmingham City to Wembley glory under the Blues extrovert manager, Barry Fry. Sadly, when he retired from the game Ward's life began to unravel. His marriage collapsed and various business ventures failed. In May 2005, Ward was arrested at his home in Liverpool for possession of large quantities of cocaine. He pleaded guilty and received an eight year jail sentence, which he served in the notorious Walton Prison in Liverpool. Ward was released after serving four years of his term. Howard Kendall visited his former player in Walton and was impressed with the way he coped with imprisonment and the way he was planning for his future.

Since leaving prison Ward has attempted to rebuild his life, not without difficulty. His former West Ham teammates have been helpful, with Alvin Martin and Tony Gale involving their former teammate in the Boys of '86 programme. In his autobiography, Hammered, Ward talked fondly about his time in East London:

'I shouldn't have left West Ham as early as I did. If Billy Bonds – and not Lou Macari – had succeeded John Lyall, I wouldn't have gone anywhere. Who knows, I could still have been living near London and maybe even working at West Ham now.'

The manager, coaching staff and players welcomed the chirpy Liverpudlian and the fans took him to their hearts. West Ham supporters who remember his outstanding contribution to the great season of 1985/86 will wish Wardy all the best for the future.

In their book, Boys of '86, McDonald and Francis offer some interesting insights into the dynamics of Lyall's squad and the relationship between the players and their manager. As the authors of the book point out, Alvin Martin was the squad's natural leader and picked up that some of the team were unhappy with one of the club's premier players, Tony Cottee. Martin asked John Lyall if he could hold a players' meeting to clear the air. Lyall agreed and the players had a positive get-together. Cottee accepted the criticism and got on with his game. It says something about Lyall's leadership qualities that he was happy for a senior player to deal with a potential dispute. At no time did Lyall see Martin's actions as undermining his authority. As McDonald and Martin remarked:

'Tactically, Lyall had the full respect of his players and was rightly regarded then as one of the best tracksuit managers in the game.'

Lyall declined to be interviewed for the Boys of '86 book, although he always treated the authors' requests with his customary politeness and good humour. There are good reasons why he chose not to be involved. The most persuasive is that Lyall had written his own autobiography on his years at West Ham and had nothing further to say about his team of the '80s.

A new challenge

Given the disappointment of the previous season, Lyall knew his job over the summer was to raise the spirits of his players and lead them into another successful season. There were the standard personnel changes. Following six successful seasons at the Boleyn, Paul Goddard left to further to his career in the north east with Newcastle United. Lyall brought in defenders, Gary Strodder and Tommy McQueen from Aberdeen, and more significantly, Stewart Robson from Arsenal for a fee of £640,000. The public school-educated Robson was not a classic West Ham type player, but was physically strong and a box-to-box midfielder in the manner of Bryan Robson and Steven Gerrard. Robson was a good friend of Tony Cottee and the two youngsters had forced themselves into Bobby Robson's England squad. The Arsenal player's opportunities had been restricted at Highbury and George Graham was reluctant to lose such a promising player, but knew he wanted first team football.

His whole-hearted playing style made Robson popular with the fans, before he succumbed to the injury problems that blighted his career. However, his arrival didn't go down too well with the senior players at the club. In an interview for the McDonald and Francis book, Alvin Martin spoke for his team:

'Robson... was just not a West Ham player. Playing for West Ham was all about one and two-touch passing but Robson couldn't play that way. We didn't need Robbo.'

Martin's assessment of Stewart Robson can be taken as implied criticism of his manager. The club failed to build on their high League placing of 1985/86 because, Martin argued, Lyall failed to sign the quality players needed to mount a second assault on the 1st Division title. Martin continued:

'I don't like having a go at anyone but if you're being ruthlessly honest, the manager has to take responsibility. I'm not being nasty but bringing back Billy Bonds – as fit as he was at 40 – was not the thing to do and didn't send out the right message to our fans.'

Cracks began to appear in the previously rock solid relationships at Upton Park between manager and players and between the players themselves. They believed that if they were going to win the League they needed to bring in players with the physical qualities of Graham Souness, Steve McMahon or Mick Harford, as Ray Stewart explained,

'...we lacked the steel of a Souness in midfield... but it wasn't for me to tell John his job.'

This is all very well from the safety of reflection and it is unlikely the players spoke up at the time – they had too much respect for Lyall. The manager made his own thoughts clear to Michael Hart of the Evening Standard:

'There is no point in buying players of similar calibre to the ones we have already because that simply closes the avenue to our youths.'

There you have it! Today a Premier League manager wouldn't hesitate to introduce new players at the expense of his youngsters – it would never occur to him otherwise. West Ham had always looked to local young players as the future of the club and Lyall was part of that tradition. Now this precious principle which underpinned the club's whole raison d'etre was under threat.

The new season was notable for the emergence of the club's most promising young player for a generation, the precocious Paul Ince. The 19-year-old scored on his debut in the 3-1 win over Southampton at Upton Park. It was immediately clear that Ince was something special. Here was a young player who could become one of the West Ham greats. But the Ince and Robson midfield partnership was never going to provide the steel the team supposedly lacked and Ince's career at Upton Park was to be short-lived.

Alvin Martin argues that Lyall's reluctance to spend money to improve his team was because:

'John ran the club's finances as if it was his own money... It was his club and he wasn't going to bankrupt it. That's the way he did his job.'

The authors of The Essential History of West Ham United, Blows and Hogg, have very definite views on Lyall's reluctance to make big money signings in 1986:

'It's something that West Ham criminally ignored during the summer of 1986, negligently sitting dormant while others improved their squads.'

'Criminally ignored' seems harsh, but the authors appear to point the finger at the board rather than the manager. The fact remains that the summer of '86 came and went, leaving Lyall with much the same squad that completed the previous season.

But the manager had faith in the squad that very nearly won the 1st Division title and saw no reason to gamble on new players. The Hammers started the new campaign in good form, but fell away in December. The second half of the season was disastrous. Serious injuries to key players robbed Lyall of the continuity he enjoyed the previous season. Skipper, Alvin Martin, Ray Stewart, Tony Gale and Alan Devonshire were all absent for long periods. No team, least of all West Ham, could afford to lose players of this quality for any length of time. The Hammers won just five League games from the beginning of February to the end of the season – hardly championship winning form. Lyall's team reached the quarter-final of the Milk Cup, but suffered a humiliating 5-0 defeat at the hands of local rivals Tottenham in a replay at White Hart Lane. Following the euphoria and promise of the preceding season, the Hammers finished in a disappointing 15th place. No wonder Lyall titled his autobiography, Just Like My Dreams.

There were compensations. Alan Dickens continued his improvement; Mark Ward enjoyed another good season and Tony Gale began to look like a top defender. Cottee continued his goal-scoring exploits with 28 in all competitions. In a total of 45 matches that season, Frank McAvennie managed just 11 goals – a major disappointment for his manager. Expectations that season were understandingly high, but instead of a further assault on the League title, Lyall faced a crisis. In March, he brought in veteran midfielder, Liam Brady from Juventus for £80,000, but even the magical Irishman couldn't turn the tide, despite scoring on his debut.

The sense of crisis deepened in May '87 when star player Tony Cottee handed in a written transfer request. Cottee was ambitious and felt a move to one of the top clubs would help his international career. Lyall knew the value of this prolific goalscorer:

'His goal-scoring had been one of the few consistent things of 1986/87 and I considered him an invaluable member of the first team.'

Fortunately for Lyall, West Ham did not receive a single offer for their top marksman. At the end of this frustrating season, Cottee and his manager sat in Lyall's garden and the two men chatted through the afternoon. Lyall told the youngster to concentrate on working on his game and ignore all the transfer speculation. Cottee agreed and set about preparing for the new season. Lyall had handled the delicate situation with his usual sensitivity and secured the services of his top scorer for at least one more year.

Bonzo's last season

Lyall lost his long-serving skipper, Billy Bonds, when the great man finally retired in 1988 at the grand old age of 41. In addition, McAvennie finally got his move to Celtic, something he had long cherished. Geoff Pike left to see out his playing career at Notts County, and Neil Orr was granted his wish to return to Scotland with Aberdeen. But it was the buccaneering Bonds who was missed most at Upton Park, particularly by his manager. The two had stood side-by-side during the successful years of the early 1980s and the great defender had been the Hammers' skipper since 1974. Lyall completely trusted Bonds' judgement and the two men met every Friday to discuss tactics and team selection ahead of Saturday's match.

Billy Bonds MBE joined West Ham in 1967 and made 795 appearances for the club, scoring 59 goals. Bonzo captained the Hammers to two FA Cup final victories and led the club to the 2nd Division Championship in 1981. The fans absolutely adored Bonds and rewarded their favourite player with four Hammer of the Year awards, while the club recognised his tremendous service with two testimonial matches. Patsy Holland remembers his former teammate:

"Billy was my role model because everything he achieved was through hard work."

Completely dedicated, Bonds was also a supremely gifted footballer and despite receiving a record number of England Under-23 caps, must have been hugely disappointed not to have been awarded full international honours. Bonds appeared in the same side as Moore, Hurst and Peters, and of course, his great friend, Trevor Brooking. He played his final game for West Ham against Southampton at the Dell on 30 April 1988. On Bonds' retirement, Lyall repaid his captain's loyalty by offering him a job coaching the club's youngsters. The managerial career of Billy Bonds, including the turbulent years at the Boleyn, is well-documented. Today Bonds lives in quiet retirement in Kent where he continues to indulge his passion for the novels of Charles Dickens. It is probably true to say of Billy Bonds, 'they don't make 'em like that anymore.'

Where do we go from here?

The team of '86 was slowly dismantled and change was in the air at Upton Park. But it was not the kind of change that got the fans excited. Expectations had been raised by the Boys of '86 who had kept the crowd on the edge of their seats in the electric atmosphere of that season. Mid-table mediocrity was not going to be accepted with good grace by the claret and blue faithful. Unfortunately, they were going to have to accept much less.

The Boys of '86 were a close-knit group of players who responded to their manager's coaching methods and subtle man-management techniques. The club needed to build on their achievements. But, once again, West Ham proved their credentials as a selling club when both parts of the goal-scoring machine of McAvennie and Cottee were shipped out, the latter for a record British transfer fee. Although he returned to Upton Park for a second spell, the Hammers missed Cottee's goals. Injuries piled up as they had in the previous two seasons, but could not be used as an excuse. Finishing 15th and 16th in the two years following the heroic exploits of '86 was a huge disappointment for everybody at the club, particularly for the much-loved, but now under pressure manager, John Lyall.

Following Cottee's departure to Everton for £2.2m, Lyall acted to strengthen the team when he brought in full-back Julian Dicks from Birmingham City and a centre-forward who became a cult figure at the Boleyn, Leroy Rosenior. The ex-Fulham striker scored on his debut in the 1-0 win over Watford, the club he rejected in favour of West Ham. Lyall paid £290,000 for Rosenior, not an insubstantial sum in the late '80s. At the time Watford was desperate to capture the Fulham centre-forward to help them in their desperate relegation battle. The West Ham manager remembers seeing Elton John, the Watford chairman, hanging around the corridor outside the dressing rooms before the game. Spotting the somewhat forlorn figure, Lyall invited him for a cup of tea in his office. The singer replied:

"No, John. You've got a game to worry about. Thanks all the same."

Lyall insisted and the pair talked for about 15 minutes before the West Ham man realised there was something other than football bothering the great pop star. At the time John was being subjected to some pretty harsh treatment by the press for his eccentric and controversial lifestyle. "Go for the jugular," Lyall told the Watford chairman, "fight back." The Hammers' manager must have said the right thing, because the following Christmas a case of champagne arrived at the Chadwell Heath training ground, marked for the attention of John Lyall. Inside was a note which said simply: 'Thanks for the chat, Elton.'

Lyall's former teammate of the early '60s, Bobby Moore, had rather a different experience of the celebrated Watford chairman. Following his retirement, Moore applied for the vacant manager's job at Vicarage Road. Following two lunch appointments and lengthy contract negotiations, Moore assumed he had secured the job. The West Ham and England legend went off on holiday looking forward to working with his new boss the following season, only to read in the Daily Mail on his return that the Rocket Man had offered the post to Graham Taylor instead. Moore never received an explanation and the two men never met again.

Elton John's loss was John Lyall's gain as Rosenior became a big favourite with the North Bank, and was immortalised in a NUSound track recorded in his honour. Rosenior was the club's main source of goals in his first full season, but it summed up Lyall's predicament when his new striker top-scored with just 11 goals in all competitions.

But it was all too little too late as the fans looked on in horror. Lyalls' beleaguered team raised the fans spirits in 1989 by two good cup runs. A victory against Arsenal in the FA Cup and a 5-0 drubbing of Derby in the 3rd round of the Littlewoods Cup were among the few highlights of a dismal season. The victory over Derby brought the mighty Liverpool to Upton Park. The boys in claret and blue were on top form that November evening and hammered the Reds 4-1. The Daily Express reported:

'Liverpool were humbled beneath an avalanche of attacking football.'

Two goals from Paul Ince, an own goal, and a tremendous free-kick from Tony Gale destroyed Liverpool. The fans would have enjoyed these few highlights, and the emergence of Ince, Steve Potts and Kevin Keen brought them some hope. But the bright spots were few and far between. After eight seasons in the top flight, Lyall's team was relegated on 5 May with a meagre 38 points. West Ham was back in the 2nd Division. The bubble had well and truly burst and the West Ham manager was facing the biggest challenge of his distinguished career.

Chapter 12
John, you're fired!

Through the 1980s, with John established as one of the top managers in English and European football, the Lyall family began to prosper. They sold their Abridge home of 23 years and moved to Stanford Rivers, just outside the little Essex town of Ongar, where they acquired the handsome Old Rectory. John's career at West Ham went from strength to strength until the relegation season of 1988/89. Up to this point Lyall's career trajectory had been on an upward curve, punctuated by FA Cup victories, high League finishes and exciting European adventures. The lad from Ilford had come a long way from his time as Boleyn office boy and youth team footballer.

They say that every politician's life ends in failure – the same might be said of football managers. Relegation in football is failure. Lyall knew this and accepted the blame. But he must have been frustrated that the group of players who achieved the highest League finish in the club's history, took the club down into the 2nd Division a season later. There had been injuries, but every club has injury problems. Senior players like Alvin Martin criticised the manager and his board for not buying the quality players he believed West Ham needed to compete with the top clubs. But did Martin seriously believe the top players in the country would leave their clubs for Upton Park, just because they had one outstanding season?

It didn't help that Bonds, Brooking and Lampard – great stalwarts of the 1970s and '80s all came to the end of their careers around the same time. The sale of Cottee and McAvennie was regrettable. Tony Cottee was one of the best young players to graduate from Tony Carr's academy. In the capricious Scot's case, his move was unavoidable – seemingly, his sole ambition in football was to play for Celtic. But Cottee and McAvennie were difficult to replace, and the goals dried up. But Lyall had outstanding youngsters like Ince, Keen, Dickens and the promising Stuart Slater desperate for a run in the first team – bringing on young players was an enshrined part of the West Ham way. But no sooner had Ince and Dickens established themselves in the side than they were sold to rival clubs – as were Joe Cole, Rio Ferdinand, Michael Carrick and Frank Lampard of the next generation. The selling club mentality is a regrettable trend which began in the latter stages of Len Cearns chairmanship and continues up until the present day, despite the empty rhetoric about the importance of the club's Academy. Tony Carr's youngsters were being sold to fund stadium development, pay inflated salaries, or reduce debt. By the summer of 1989 West Ham had begun to lose its way and Lyall was a victim of the club's changing values rather than the architect of its demise.

Ultimately, the players have to take responsibility for the team's performances in 1988/89 rather than look around for people to blame. New goalkeeper, Alan McKnight shouldered most of the blame following a series of dramatic errors in the relegation season. But, as the Irishman reflected later: "I was also taking the rap for other people's blunders and found that difficult to handle."

Former players were quick to criticise. Lyall's former teammate, John Bond, was quick to jump on the bandwagon: "It's time John Lyall stepped down," fumed the club's former full-back, "there are too many old faces at the place and changes need to be made."

The former Hammers' full-back's views should be respected, he was a great club servant and his criticism was well-intended. His veiled attack on the club's management came as a shock. Bond was a popular figure at West Ham and his sad death in 2012 was marked by a minute's silence at Upton Park, and hundreds of tributes from former players and supporters.

Lyall found himself in an extremely vulnerable position, with the Hammers back in the 2nd Division and with just one year left on his contract:

'I was bitterly disappointed. So, too, were the players. You can't complain though, if you have played all your games and failed. There were

235

mitigating circumstances, but I was never a manager who liked to offer excuses for defeat and failure.'

At the end of the season Lyall returned home to Essex to spend some precious time with Yvonne and the family. As he settled into the summer his thoughts would have turned to the forthcoming season and his contract discussions with his chairman, Mr Len. Back in April, with relegation staring the Hammers in the face, Len Cearns pledged his guarded support for his beleaguered management team:

'Whether we stay up or not will not alter our considerations about John's contract.'

Up until 1989, with just five managers in their history, the West Ham board had an enviable reputation of showing faith in their managers. Lyall never gave a second thought to the possibility of leaving the club – that was not the West Ham way. But football and its old values were changing fast.

One Saturday morning early that summer, Lyall was mowing the lawn at the family home in Ongar when Yvonne took a call from Len Cearns. Naturally she asked if he wanted John to return the call. The chairman replied, "No that's quite alright, please tell him I shall want to speak to him when I return from Aldeburgh," (the chairman's country retreat) "in ten days' time."

On Monday 5 June, Lyall drove down to Chadwell Heath to begin his preparations for the new season. He needed to sort out some pre-season fixtures, training schedules and catch up with the coaching staff. Glancing at the papers over breakfast that morning I'm sure he would have noticed that Bobby Robson's England team were flying out for a pre-season friendly with Denmark. But his thoughts were with West Ham and the coming season. He met Tony Carr down at the training ground and the pair chatted about possible transfers and if any of Carr's young academy prospects were ready for the first team. Suddenly the telephone rang. It was the chairman asking if John could come over to the Cearns' family home in Chigwell later that morning. It was important. Lyall agreed, and thought little of it as he often visited the chairman at his home to discuss club business.

Lyall arrived at Cearns' luxury Chigwell villa about an hour later, blissfully unaware of what lay ahead. The West Ham chairman came straight to the point and without even offering his manager a cup of tea, brutally sacked him on the spot.

Cearns was well prepared and presented John with a deal. The club was offering a testimonial match, a regular monthly payment until he secured another job and a lump sum. Lyall was stunned, but kept his nerve. He was an immensely proud man and told his chairman in no uncertain terms what he could do with his deal. As Yvonne remembers, Cearns' offer of a testimonial match brought an angry response from Lyall: "If you think the fans are going to pay for my redundancy out of their own pockets, you've got another think coming."

Lyall also rejected the monthly golden handshake and stayed calm enough to tell Cearns:

"I came here in the club Mercedes, the keys are in my pocket and that's where they are staying."

Mr Len then wrote the following on a sheet of notepaper:

'Club car given to J. Lyall on termination of contract.'

The chairman tore off the note from his sheet of paper and handed it to the exasperated Lyall. Yvonne retained the note and it remains in her possession to this day.

After a very short exchange Lyall left. He was stunned. Cearns failed to thank his former manager for 34 years of dedicated service and made no attempt to acknowledge his achievements at West Ham. Lyall explained later: "I didn't get a cup of tea. We didn't shake hands. I left the table and let myself out the front door."

As Lyall drove down the gated mansion's driveway, he thought to himself, Well, that's over. What's next?

Today, club chairmen probably do this kind of thing by text

message. Lyall drove back to the training ground to inform his staff about his dismissal. Ronnie Boyce and Eddie Bailey were away on holiday, but Billy Bonds was there working with some youth team players and Mick McGiven and Tony Carr were in the office. Lyall called them together in the room where he discussed team tactics with Bonds on Friday afternoons. Their response to Lyall's news was predictable. McGiven was deeply shocked and resigned within a few weeks. It was typical of Lyall that he thought more of his staff than himself at this difficult time. He told them the chairman planned to speak to them during the afternoon and they should listen to what he had to say. "Don't do anything hasty – your livelihoods are at stake," urged Lyall.

Later that morning, the now former West Ham manager left Chadwell Heath for the final time. As he drove through the streets of East London on his way home to Ongar, Lyall had time to reflect on the past 34 years. He thought about the players, coaches and great friends he made during all those years at the club. His two FA Cup final victories and glory nights at Upton Park drifted into focus. He might also have given a passing thought to the QPR offer and how West Ham had denied him the opportunity of a lifetime.

When Yvonne returned home from shopping later that Monday afternoon, she spotted John's car in the driveway. "Hello," she said, "lovely to see you home so early."

John replied, "I've been sacked Von," to which she replied,

"... are you joking? I can't believe it. They wouldn't do that to you would they?"

Thinking of all those years of John being away from home, Yvonne reacted with understandable annoyance. She was furious. After so many years of loyal service to the club he loved, her husband had been summarily dismissed with little thought of the depth of his loyalty, or the extent of his achievements. She was particularly angry because Len Cearns knew he was going to sack her husband before he went on his 10 day break to Aldeburgh – Yvonne had taken the call. But John was more circumspect and told Yvonne, "Well, at least we'll have more time together."

The news of Lyall's dismissal was released that afternoon. John's mother saw her son's picture on the TV and thought he had had an accident. Later that day John received calls from Ray Stewart, Stewart Robson, Paul Hilton, Graham Paddon and Bobby Barnes. Trevor Brooking contacted his old friend and manager, as did Ernie Gregory. Fellow managers Alex Ferguson, Terry Venables and Don McKay all called offering their support. Mackay told Lyall, "If this could happen to you, what chance has the rest of us?"

That afternoon, Ronnie Boyce drove out to the Lyall's house and was joined by John's son, Murray, West Ham secretary, Tom Finn, and Colin Wines, an old friend and Hammers' supporter. This little cluster of West Ham people sat quietly in the garden with a consoling cup of tea while Yvonne dealt with a constantly ringing telephone.

The press were soon hot on the trail and one national newspaper immediately offered Lyall £10,000 to tell his side of the story. Of course, they were wasting their time. John said later:

'I had never done that sort of thing and could see no point in doing it then.'

Lyall dealt with the press in his own time. He told them he was grateful to the staff, players and supporters at the club for their loyalty over the past 34 years. The one thing he did not want to appear was bitter, as he revealed in his autobiography:

'Bitterness is a negative and destructive emotion, and I didn't want it gnawing at me for the rest of my life.'

One man who will be pleased that Lyall remained in a positive mood, in spite of what he must have been feeling, was David Cross. The man who Lyall transformed from a keen, but limited, centre-forward into the one of the most feared strikers in the 1st Division, refused to read his former manager's autobiography. This fine Hammers' goalscorer didn't want to read about the man he so admired telling everybody how bitter he was. Cross need not have worried. Lyall said he felt no anger or bitterness, just an overwhelming feeling of sadness.

The telephone continued to ring at the Lyall house until long into the evening. Paul Allen and Frank Lampard were the last to call at around midnight. Ever positive, Lyall was comforted to know he had so many friends in football: "It was one of the nice things about the day." As he tried to sleep the 49-year-old reflected on events: "For the first time in 34 years I would wake up the next morning not working for West Ham. I had started the day very much like every other during those years. I finished the day as an unemployment statistic."

The following day Mick McGiven collected John's personal possessions from the ground, while his former boss spent the day at home pondering his future. Lyall knew he wanted to stay in the game and thought about managing a different club. But he knew it would be difficult to find an environment where he could build a team in the West Ham tradition. A tradition he had learned from his mentor, Ron Greenwood. For Lyall, West Ham and all their dedicated fans, it was the end of an era.

When they heard the news of Lyall's abrupt dismissal, the fans were horrified – West Ham just did not behave like this, we are a family club. Later that week the board issued a terse 70-word statement announcing they had sacked the man who had served the club as player, coach and manager for over three decades. There is no question that Lyall was shocked by the club's behaviour and later wrote:

'You tend to look at other factors... success in the FA Cup... loyalty... long service... I couldn't say I noticed much sympathy, reluctance or any other emotion as he terminated my 34 years at the club.'

The West Ham manager for the past 15 years walked away with a one-off payment of about £100,000 and in regrettable circumstances. This essentially human and caring man was universally popular at Upton Park and at the training ground. Not just with the players, but everyone, including the car park attendants, ground staff, catering people and even the postman. Lyall never forgot his roots and ensured that everybody visiting

Chadwell Heath got a warm welcome and a cup of strong tea. He led the club by setting an example with his impeccable manners and behaviour.

Lyall left West Ham before the introduction of the Premier League. Football was changing fast and men with the values of Lyall and Greenwood were becoming an endangered species. The club could easily have managed an orderly transition with Lyall promoted to the position of Director of Football, with perhaps Mick McGiven or Ronnie Boyce appointed as team manager. Instead they decided to throw away 100 years of tradition. Changes in the boardroom and in the ownership of the club soon followed the shambles of Lyall's departure. The patrician Mr Len was soon gone to be replaced by his son, Martin Cearns. Over the next few years the club was sold and resold, trading its reputation for cash, before sliding into levels of debt unimaginable to the club's ancestral figures like Arnold Hills, Syd King and Ted Fenton.

It's true, as Yvonne admits, that Lyall had ostracised himself from the board following the QPR affair. The director of football suggestion was never going to happen. As both Phil Parkes and Pat Holland have pointed out, Lyall became too powerful a figure in the club for a modern chairman to accept. He knew every nook and cranny of West Ham, and controlled every aspect of the club, including decisions on transfers, catering arrangements, player contracts and wages. He was a manager for his time and that time was up.

West Ham could have made better use of the long-serving Lyall, as they could have done with the man who is generally regarded as the soul of the club, Bobby Moore. Since Lyall's departure the West Ham way, inspired by Greenwood and beloved of the fans, has all but disappeared into memory. What precisely was the West Ham way and why was it worth defending? It was a commitment to an open style of attacking, exciting, purist football that everyone in the game admired. But it was also a set of values enshrined in the way the club always did things – a genuine and caring compassion for other people, commitment to the local community and its young footballers, and a sense of belonging that was unique to this particular part of London. These were all essential values that managers from Syd King to John Lyall upheld. These values were abandoned the day that Len Cearns sacked John Lyall. It says it all that Lyall was only the fifth West Ham manager since Syd King's appointment in 1902 – there have been 10 in the 23 years since his dismissal in 1989.

With nothing in the Boleyn trophy cabinet since the FA Cup final of 1980, West Ham has been badly managed and poorly governed for the past 30 years. The one thing that doesn't change at this once proud club is the passionate fans, who can only dream of the days when the Hammers were conquering Europe and producing Word Cup-winning footballers.

Building on Greenwood's fine work, Lyall enjoyed 708 games in charge at West Ham. His record speaks for itself: two FA Cups, the final of the European Cup Winners' Cup, the final of the League Cup, triumph in the 2nd Division championship by a record 13 points, and in 1986, he took West Ham to their highest ever League position in the top flight.

The players close ranks
It is right that we should let the players and fans have the last word on John Lyall's outstanding career at Upton Park. Tony Gale, lynchpin of the Lyall's Boys of '86 side spoke for most of the players and fans when he said:

'The club has never recovered from John Lyall's departure... the family feel... it was all down to John.'

Kit-man, Eddie Gillam said at the time,

'...as soon as the board sacked John Lyall, West Ham United became an ordinary football club. We were the family club but once John went we became just like all the others.'

Close colleague, Mick McGiven remembers how he felt at the time about his good friend's departure from the club he loved:

'His leaving ripped the heart out of me. I cried when he left.'

One of West Ham's greatest signings, Phil Parkes, remembers a good friend, with whom he regularly shared his love of carpentry as:

'Not just a manager, but a very special person.'

Recently in his office at the club's Academy, Tony Carr, who Lyall appointed as full-time coach at Upton Park, spoke eloquently about his former boss for an hour in the middle of a very busy Friday afternoon. He remembered how Lyall gave him a chance after injury ended Carr's playing days:

'I will be eternally grateful to John – he brought me back to West Ham.'

Tony Cottee recalls his former manager:

'John was a headmaster-type figure, someone I respected and looked up to. He had looked after me on and off the field since I was 14-years-old... I felt highly of him as a person and a coach... he made it clear his door was always open.'

Cottee experienced both sides of John Lyall; the human, caring person and the tough negotiator on wages and contracts. Cottee continued:

'Although he was renowned as one of football's gentleman, he also had a tough side of his character – as I discovered when we met for contract talks. John's reaction to my demands scared the life out of me.'

Reflecting on his years at West Ham recently, Ray Stewart revealed that the only manager who approaches John Lyall in terms of honesty and trust is Sir Alex Ferguson. The legendary Hammers' full-back continued:

'I had enormous respect for John. He looked after me as a teenager,

regularly visited me in hospital when I was injured and offered me a contract at Ipswich, when he knew I was struggling with injury. He demanded loyalty and respect.'

Like Ferguson, Lyall built a club, rather than just a team and he knew and understood the local community as Stewart explains:

'John knew all the local police officers. He told the players – if you are out and have drunk too much to drive, then don't. Call me or Eddie, whatever the time of day or night and we will come and get you.'

When players did get into trouble, as the young Paul Ince did on one occasion, Lyall was able to talk to the police and resolve the matter, while reminding the player of his responsibilities to the club, his family and the local community. It is a rare manager who will go to these extremes to protect his players.

The fans' view
If the players were shocked by Lyall's sudden departure from Upton Park, most Hammers' fans were outraged by the club's treatment of their most successful manager. Reflecting on Lyall's crude dismissal, Stuart Allen, huge West Ham fan and devoted club archivist, said simply:

'John was the first manager I could relate to. His sacking horrified me. He inspired support in all of us.'

Lifelong supporter, Clare Horgan from Abridge, who went to school with Murray Lyall, has fond memories of John:

'His house was on my paper round – he was a top man.'

Clare shared this particular childhood memory:

'I went to school with Murray and we both lived in Abridge. John was so gracious when a young kid knocked on his door asking for 1980 Cup

Final tickets. He stood on the doorstep and explained how he didn't have enough tickets to go round – he could have just shut the door, but it marks the calibre of the man that he took the time to explain.'

Clare was one of many fans who willingly came forward to share their thoughts about Lyall. Colin Cousen spoke for most when he said:

'Great man – should have been the England manager.'

Jaywat Parkboo, admired Lyall's tactical acumen:

'John Lyall always came across as a gentleman. He brought steel into the defence, but still allowed the flow of West Ham to continue – I think we only used 14 players in that great season of 1985/86.'

Many fans remember the camel-coloured Crombie Lyall wore on the touchline during the winter months, while others joked about the way he urged his team to play West Ham football with their boots stuck deep in the Upton Park mud. For many of the faithful, Keith Taylor offered the most poignant comment on Lyall's time at the Boleyn:

'It's very rare to hear a former manager's name chanted in the stadium 20 years after he left – amazing man. John Lyall's claret and blue army.'

West Ham fans both respected and loved their former manager. Distinguished club historian, John Northcutt remembers the Hammers' boss as,

'...a warm, genuine and honest person.'

Northcutt wrote to Lyall asking if he would be kind enough to contribute a short article for the 50th issue of the West Ham Statisticians Group monthly newsletter. Within days he received a handwritten letter outlining a typical week in the life of a football manager. The letter illustrates the detail of Lyall's everyday working life at West Ham. This is the letter printed in full.

Dear John,

Once again I have the pleasure of contributing an article for the magazine which I hope will be of interest to all the members. It was suggested I relate to a typical week in my life as a manager. I can fully understand football supporters wondering what a manager actually does between each game and how fully he is involved in the activities of the club.

In this day and age we read much of the modern manager not being involved in training and not being involved in the administration of the football side of the club, and continually going off for holidays to recharge the batteries. I can assure you that is not the case and over the years I have noted that the great majority of managers are simply hard-working people.

My week is typical of the effort offered at most football clubs throughout Britain, although the content is controlled by the individual manager. Monday began at the training ground at 9.00 am with a discussion on Saturday's performance with my staff. Our normal chats last about an hour and the content is varied, i.e. training session to be prepared, form of individual players, and analysis of future opposition.

At 10.30 am we trained for over two hours with the senior players which involved the correction of problems from the Sunderland match together with certain physical and technical practises. After lunch my staff and I patterned out our training schedules for the week with obvious emphasis on Luton Town.

I returned home at 4.00 pm and then left again to attend a youth cup final against Brighton at Upton Park. With the preparation for the game done by our youth manager Tony Carr, I had the opportunity to talk to scouts and parents prior to the game which is an important factor as the youth development section of the club is the future. Having drawn the match we felt it necessary to discuss the team's performance and we spoke to the young players for 45 minutes after the match with reference to their strengths and weaknesses. I returned home at 11.00 pm.

Tuesday is a day off for the players and I am spending the morning at the ground dealing with my correspondence and various other admin problems. Fortunately, I have a highly efficient aide in Mrs Moss who takes much of the time consuming work for me.

This afternoon I will return to the training ground for a Reserve game and then come back to Upton Park for a Board Meeting which will finish around 8.30 pm. Tomorrow we will be training with the senior players and in the afternoon, as per usual, my staff and I will work with the youth players on their individual techniques. In the evening I intend to watch the Luton game in preparation for our own game with them on Saturday.

Thursday brings a trip to Holland to watch a couple of players who have been recommended to us by our contacts on the Continent. These trips are always worthwhile, not only to watch individuals but to observe and note the tactics and new innovations of continental football.

My chief representative, Eddie Bailey, always accompanies me on these visits as he logs our comments and opinions and can offer much useful information when we make our comparisons with a similar British player.

We will return on the first flight on Friday morning and travel directly to the training ground for our final preparations for Saturday's game with Luton. The morning will involve training and a team meeting with discussion and debate, and of course the selection of all our teams for Saturday's fixtures. In the afternoon I will return to Upton Park and make an effort to be home at 5.00 pm. I usually try to spend the evening relaxing at home as I always feel the night prior to a game should be used to charge the batteries. On Saturday morning I usually relax and try to be at Upton Park around midday. This gives me time to deal with any emergencies and also to make further tests on any injured players with our physio Rob Jenkins. And so to the game, a win we hope. Following the match I meet the press and usually find myself leaving the ground around 7.30 pm in the evening.

As you will be aware the week is fairly busy but if you read the detail you will see the great variety and stimulation involved in my weekly routine. As I stated earlier this is typical of the involvement of football people and I am certain very few would alter their lifestyle for the conventional 9 to 5. Finally, on behalf of all at the club thanks not only for your support but for your efforts in maintaining and producing the facts

which help write the history of West Ham.
Best wishes, John Lyall
October 1987

'Fairly busy' is a huge understatement – in this typical week Lyall is rarely at home. The letter provides a wonderful insight into the life of a top manager and highlights Lyall's total commitment to his job. And, as Northcutt says, he was always unfailingly polite and generous with his time:

'To spend the time writing the article in a busy week was a lovely gesture and was much appreciated by our readership. He kindly invited me to meet him at Chadwell Heath and I spent a pleasant time listening to his many stories. He made me feel important. I left the meeting thinking... how lucky we were to have him as our manager at West Ham.'

Steve Marsh, of Hammers' memorabilia site, theyflysohigh, first met Lyall when he arrived early for an evening home match. Marsh strolled across the car park to wish the newly appointed West Ham manager good luck. The pair chatted for a few minutes before Lyall gave Marsh his autograph, the first of an exhaustive collection of West Ham players' autographs compiled by Steve since the day he met John Lyall. He has never forgotten the occasion.

Hammers' fans clearly adored Lyall and were quick to applaud his achievements. They would have appreciated Lyall's own reflections on his time at Upton Park:

You cannot devote 34 years to a club and not still retain some affection. For me the bubbles will never fade and completely die.'

Lyall's abrupt dismissal was a hammer blow to the players and fans. His name has never died at Upton Park on the contrary it has reached almost mythical proportions since the day he left the club.

Time to move on
In the end, John Lyall was no longer the manager of West Ham United. At the age of 48, he could look back on his 34 years at Upton Park with genuine pride in a job well done. It was now time to wash the Hammers' claret and blue from beneath his fingernails

and look forward to his next project – perhaps building a new extension to the house or, who knows? Perhaps, even managing a new football club.

Chapter 13
Time for reflection

After the traumatic events of June, 1989, Lyall took a welcome five month break. He spent time with his family, enjoyed a little fishing and caught up with work on the house and garden. John was an accomplished handyman and loved nothing more than making and fixing things. Some of the skills he brought to management – close attention to detail, persistence and the desire to get things just right, served him well in doing jobs around the house. Lyall enjoyed the break, but even if he never showed it, must have been wounded by the way he was treated by his old club. However, despite the disappointment and some loss of pride, he managed to retain a sense of perspective.

When he was appointed as manager at Upton Park in succession to Ron Greenwood, we know Lyall promised his wife that he would retire at the earliest opportunity – no lifelong Sir Alex-type devotion for John Lyall. He knew full well that he owed Yvonne a long retirement. Although professional football had given the family a comfortable and interesting life, it was never far from John's mind that Yvonne often had to endure long periods alone at home. As we see from Lyall's letter to John Northcutt, time pressures on football managers are immense. The after-match media circus, players needing a consoling word, foreign travel, all ensure consciousness people like Lyall are kept away from their families for long periods. Yvonne never went to matches. "I wouldn't go with him if he worked in a bank," she always said. Fortunately, the Lyall marriage was an unusually strong one and able to withstand the pressures of modern professional football. John wrote about this reassuring element of his life in his autobiography:

'We have always been a close family, and we enjoyed our time together. Yvonne, Murray and I decided to make the best use of each day.'

But Lyall knew the summer of 1989 was just a break from the game, not his retirement:
'Yvonne and I know there will be a day when I go back into football. We both know I'll go back.'

Precious thinking time
Lyall was greatly respected in the game and was soon invited to join various committees and advisory groups. He was delighted to be asked to sit on the appeals tribunal of the Football League Executive Staffs Association and enjoyed working with Prof. Sir John Wood, Gordon Taylor and Brendan Batson. He had time to think about the game and what was happening internationally – English clubs were still banned from all European competitions at this time. Like Trevor Brooking, Lyall believed the ban set English football back a generation, as the national side retreated into a negative insularity from which it has never fully recovered. Lyall was an internationalist by instinct and welcomed the introduction of foreign players into English club football. He understood Ossie Ardiles, Ricardo Villa, Arnold Muhren and Frank Thijsenn brought something new and fresh into the 1st Division and his views on the development of the domestic game resonate down the years:

'We must do more to learn about changing style and patterns of play in the rest of the world... England's three successive defeats in the 1988 European Championships in West Germany were a warning shot.'

However, Lyall's support for foreign players was balanced by his concern that two or three rich clubs would come to dominate the English game, to the detriment of the rest. He could not have imagined in 1989, with the Premier League still three years away, to what extent his fears would be realised. This thoroughly decent man would have found the mountainous levels of debt in the Premier League deeply disturbing, and the salaries of Premier

League players beyond belief.

If Lyall lived by what some may consider old-fashioned values, in many respects he was ahead of his time. Mick McGiven, Eddie Bailey and Ronnie Boyce attended physiology and sports science courses at Roehampton and understood the need for testing players' balance and reaction, blood pressure, aerobic level, stamina and strength. Lyall logged all this information on detailed player profiles. The West Ham way was not just a style of football, but a systematic approach to training, coaching and players' welfare. As McGiven says, "The West Ham way was a whole philosophy of football."

Lyall added a sports physiologist to his staff, years before such appointments became routine. The injury list at Upton Park was worryingly high and the rate of recovery of those under treatment was a serious concern. Lyall appointed the American, Angela Cannell to look at what he perceived as the changing pace of the game:

'The speed of football has outgrown most other facets in the evolution of the game and as a direct consequence of this players are increasingly susceptible to stress injuries, particularly in the pelvic region.'

Cannell advised on the balance of the club's training. She examined the players' running styles and stressed the importance of stretching after intensive work-outs in order to increase flexibility. The growing injury list began to dwindle. In appointing Cannell, Lyall was way ahead of his time. Alas, he was not at the club long enough to enjoy the results of his innovative thinking. But one thing was certain – Lyall was going to be an extremely hard act to follow.

At the time of his departure from West Ham, Brooking believes Lyall became disillusioned with the English game, partly as a result of the EUFA ban. He witnessed the game turn inward ignoring the exciting developments in Europe and South America. For example, as part of the trend towards long ball tactics, goalkeepers began to kick the ball downfield rather than trust their defenders to bring the ball out, as Bobby Moore always loved to do. When defenders had possession they moved the ball back or square, rather than playing it forward quickly to creative midfield players like Brooking and Devonshire, who worked tirelessly to find the right angles. Route one football encouraged idle thinking as defenders were urged to belt the ball upfield, relying on big forwards to win the resultant rebounds, or what the coaches called second ball. It was a pressing, percentage game which Lyall would have found abhorrent. There was no room in this direct approach for subtle angles, bewildering little triangles and exciting wing play which is the essence of the beautiful game.

Pat Holland, as a graduate of West Ham's famous academy, deplores the negative tactics that have become part of the DNA of English football. He said recently,

> '... coaches like Frank Clark and Charles Hughes encouraged the longball, percentage game. I hated all that win the second ball and get in their faces rubbish.'

Holland saw the FA-inspired approach as lazy and negative in contrast to the endless skills practice and ball work employed by more intelligent and thoughtful coaches. Clubs who employed these tactics narrowed their pitches, allowed the grass to grow and conveniently neglected to use the roller. All of this prevented sides like West Ham from playing their more subtle, passing game.

Brooking believed Lyall struggled to adapt to this negative revolution and his team's results suffered as a consequence. Lyall did attempt to balance the two essentially opposed styles, but hated compromising his purist instincts of playing through the three-thirds of the pitch. Speaking in his busy office in the FA's Wembley headquarters on the day Fabio Capello resigned his post as the England manager, Brooking agreed that the 1980s was a dark age for English football. It wasn't until the EUFA ban was lifted that football in England began to take a long, hard look at itself. Brooking's appointment as Director of Football at the FA was an admission that English football's obsession with percentage tactics was misguided and wrong. Current world champions Spain have demonstrated just how far England has fallen behind in international football. John Lyall would have cherished the wonderful passing game of Xavi, Messi and Iniesta. Spain's outrageously skilled and beguiling style vindicates every principle he stood for in the game of football. John Lyall's ideas on football have heavily influenced Brooking's aims to improve skill levels in the English game. Brooking believes the standard of the country's best 16-year-olds is simply not good enough. One of the contributory factors to this worrying state of affairs is the quality of coach education which, Brooking says, must improve. What the Director of Football refers to as ball mastery, brilliantly demonstrated by Xavi, Iniesta and their Spanish teammates, is not a priority for English coaches at youth level. The FA coach education programme aims to place skill acquisition firmly at the top of its list of priorities and redress the imbalance between skills and sheer physical effort. The current academy system is clearly not working for the national side. With foreign players making up around 60% of the Premier League, there is little incentive for clubs to commit to developing local young footballers. At the heart of Brooking's blueprint of a brighter future for English football are: age-appropriate coaching, small group matches where players are encouraged to develop their skills, a stress on the importance of movement and creating angles, work on ball mastery, and crucially, improve their decision-making. Another plank of the FA's policy for improving the skill levels of home-grown youngsters is to increase the number of English players in the Premier League to 65% within the next five to 10 years. This will help, and the performances of the England Under-17 team have been encouraging in this respect.

Brooking is also keen to change the culture of youth football within the professional clubs. The ex-West Ham legend laments the lack of desire in many of our young players and stressed the importance of character in achieving success at the top level. It is vital, he argues, that young players are prepared to make sacrifices in order to achieve their full potential. Repetitive practice makes perfect in most sports, particularly practice under pressure. Youngsters are quick to boast they have reached Level 10 on their

Play Station, the Director of Football laments, but less keen to spend the equivalent hours honing their skills on the practice ground. The basis of Brooking's criticism on the current state of English football is the principles he learned under Greenwood and Lyall on the training ground at Chadwell Heath. The architects of West Ham's success and reputation for exciting, attacking football, instilled in their players the importance of practice, good habits and desire to improve as professionals. Reflecting on the aftermath of Team GB's glorious showing in London 2012, Clive Woodward, the former England rugby coach and Olympics performance guru, argues that too many coaches are obsessed with coaching teams, rather than improving performance of what he refers to as podium players. The team coaching approach, claims Woodward, is easier and requires less effort. Both Lyall and Greenwood were brilliant at improving the performance of individual players, as many have testified. Trevor Brooking takes the same approach at the FA and is clearly passionate about his role and we can only wish him well – the future of English football is at stake.

Back to work
In 1990, after a few months of much-needed rest and reflection, Lyall and Dave Sexton were invited by Bobby Robson to cast an eye over the opposition and prepare team reports for the Italia '90 World Cup. This was a welcome gesture by Robson, but in Lyall and Sexton the England coach knew he had two of the best minds in European football on his team. Lyall would have enjoyed the environment of international football, away from the day-to-day pressures of running a club.

A more substantial offer for Lyall's services came from an old East London buddy. Late in the summer of 1989, the Tottenham manager, Terry Venables asked his old friend to join his coaching team at White Hart Lane. Lyall quickly agreed and spent 18 happy months with Venables, coaching, writing team reports and generally helping out at the club. Venables couldn't believe Lyall was out of the game following his dismissal by West Ham and said, very generously:

'I always wanted to work with people who were better than me. It

enhanced my think tank – and there was nobody better than John. He was a special bloke.'

The Tottenham manager had been an Under-21 team coach under Ron Greenwood and was aware that both Greenwood and Lyall were hugely respected in the game. Venables was also familiar with the way things worked at West Ham. As a teenager in the late '50s, he worked under Malcolm Allison and Noel Cantwell at Upton Park knew what West Ham was all about. Sadly, the Dagenham boy chose Chelsea over his local club. With such similar backgrounds, Venables and Lyall appeared a perfect match.

Venables was a brilliant tactician, as his record shows. He confirmed his early promise by achieving a distinction in the FA Full coaching badge, gaining an impressive 96 out of 100 in the examination. Like Lyall, Venables was a great thinker about the game. His greatest influence was Johann Cruyff's total football Dutch team of the 1980s, with their creativity, mastery on the ball and speed of movement. Venables was a good judge of character and as he said:

"John understood the game and his knowledge was second to none.

He was also an excellent man manager and a joy to work with."

On his return to English football after three successful seasons at Barcelona, Venables had put together an exciting group of players at White Hart Lane who, despite their undoubted talent, were proving difficult to manage. Paul Gascoigne, Paul Allen, Mitchell Thomas and Gary Lineker were all part of the side that won the FA Cup in 1991. Pat Holland, who joined Spurs as youth and reserve team coach in 1988, described this group of players, perhaps euphemistically as, 'an interesting bunch.' Venables was a shrewd operator and knew that Lyall was a good communicator and no pushover. If anyone could get the best out of a difficult group of players it was the ex-West Ham manager. Venables introduced a zonal defence at Spurs, deployed creative players like Gascoigne and Allen in midfield, and two wingers who could track back and support the midfield. With his knowledge of this system and his ability to get to get the best out of individual players, Lyall was the ideal person to help Venables mould this team of disparate individuals into an efficient unit.

There is no question that his time at Tottenham helped Lyall overcome the trauma of leaving West Ham. Murray Lyall remembers Venables being 'very good to my dad at this time.' Fortunately, Lyall was able to return the favour when he helped the ex-Tottenham man to plan England's tactics in the wonderful 4-1 demolition of Holland at Wembley in 1996. Lyall enjoyed his time working with Venables and left feeling refreshed and ready for a new challenge. It came from a surprising source.

Chapter 14
A new challenge up the A12

In May 1990, completely out of the blue, the Ipswich chairman, Patrick Cobbold, called John at home and asked if he would be interested in applying for the manager's job at Portman Road. Naturally, there would have to be an interview and things needed to be done in the correct way. The interview took place in the Cobbold ancestral home, Glemham Hall, in the delightful Suffolk countryside just north of Ipswich. After laying out his terms to the interview panel, Lyall took a stroll round Glemham's spacious grounds where he enjoyed his customary cigarette. The Ipswich board didn't need much time to deliberate. They took to John straight away, accepted his terms and offered him the job.

He discussed the offer at length with Yvonne, who knew if her husband accepted, it would probably mean selling the Old Rectory at Ongar where the Lyalls lived close to friends and family. Ipswich Town had been in the same family for generations and John enjoyed a great rapport with the Cobbolds from his West Ham days. They did things the right way and were highly respected Suffolk people. With its perfect playing surface and family feel, Portman Road was the ideal new job for John Lyall. After the turmoil at Upton Park, he was happy to begin a new challenge in the peaceful environment of East Anglia. Lyall accepted the Ipswich offer and became the new manager of Ipswich Town FC.

The Town, as Ipswich is known locally, is a football club with a distinguished history. Lyall was proud to join an illustrious list of managers which included two of the greatest names in world football; Sir Alf Ramsey and Sir Bobby Robson. The old West Ham boss was fully aware of the club's tradition and relished the prospect of following in the footsteps of such celebrated football luminaries.

Ipswich FC was launched at the end of the 19th century by a group of determined people attached to Ipswich School and the club's gentle origins provide a stark contrast to the harsh industrial beginnings of West Ham United. Despite its semi-rural setting, the fans are as passionate as any. The Ipswich supporters love their club, but perhaps Portman Road lacks the fanatical intensity of the emotional cauldron that is Upton Park. This would have suited Lyall at this time in his career, although as he was to discover to his cost, some Ipswich fans could be as damning in their criticism as the most die-hard members of the North Bank at the Boleyn Ground.

New broom
John Lyall arrived at Ipswich with nothing to prove. He had enjoyed a long and successful career at West Ham and had the respect of the best managers in the country, including Robson, Clough and Ferguson. The new Ipswich manager pitched into his job with characteristic enthusiasm. The months he spent with Terry Venables at Tottenham gave him time to adjust and he was eager for the challenge awaiting him at Portman Road. Lyall arrived at Ipswich and set about the task of rebuilding the club, following the dismissal of John Duncan. An exciting new chapter in the history of the Town was about to begin.

Lyall decided to reshuffle the staff team, eventually bringing in Mick McGiven from West Ham as his first team coach. As McGiven recalled recently:

'There was no decision for me to take. I would have gone anywhere with John. I knew I would enjoy every day at Ipswich.'

Peter Trevivian went back to running the youth team, while Lyall appointed Charlie Woods as his assistant manager. The highly experienced Woods was a key figure at Portman Road. He was the first team coach under John Duncan and won the FA Youth Cup for Ipswich on two occasions during his time in charge of the club's juniors. The new manager trusted Woods and remarked later, "Charlie Woods was one of the nicest people in football."

During Lyall's first week at Ipswich he took Woods to one side and said to him, "What do you think about Eddie Bailey coming here Charlie?"

The somewhat puzzled Woods replied, "Look John, you're the boss – you decide." Of course, it was part of Lyall's inclusive leadership philosophy to seek advice from his staff and Woods appreciated being consulted.

With Woods settled in his new role, the new boss completed his staff reshuffle with the arrival of McGiven. Their first priority was to stabilise things at Portman Road, both on and off the field. Lyall had control of most aspects of business at Upton Park – he knew how much money each turnstile took on match days, the detail of the catering contracts and made decisions on players' wages and length of contracts. There was nothing about the club he didn't know. This was not how Ipswich Town was run and the new manager had to learn quickly that the team, rather than the club, was his sole priority. The manager at Portman Road was a much less powerful figure than Lyall was at West Ham. It could not have been easy adjustment for him to make.

A day out at Portman Road

I stepped out of Ipswich Railway Station on a beautiful July morning. Inside the station hundreds of Suffolk folk were bustling about, thrilled to be heading down to Stratford for the 2012 Olympic Games. The place was buzzing – full of excited anticipation. Leaving the station behind I headed towards the town centre, I was immediately confronted by the splendid Portman Road stadium, home of Ipswich Town FC. Freshly painted and looking its best, the ground was a hive of activity in preparation for the new season. I was there to meet Pat Godbold, former personal assistant to a succession of Ipswich managers, including Ramsey and Robson.

Now retired, Pat has been part of the Suffolk club for over 50 years. She still attends home matches and keeps busy organising the club's extensive archive. Pat was secretary to Lyall at Portman Road in the early 1990s and remains a close friend of John's wife, Yvonne. Pat had arranged a full schedule which included interviews with some of John's old colleagues and former players, including Charlie Woods and long-serving stalwart of the Tractor Boys, Simon Milton, both key figures in Lyall's promotion team of 1992. It promised to be an exciting day.

As you approach the stadium you pass statues of Sir Alf and Sir Bobby and quickly get the sense that this club is a bit special. The feeling is confirmed by the friendliness of the staff and their willingness to help. Over coffee, I asked Pat if she could recall her impression of John Lyall. She explained that her first contact with John was in 1986, the year Ipswich were relegated from the old 1st Division under manager, Bobby Ferguson.

In their must-win, penultimate game of that season the Tractor Boys lost 2-1 at Upton Park to Lyall's great West Ham Boys of '86 team. After the final whistle, the Ipswich skipper, Terry Butcher, normally the mildest of men, stormed down the players' tunnel and in his frustration, kicked a hole in the door of the home team's dressing room. On the way back to Suffolk, Butcher began to regret his violent outburst. The next day he asked Pat if she would call the West Ham manager and apologise on his behalf. Butcher was at London airport with the England squad and about to fly off to play in an international match. Lyall willingly accepted Butcher's apology. Pat found her boss-to-be extremely polite and understanding, agreeing that the incident was out of character for the Ipswich and England captain. The matter need go no further. The next time Pat spoke to Lyall was four years later when he was introduced to her as the club's new manager.

Later that day I met Simon Milton. We sat together in the Director's Box at Portman Road watching the ground staff prepare for the first match of the new season. Milton was born in Fulham in 1963, but moved to East Anglia as a teenager. He played non-League football with Thetford and Bury Town before being offered a professional contract at Ipswich by Bobby Ferguson. The midfielder made his debut in December 1987 and in his 11 years at the club went on to make over 300 appearances for the Tractor Boys. The highlights of a distinguished career were promotion to the Premier League in 1992, three seasons in the top flight of English football and winning Ipswich Player of the Year in 1996.

When Lyall was appointed new Ipswich manager in the summer of 1990, Milton was 26-years-old. He looked back on Lyall's arrival at the club:

'We had a core of players in their mid-20s who were good professionals and desperate to improve and be part of a successful team. The club took off when John arrived.'

Long-serving Milton, now commercial manager of Ipswich's successful youth academy, warmed to his theme:

'The training was different. We trained flat out and were an enthusiastic group, receptive to new ideas – it was a perfect marriage. He improved every player at the club. He also had a presence about him – he commanded respect from day one.'

Milton, who had his testimonial against West Ham in 1989/90, was clearly impressed with his new manager:

'He was very honest and his door was always open. He was the best manager I played under and it was my best time as a player.'

The ex-midfield player gave an example of Lyall's insight and thinking about the game:

'When I played on the right or left of midfield I always came off the pitch feeling frustrated that I hadn't been fully in the game. I much preferred to play central midfield where I was in the game for the whole 90 minutes. One day I went to see John and told him how I felt.'

Lyall's response was characteristically persuasive:

'OK Milts – let's look at your last 40 games. You played 10 games on the right and scored six goals, 15 on the left and scored seven goals. That leaves 15 games in central midfield where you never scored once. Now do you understand why you will be playing out wide for me this season?'

Milton left the meeting feeling much better about his game and his value as a player. The midfielder went on to score important goals in Ipswich's 1992 promotion year and in the club's three-year spell in the new Premier League. Lyall helped Milton in other ways, as the midfielder remembers:

'In the early '90s we were a mixture of senior professionals and young lads making their way. John understood this and gave older players like myself, responsibility for looking after the youngsters. By doing this he brought the team together.'

Milton has a memory of Lyall which, he believes, sums up the kind of manager he was. It's also an example of Lyall's close attention to detail:

'I came in one day during the summer break and there was John and the rest of the coaching staff, down on their hands and knees painting the skirting boards in the players' tunnel. What other top manager would do that? This was John Lyall.'

When Simon left to return to his work at the Youth Academy, I spent a pleasant hour in the company of the delightful Charlie Woods. The former midfield player enjoyed spells at Newcastle United and Crystal Palace, before joining Ipswich Town. Cumbrian-born Charlie, now 71-years-old, has a long association with the Suffolk club both as a player and coach. When Lyall was appointed manager in 1990 he quickly realised he needed someone with local knowledge on his team. Lyall promoted Woods to Assistant Manager. It proved an inspired choice:

'John changed everything. He gave everyone responsibility, including the senior players. The players responded to the new training. In many ways he was like Bobby Robson as a manager – we all had the greatest respect for John.'

Charlie Woods retired a few years ago, but remains active. Like Pat Godbold, he is still a regular at Portman Road and plays golf to an impressive 5 handicap.

Woods was a great ally to Lyall in Ipswich's promotion drive in 1991/92. The pair worked closely together, scouting, weighing up opponents and having endless discussions about players and tactics.

I left Portman Road that day with a new enthusiasm for my subject and a deeper understanding of John Lyall, both as a manager and a person. I had met some wonderful people and was privileged to be at the centre of a proper football club – even if it only was for one day.

Laying the groundwork

Like any good manager starting out with a new club, Lyall was keen to assess the players he had inherited, rather than plunge straight into the transfer market. However, there was some transfer activity that summer. John Wark left the club for the second time, on this occasion to Middlesborough for £500,000. Wark was unable to agree terms with the new manager, showing once again, how tough Lyall could be negotiating players' contracts. He never lost the value for money instincts his Scottish parents taught him as a youngster. Most managers take players with them from their previous club, and Lyall was no different in this respect. His first signing was Phil Parkes, the veteran Hammers' goalkeeper. Parkes was close to his 41st birthday when he signed for Ipswich, and played the last three games of the 90/91 season before he finally retired.

Lyall also attempted to lure the Hammers' full-back Ray Stewart to join him at Portman Road, but the veteran full-back turned down the move. Stewart had suffered career-threatening injuries the previous season and knew in his heart he would never be the same player again. There was no question that Stewart appreciated the gesture, but didn't want to let down his old manager and friend. Lyall did make two signings in his first season which helped to transform the club's fortunes over the next two years.

In January 1991 Lyall paid Sheffield Wednesday £150,000 for Steve Whitton, who he signed for West Ham in 1983. Plaistow-born

Whitton played three seasons for the Hammers in the mid-'80s, making 46 appearances in which he scored just eight goals. He usually played wide on the right and possessed great power, pace and no little skill. Lyall knew just what to expect from his new signing. Whitton more than repaid Lyall's trust in him, making a 130 League appearances for Ipswich, scoring an important 23 goals. The winger was a key part of Lyall's 2nd Division championship side of 1991/92.

For his second major signing Lyall brought in another ex-Hammer, Paul Goddard, who was without a club having been released from his contract at Millwall. Goddard had been a sensation at Upton Park in the mid-'80s. His goal-scoring partnership with David Cross almost carried the Hammers to the 1st Division championship in 1986. Lyall later sold Goddard to Newcastle for £415,000 to make way for the emerging young striker, Tony Cottee. Diminutive in stature, Goddard possessed real strength and surprised many a top centre-half with his pace and power and more than repaid his old manager's faith in him. The England international settled into Lyall's new team quickly and formed a lively and effective striking partnership with both Chris Kiwomya and Jason Dozzell.

In Kiwomya and Dozzell, Lyall had inherited two strikers with enormous potential. Kiwomya was the club's top scorer in the promotion season and was a key figure in Town's Premier League adventure. The Huddersfield-born youngster signed for Ipswich in 1987 and made 230 appearances for the Tractor Boys, scoring a total of 64 goals. I was fortunate to speak to Kiwomya as part of the research for this book. He spoke about his time with Lyall at Ipswich with great fondness and affection When Lyall arrived at Portman Road in 1990 Kiwomya was in his third year with the Suffolk club and keen to return to his northern roots. He asked for an early meeting with his new boss to explain his feelings. Lyall listened to his young striker patiently before replying: "Why would you want to go to Barnsley or Doncaster or somewhere? You are only half a player at the moment. If you stay here we can turn you into a top striker, but you will need to listen and work hard."

Kiwomya explained: "Mr Lyall won me over – I loved his mixture of humour and seriousness. I could see he cared about his players and wanted us to improve as professionals. I trusted him from the start and decided to stay."

As part of his education, Lyall sent young Chris to watch Liverpool and Manchester United. "Watch their forwards Chris – look closely at their game. You will learn so much."

Kiwomya responded to this kind of responsibility and became a better player: "John was always demanding, always pushing for more." He remembers one occasion, following a match against Middlesborough when his manager took him to one side and said:

"Grab a coffee and come and sit down for ten minutes." Two hours later, after taking Kiwomya's game apart piece by piece, Lyall told him to go and join his teammates.

"He killed me that day," said the striker, "but I learned so much from these meetings and appreciated the time he gave me."

Kiwomya's remarks are a wonderful illustration of Lyall's encouraging man-management style: "I was always in his office, discussing games and my own performances. He had time for us and really cared. Sometimes he made me feel I was the best player in the world."

If he was by instinct a compassionate individual, Lyall had his tough side, as Kiwomya confirms: "We played Leeds away one Saturday in our first season in the Premier League. After the game the boss said to me, 'go home for the weekend, take Monday off and come back for training on Tuesday.' I really appreciated the gesture. When I got back the following week for training, he made me work twice as hard as usual – he was making a point – you never messed with John Lyall."

Kiwomya also admitted he over-stepped the mark a few times as a youngster, but Lyall dealt with him firmly and fairly and the youngster soon learned his lesson. The time and care Lyall invested in young players like Chris Kiwomya was to pay huge dividends for Ipswich over the next few seasons as the squad gained in confidence and strength under his perceptive and inspirational leadership. Chris Kiwomya's improvement under Lyall was rewarded with selection for the national side at Under-21 level, and eventually a £1.2 million dream move to Arsenal.

Management on a shoe-string

When Lyall was appointed to his new job, the Ipswich chairman, Patrick Cobbold, explained that there was no money available to spend on big name players. Lyall accepted this and put together a team of tried and trusted professionals who could get his new club into the Premier League.

Lyall's new team started their first season in disastrous fashion. In the opening game at Portman Road the new manager received a tremendous ovation, and expectation among the Ipswich faithful was sky high. Unfortunately, the players hadn't read the script and the Tractor Boys were well beaten by Sheffield Wednesday. The new manager bounce had failed to materialise and things got worse when Lyall's men lost their second game, away to Swindon Town. However, the side rallied and by Christmas were settled in mid-table, a position they occupied for the rest of the season.

Ipswich eventually finished in 14th place in 1990/91, a full 30 points behind runners-up, West Ham United. The new signings took time to settle in and the team looked disjointed and lacking in confidence. But Lyall knew his first year was going to be the most difficult. At the end of that season Chris Kiwomya told his manager, "Don't worry – we'll finish higher next season John."

To which Lyall replied with characteristic resolve, "Next season Chris, we'll be promoted."

John Wark returns to Portman Road

For his second season Lyall made further adjustments to his squad. John Wark returned to Ipswich after failing to settle at Ayresome Park. Against the wishes of his manager, Lennie Lawrence, the Scottish international refused to move to Teeside and continued to live in the Ipswich area. Wark's reluctance to move led Middlesborough to release the ex-Liverpool star from his contract. Without a club, he asked Charlie Woods if he could keep himself in shape by joining the training at Portman Road. Woods readily agreed and before long, as a result of a series of injuries, Wark found himself filling in for the reserves and eventually gaining a first team place.

Lyall and Woods knew the value of Wark's experience and positive attitude. The Scot was a key member of the Liverpool side that triumphed in the 1978 FA Cup and the UEFA Cup three years later. Wark's career reached its peak in 1981 when he won the coveted Footballer of the Year award. With 29 senior Scottish caps and an outstanding goal-scoring record, he proved a valuable addition to the Ipswich squad. Wisely, Lyall chose to deploy Wark in central defence where he was outstanding alongside David Linighan. The revitalised Wark repaid his manager's faith when he won the Ipswich fans coveted Player of the Season award. Despite suffering a few years with injury, at the age of 33 the veteran remained a very useful player. His fragile condition meant that he rarely trained, as Wark admitted:

'John knew how to treat me. I didn't train a lot – mainly came in for 5-a-side Friday. But he knew I was coming to the end of my career and he trusted me.'

With the defensive rock of Wark and Linighan at the heart of his side, Lyall was confident the Tractor Boys could challenge for promotion in his second season.

The club's supporters were anxious to return to the top flight and would have been disappointed with their team's performances in the previous campaign. But the majority of the die-hard fans trusted the new regime and remained patient, although they expected significant improvement. However, the more fickle supporters were less patient. Seasons ticket sales were well down in the summer of 1991 – a major concern for any club. A depressingly low crowd of just 8,937 turned out for the first home match against Port Vale, the lowest attendance for any opening home game in the club's history. The Ipswich faithful need not have worried as their team came charging out of the traps winning three of their first four games, which included a 2-1 victory in the match against Port

Vale. Slowly, the team won over the Ipswich faithful and the Portman Road attendances began to soar, reaching over 20,000 on four occasions during the 1991/92 season. As Mel Henderson and Paul Voller wrote in The Essential History of Ipswich Town:

John Lyall began to exert his influence and his coaching prowess was never in doubt as he masterminded a remarkable turnaround.'

They recognised that the new Ipswich manager,

'...was far from the spent force West Ham suggested he was when they dismissed him three years earlier.'

Lyall inherited a decent, if dispirited group of players languishing in the lower reaches of the 2nd Division. Led by skipper Linighan, the defence including goalkeeper, Craig Forrest, Wark, local legend Mick Stockwell and left-back, Neil Thompson who dealt comfortably with most 2nd Division attacks. Milton, Romeo Zondervan and Suffolk boy, Gavin Johnson provided skill and industry in midfield, and in Milton's case important goals. Chris Kiwomya proved a revelation up front with Whitton and Dozzell, the trio scoring 55 League and cup goals between them in Lyall's second season. Paul Goddard was restricted to a total of 21 appearances, but his presence would have inspired the other strikers and lifted the squad with his undoubted class and experience. Lyall knew that his primary task was to lift the spirits of the other players and get them to believe in themselves.

By Christmas '91 the manager knew his team were capable of making a run for promotion. A series of draws through October and November threatened to derail all Lyall's good work, before an impressive run of six successive wins in December, January and February steadied the ship. It was a Happy Christmas for Ipswich's fans when two goals from Chris Kiwomya sealed a good home win against Charlton on Boxing Day. The following Saturday over 17,000 crammed into Portman Road to see their new heroes beat Blackburn Rovers 2-1 with goals from Johnson and Dozzell. The first two months of 1992 were a wonderful time to be an Ipswich

Town supporter. Goals from Milton, Kiwomya, Dozzell and Whitton gave the Tractor Boys FA Cup wins over Hartlepool and Bournemouth and a bumper home 5th Round tie against Liverpool.

Over 26,000 crammed into Portman Road to see their heroes held to a 0-0 draw by the mighty Reds. On the Saturday prior to the replay Town travelled up to Merseyside for a League match against Tranmere Rovers. A sound display brought Lyall's men a 1-0 victory thanks to a stunning Milton strike, stretching their unbeaten league run to seven – six wins and a draw. A feature of the Tranmere match was John Wark's vice-like grip on the old Anfield favourite, John Aldridge. After the match the Ipswich manager was typically upbeat about the FA Cup replay the following Wednesday:

'Hopefully, Merseyside will be lucky for us. We can draw great strength from this win. We know it will be difficult in the cup replay, but a good away win behind you is a marvellous boost, particularly one in the same area.'

In a titanic battle at Anfield, Jason Dozzell raised the spirits of the away supporters when he scored in the first period of extra-time to put his side 2-1 ahead. But Liverpool struck back twice to send the Reds through to the quarter-final. That evening millions of TV viewers saw Ipswich Town give the mighty Merseysiders the shock of their lives. The matches against Liverpool gave the players a tremendous confidence boost and they returned to their promotion bid with renewed self-belief.

Lyall's trust in his players and his own ability was winning through as Town began to take the 2nd Division by storm. The pre-season sceptics were converted as Portman Road turned into a cauldron of hope and expectation. Their FA Cup heroics and the side's impressive League form earned Lyall the Barclays 2nd Division Manager of the Month for February. He was the first Ipswich manager to be honoured in this way since Bobby Robson won the 1st Division Bells award, just before going off to manage England. Lyall accepted the award with characteristic modesty. He said:

'Great credit must go to the players who have responded so well to my talking – sometimes moaning. Charlie Woods has done a marvellous job and so have Mick McGiven, Bryan Klug and Peter Trevivian.'

Lyall continued:

'These coaches are not just solely involved with their individual teams but also muck in and help out at all levels.'

John Kerr, the new Ipswich chairman paid this tribute to his manager:

'Our manager has worked very hard and I am delighted he has won the award. It is richly deserved.'

But Lyall was not much interested in winning personal awards. We know that he shunned the traditional manager's office for a boot room style space where all the coaches worked together as a team. This encouraged camaraderie, staff morale and fostered the belief that 'we are all in this together.'

It may be a cliché, but the Anfield FA Cup defeat meant that Lyall could concentrate fully on his aim of winning the 2nd Division championship, without the distraction of a cup run. Following a shock 2-1 home defeat at the hands of Watford on the 17 March, Town won five games in succession – a run which included notable home wins over promotion rivals, Derby County, Wolves and Newcastle. Goals from Whitton, Wark and Kiwomya ensured the 3-2 victory over Newcastle. On that day, 20,000 excited fans packed into Portman Road – a sure indication that the locals were, at last, getting fully behind their team. The sense of excitement in the town reached new levels as Blues faced the crucial, last few games of the season.

Promotion to the Premier League

The impressive run of victories in March and early April provided Town with a 10 point cushion at the top of the 2nd Division. However, like a batsman in the '90s, Lyall's men faced the last few games of the season in a state of nervous anticipation. The fans

271

could only look on in disbelief as the lead dwindled to just four points. But with three games to go, the championship remained in their own hands, despite consecutive defeats at the hands of Sunderland and Bristol City. Grimsby Town arrived on 21 April with the Tractor Boys needing a win to clinch promotion. A bumper crowd of 22,393 squeezed into Portman Road ready to get the promotion party started. But a stuttering, oddly subdued performance by the home side led to a frustrating 0-0 draw.

With just two games to go Town remained promotion favourites. But the nerves were jangling as staff, players and fans travelled the short distance to Oxford for the penultimate game of the season. Lyall needed all his vast experience to calm the players and prepare them for the match that would determine their destiny. When veteran Jim Magilton scored for Oxford, the travelling supporters could hardly believe their eyes. But they needn't have worried. Within two minutes Suffolk lad, Gavin Johnson equalised and Town held out for a creditable 1-1 draw, earning the single point that gave Lyall's team the promotion they had worked so hard to achieve. The Tractor Boys were back in the big time.

The local Evening Star, often grudging in its appreciation of London boy Lyall's work, was unusually generous in its praise:

'A season that started with a boycott from fans at the season ticket office and rank outside odds of 25-1 for the title has ended in great glory for a team coached into a quality outfit by manager, John Lyall and his staff.'

The championship trophy was presented after the final game of the season – a 3-1 home win against Brighton. Goals from Whitton and Johnson sent the Town supporters into dreamland. The Tractor Boys had won the 2nd Division title with a total of 84 points, four ahead of runners-up, Middlesborough. The players paraded the trophy through the town the following day, in the customary open-top bus. John Lyall must have experienced a huge sense of relief and satisfaction. Hopes were understandably raised when he was appointed and his first season had ended in disappointment. Job done, the ex-West Ham man could now prepare his side for the newly-formed Premier League. As Henderson and Voller wrote:

'It was a fantastic achievement on modest resources.'

West Ham must have seemed a distant memory as Lyall enhanced his considerable reputation even further with his success at Ipswich. Despite a lack of money he had put together a strong side and an excellent back-up team. The players had tremendous respect for their boss and loved working with him. They accepted it when he told them, "Don't ever take my friendliness for a weakness – in any argument there will be only one winner." In many respects he was the perfect manager – great people skills, an inspirational coach full of new ideas, and friend and confidante to his players. Lyall had accepted a new and exciting challenge after 34 years at Upton Park. If he looked back over his shoulder, it never showed.

The Evening Star reporter wrote:

'Lyall has taken justifiable acclaim for his work, on and off the field. To his credit he remains the same chirpy Londoner (sic) as he was at the start. Success has not changed his manner one bit.'

Two days after their visit to Upton Park to play in Ray Stewart's testimonial match, the players flew out to sunny Portugal for a golfing holiday at the club's expense. The players enjoyed the opportunity to relax for a week or two after a successful, but very tough season. Preparation for life in the Premier League began would soon begin in earnest.

The promotion season saw genuine heroes emerge at Portman Road. Club captain David Linighan, of that wonderful football family, was a tower of strength at the heart of the Ipswich defence. Full-back, Neil Thompson was described by TV commentator, John Motson as 'the best left-back in the 2nd Division' and John Wark was an inspirational presence at the heart of the defence. Forwards Chris Kiwomya and Jason Dozzell were a constant goal threat and always played their hearts out. When required, Dozzell, acting skipper in place of the injured Linighan over the last few matches, was as effective in midfield as he was in his customary place at the point of the attack. Dozzell spoke with real pride and emotion of his side's achievement:

'This is the greatest day of my life. I am an Ipswich boy and to lead the side at this time is like a dream. I have never looked forward to a season more than the next one.'

Linighan, Thompson, Wark, Kiwonya and Dozzell are just a few of the stars of the promotion team, but the whole point of Lyall's leadership is that this was a combined effort involving everyone at the club. Lyall wanted to see Portman Road, 'full of fans enjoying their football.' By the end of the season he got his wish. On 27 April 1992, under the headline 'LYALL ACHIEVES AIM AS FANS FLOCK BACK', were the words,

'...Town's return to the top flight is due to brilliant coaching and man-management of someone whose biggest thrill in life is to get the very best out of players on the training ground. John Lyall put in countless hours training and coaching.'

It was a fitting tribute to this most modest and unassuming of public figures. At the end of that memorable season, in a typical act of generosity, Lyall bought each member of his staff a commemorative watch to thank them for their hard work and support. After the frustration of his first season at Portman Road, John Lyall was back where he belonged in the top flight of English football.

Chapter 15
The Premiership comes
to Portman Road

The English Premier League was formed in 1992 following the Taylor Report into the 1989 Hillsborough disaster. The FA Cup semi-final between Liverpool and Nottingham Forest was abandoned when it became clear that a tragedy of catastrophic proportions had occurred in the Leppings Lane end of the ground. Hundreds of fans spilled onto the pitch as the magnitude of the disaster became evident. A total of 96 people died that April afternoon. The Taylor Report found a 'failure of police control', too few turnstiles for a crowd of 30,000 or more and inadequate crowd barriers. By the end of the 1980s British football stadia had become dangerous places.

An independent report in 2012 revealed that police had altered witness statements and falsified key evidence in their attempt to blame Liverpool supporters for the Hillsborough tragedy.

The Taylor Report, published in 1990, recommended the abolition of all standing terraces, the introduction of all-seater stadia, improved stewarding and police control, and the removal of all fencing. New stadia were required to be all-seater and it became obligatory for clubs to improve existing grounds in line with Taylor's recommendations. The first new stadium to be built under the Taylor Report guidelines was Millwall's New Den and today there are dozens of new football stadia up and down the country. Most modern grounds have been transformed beyond recognition from the ancient structures of the industrial age.

Portman Road was no exception. In the summer of 1992 the old ground was transformed into an all-seater stadium as both main stands were converted to comply with Taylor. A few coats of blue and white paint and the ground looked fresh and ready to entertain the likes of Liverpool and Manchester United. Of course, everyone associated with Ipswich Town was thrilled to see their club in the Premier League in its inaugural season. Membership of the strongest League in Europe brought with it healthy revenue streams in the form of the BSkyB largesse, but it also brought increased responsibility.

If the ground was ready, the players and staff couldn't wait for the season to start. After two years in the job, the Ipswich manager knew his players well enough to know they would give their all in the Premiership. Just as he did when the Hammers were relegated at the end of the 1980s, Lyall kept faith with the squad that won promotion. But he would have asked himself the question. Can this team of decent professionals and local boys from non-League football survive in the Premier League? He would soon get his answer. But, in some respects he had little choice but to trust this group of players. It had been made clear to him from the start that there was little money available for new players – he was operating on a shoestring. He allowed Romeo Zondervan to return to Holland with his family and replaced the popular Dutchman with his sole pre-season signing, midfielder Geraint Williams who arrived from Derby County in return for a fee of £650,000.

There were a few minor team changes. Clive Baker replaced Craig Forrest in goal for the major part of the season, while former Town manager, Bobby Robson suggested Lyall take a look at two of his Sporting Lisbon players, Bontcho Guentchev and Vlado Bozinoski. Both were struggling to find a regular place in the Lisbon side. Of course, Lyall trusted Robson's judgement and brought both players to Suffolk. Of the two Guentchev was the more successful and became a big favourite of the Ipswich fans. With his squad settled, the manager could look forward once again to matching his tactical skill against the best in English football. With his vast experience, Lyall knew the extent of the challenge he faced in the new Premier League – the stakes had been raised significantly. His first task was to try to improve the performance of every player at the club.

Chris *Lino* Kiwomya understood this and spent hours talking to his manager about ways he could improve his game. Lyall repeatedly said to his young striker, "Why are you doing this? Have you thought about doing it this way?" It was Lyall who nicknamed the young striker, *Lino*, because for one reason or another he was always on the floor. He remembers Friday training sessions when his manager would work with him on improving his touch and basic speed:

> *"You need to work your movement Chris," Lyall told him. "We'll work on you moving late and developing an explosive start. If you can improve this part of your game and your touch, you'll become a real player. Practice these skills every day for ten days and they will stay in your physical memory. This is the Premier League now."*

The forward was well aware that his new manager had worked with some of the greatest names in football in Bobby Moore, Geoff Hurst, Martin Peters and Trevor Brooking – why wouldn't he listen? The rapport Lyall developed with Kiwomya is similar to the relationship he enjoyed with David Cross at West Ham. The Hammers' centre-forward improved dramatically under Lyall's tutelage to the extent that he came frustratingly close to gaining international recognition. Like Cross, Kiwomya was willing to learn and desperate to improve. Lyall loved this in a player – he knew his centre-forward was happy to stretch himself to the limits of his ability. With this sheer determination and Lyall's attentive support, Kiwomya soon gained full control of his game and became a key figure for Ipswich during their spell in the Premier League. The new Portman Road hero quickly agreed to sign a new contract because, as he said:

> *'To leave Ipswich would be interrupting the finest football education there is. Mr Lyall's door is always open and he's a great coach who has done so much for me.'*

Even a seasoned international player like John Wark, with all his European and World Cup experience, benefitted from Lyall's coaching methods:

'John's training sessions were a revelation. I was coming to the end of my career but I was still learning. He worked with us on making quarter and half-turns, which really helped the forwards. John was way ahead.'

Lifted by Lyall and his staff, the players were full of excitement and anticipation for the new season. As Simon Milton commented, "It was the best time of our careers – we were at the top of our game and busting for the season to begin." For the first time in the English top flight, the 1992/93 season began with games spread throughout the weekend and Monday evening. But Town began the most historic season in their history with a traditional Saturday 3.00 pm kick-off, at home to Aston Villa. In front of an expectant Portman Road crowd of nearly 17,000, a 1-1 draw was not disastrous and Lyall was pleased with his side's performance – the Tractor Boys were up and running in their new elite environment.

Slowly, the players gained in confidence and began to relish their newly won status. Four points from their first two games relaxed everybody at the club, as they prepared for their third match, high-flying Manchester United at Old Trafford. As Milton has pointed out, "For most of us Ipswich players, Premier League matches at Old Trafford against Manchester United were the highlights of our professional careers."

Lyall was aware what these games meant to the players and the club in general and prepared his squad accordingly. Milton, who was among the substitutes for the Old Trafford match, remembers Lyall as a great tactician, who although purist by instinct, was not averse to sending out a team to frustrate the opposition. As the midfielder explained, "John was a flexible coach who changed our tactics to fit the other team." A further example of his flexibility is offered by Charlie Woods:

'John worked out a way to play which opposing defences couldn't handle. Neil Thompson, or someone else out on the left – would hit a long crossfield ball just inside our own half out to the right wing for Steve Whitton. Stevie would play the ball first time into the path of the on-running Kiwomya or Goddard, or take it to the byline himself –

despite his size, Whitton could also play. We scored a few goals using that move, but it wasn't classic West Ham.'

Lyall's Ipswich side needed every ounce of their manager's famed flexibility and tactical acumen as they entered one of the toughest environments in football – the Old Trafford theatre of dreams?

Old Trafford welcomes the Tractor Boys

The players and fans arrived at Old Trafford that summer Saturday in August eager to encounter the likes of Mark Hughes, Gary Pallister and 'the new George Best', 18-year-old Ryan Giggs. Lyall, who loved nothing more than to pit his wits against his great friend Alex Ferguson, picked an attacking side with three strikers in Goddard, Kiwomya and Dozzell. To the surprise of everyone at Old Trafford, the Tractor Boys were set up to try and win the game.

With Milton on the bench, the side looked short-handed in midfield. But every Ipswich player worked their blue and white socks off to frustrate United. The ever-willing Dozzell was deployed in midfield alongside Thompson and Williams and the trio worked extremely hard to close down the opposition, who were missing Paul Ince with a hip injury. Linighan, Wark, Stockwell and the young Whelan defended heroically, while up front Kiwomya and Goddard chased and harried Pallister and Bruce, who had an uncomfortable afternoon. Every player in a blue shirt had been given a specific marking job, which they executed to perfection. At the interval the sides were level at 0-0, with John Lyall by far the happier manager.

Ten minutes into the second half the 600 travelling supporters were in ecstasy. Thompson took a long throw-in down near the corner flag. Dozzell reached the ball first and flicked it over Pallister into the path of Kiwomya. The striker brought the ball down neatly with his chest and thumped it joyously past Schmeichel in the United's goal. It was a fairy tale moment for Kiwomya who had always dreamed of scoring at Old Trafford. Could the Tractor Boys hang on for an unlikely victory? They had their answer within a few minutes when Denis Irwin fired home an accurate Andrei Kanchelskis cross to equalise for the Red Devils. But the boys in blue refused to be beaten, redoubled their efforts and achieved a highly creditable draw.

Once again Lyall had out-thought one of the best coaches in the game, as he did when his West Ham side beat Arsenal in the 1980 FA Cup Final. After the match Mick McGiven said:

'I was very, very pleased with a performance full of honesty and commitment. I told Kiwomya to move out to the left away from Bruce, but because I knew the United centre-half loved to carry the ball upfield which would leave room behind him for Chris to exploit with his pace. We had two great chances at the end and could have won it.'

John Wark, fresh from a heroic display in the centre of the Ipswich defence added with typical modesty:

'I was told to watch Brian McClair. I thought we coped quite well. We got the point we deserved.'

The United boss was generous in his post-match comments:

'At least Ipswich tried to play football which is more than the two previous teams we played.'

Manager Lyall was philosophical about the result and his remarks give us an insight into the way this most perceptive of coaches thought about his job. He told the Evening Star:

'We know that there is plenty of team spirit and no little talent, but improvisation is the key to success. If we can find that little bit of tactical play then we will use it instead of lining up 4-4-2 against what is in most cases another 4-4-2 each week.'

The use of regular full-back Neil Thompson in midfield, Wark in central defence and Dozzell operating from a midfield position against United, are all examples of what Lyall meant by improvisation. He encouraged his players to take up new positions and his team to adapt to new shapes and formations. Lyall was simply trying to do what he did at West Ham – get the players to think about their game and not be locked into systems. They responded magnificently that day at Old Trafford. But not everyone agreed. An Evening Star reporter said to McGiven after the game, "That was all a bit negative Mick." The Ipswich first team coach replied in his usual, forthright manner!

With the next two games against Liverpool and Tottenham, Ipswich was experiencing a baptism of Premier League fire. As Lyall said at the time, "This is the sort of week that the fans were dreaming about. Now it is a reality."

The Ipswich chairman enthused: "This is the most exciting week the club has experienced for over a decade."

Lyall's players didn't disappoint him. Draws in their next four matches after their Old Trafford heroics, were followed by a 2-1 home win against Wimbledon. Newly-promoted Ipswich had started their first Premiership season unbeaten in eight games, which included draws against Manchester United, Liverpool and Tottenham. Before the end of December, Town had won a total of eight matches including home victories against Leeds United, Everton, Manchester City and Blackburn Rovers. A precious away win at Nottingham Forest, thanks to a Jason Dozzell goal, gave Lyall every reason to feel optimistic about the rest of the season. The Tractor Boys had taken the Premier League by storm with 42 points from their first 21 matches.

The 2-0 win against Tottenham at Portman Road in January 1993 must go down as one of the most impressive results in the club's history. Goals from long-serving Frank Yallop and Bulgarian international, Bontcho Guentchev sealed a momentous victory. If that was not enough excitement for rural Suffolk, just three days later table-topping Manchester United arrived at Portman Road for the return League match. Victory would send Ipswich up to the giddy heights of 4th place in the Premier League. For Town supporters this placed Lyall's boys into the same category as Sir Alf Ramsey's legendary team of the early '60s. No praise could be higher. Fully aware that his opponents had taken a hard-earned point away from Old Trafford in the corresponding fixture in

August, Alex Ferguson chose a very strong side, which included Eric Cantona, Paul Ince, Mark Hughes and Ryan Giggs. Knowing there was little point in second guessing his friend and rival, Ferguson simply picked his best team.

Lyall set up his team to advantage. He left out regulars Wark and Stockwell and played both Bozinoski and Guentchev, with Dozzell in midfield. The Ipswich no. 10 was detailed to tail England international, Ince and the ploy worked a treat. The 25-year-old Dozzell was so effective he found time to join Kiwomya in attack as the pair regularly combined to threaten the United goal. The Evening Star reporter wrote:

'On Saturday, Jason Dozzell was a real mastermind.'

But Kiwomya was not about to be upstaged. In the 23rd minute, Peter Schmeichal made a hash of his clearance and the young forward was on it in a flash turning the ball into the net to give his side a 1-0 lead. The 27,068 fans squeezed into Portman Road were in raptures as the home side threw themselves at their illustrious opponents in an attempt to score the important second goal. To the crowd's amazement the goal duly came, but from an unexpected source. Frank Yallop's goal in the previous game against Spurs was his first for Ipswich for four and a half years. He did it again in the United match. Yallop's strike in the 47th minute sealed the victory for his team. Brian McClair scored a late consolation goal for the Red Devils, but it was too little, too late for the eventual champions. Lyall had done it again. On that wonderful Saturday afternoon his team had shown far more desire and commitment than their illustrious opponents. Unbelievably, at the end of January Ipswich Town were 4th in the Premier League.

The Evening Star's headline screamed, 'GLORY DAYS MIRROR RAMSEY'S ERA'. Its reporter, presumably referring to Lyall's and Woods's numerous scouting missions, wrote:

'...meticulous training and use of information, plus a squad with so much respect for the management team and you have a recipe for

success...'

By Christmas Town had lost just twice, a tribute to the side's defensive qualities. The big question for Lyall, his staff and the fans was – could their team keep it up? Sadly, for the Portman Road faithful, the Tractor Boys failed to notch up a single win in the 13 games from the end of January. The magnificent victories over Spurs and Manchester United quickly became a distant memory as Lyall's men stumbled from one defeat to another. Fortunately, a late run of two wins against Norwich City and Nottingham Forest in the last three games ensured Town's survival in the Premier League. It was a close run thing. The highlight of this unforgettable season was undoubtedly those three glorious days at the end of January when everything seemed possible at Portman Road.

Late in the 1992/93 season Lyall and Charlie Woods raised a few eyebrows when they went off on match day scouting missions, leaving McGiven in charge of the first team. The pair clocked hundreds of miles watching opponents and running a professional eye over possible new signings. Woods remembers these trips with affection, "We talked football about football and life in general, but had to stop every couple of hundred miles to empty John's ashtray," he recalled.

The pair gathered detailed information to inform their training schedule for the week ahead – this attention to detail more than paid off in Ipswich's first season in the Premier League, as the January victories over Tottenham and Manchester United confirm. With a limited squad and very little money, Ipswich had punched well above their weight. It was always going to be difficult to sustain their good form throughout the season – and so it proved. But most Ipswich fans would have taken a 16th place finish at the end of that season. Lyall was encouraged by his team's performances but knew the squad needed strengthening in time for the new campaign, as Henderson and Voller later wrote:

'But John Lyall was not fooled by Ipswich's showing after an absence from the big-time for six years. He pinpointed areas of the squad that he felt required strengthening.'

At the end of May, the staff and players could reflect on a satisfactory season full of promise. They had consolidated their place in the Premiership and felt comfortable at the higher level, particularly in the first half of the season. The manager had been loyal to the players who achieved promotion, but now it was time to press the board for support.

The Lyalls go house-hunting

Lyall committed himself fully to Ipswich Town. Within weeks of his appointment, John and Yvonne began looking for a house in Suffolk. The Lyalls knew this would be their last move and were determined to find a house with a lake, where John and Yvonne could indulge their passion for fishing. As hard as they searched, they couldn't find the right house and didn't finally move to Suffolk until June 1994, when they discovered Wallers Farm in the delightful village of Tattingstone. The Lyalls' difficulty in finding the right house was interpreted by some people, who should have known better, as a deliberate decision not to make the move to Suffolk. Henderson and Voller wrote:

'Lyall and McGiven chose to make the daily journey from the London area, rather than move to East Anglia.'

This is misleading and simply wrong, as Yvonne Lyall recently explained, "We were ready to move straight away – if only we could have found the right house."

Henderson and Voller claim that Lyall and McGiven's so-called decision not to move to the Ipswich area adversely affected the pair's relationship with the local press. In their Essential History, they write:

'One area of Town's activities that seemed to suffer was their relationship with the media, neither of the two newcomers having been used to speaking to newspapers, radio and TV representatives on such a regular basis.'

This is nonsense. In his years at West Ham, Lyall developed deep and lasting relationships with both the local press and national media. He was in touch with reporters from the Stratford Express and the Ilford Recorder on a daily basis – you only have to ask the great East End sports' photographer, Steve Bacon and reporter, Trevor Smith, with whom Lyall enjoyed close friendships. It is also naive to refer to Lyall and McGiven as newcomers. English football at the top level is full of players from all over the world, as Ipswich supporters will know more than most. Older fans of the Tractor Boys will treasure wonderful memories of the great Muhren and Thijssen team of the late 1970s and early '80s. Henderson and Voller's rather jaundiced provincialism fails to do justice to a modern football club with an impressive record of acquiring top international footballers.

In their book, in which they fully recognise Lyall's coaching prowess, the authors warm to their theme. They write:

'John Lyall did not enjoy a close relationship with the Ipswich supporters. He kept his distance, chose not to appear at many social functions... He was a bit of a stranger to the fans.'

This is the man who took an ailing Ipswich side to the promised land of the Premier League in just two seasons. The two former reporters provide no evidence for their allegations. In the extensive research I undertook in the course of writing this book, I interviewed many of the club's ex-players, former coaches, club officials and fans. Tony Dable was Youth Development Officer at Ipswich Town when Lyall arrived at Portman Road. One of the most highly-regarded youth coaches in English football, Dable taught at Chantry High School and coached Ipswich and South Suffolk Schoolboys, before leaving teaching to work full-time for John Duncan at Portman Road. It was Dable who discovered Jason Dozzell, James Scowcroft, the Bramble twins, Richard Wright and Adam Tanner, the teenager who scored Ipswich's winning goal in the club's first ever victory at Anfield in 1995.

When John Lyall arrived at Ipswich, he quickly saw the value of having someone on his team with roots in the schools and local youth football. As Dable, said recently: "John accepted me and valued our good connections with the schools. He also understood that building a successful youth set-up takes time."

On the issue of Lyall's relationship with the Ipswich supporters, this loyal Ipswich servant insisted: "I can't agree that John wasn't accepted by the fans. They respected John for bringing the club on."

If Lyall won over the fans, he also quickly gained the trust of the players. Dable recounted two stories which perfectly illustrate Lyall's man-management skills. On the morning of the open bus parade following Ipswich's promotion to the Premier League in 1992, Dable stood outside the main gate with the rest of the fans to cheer the parade on its triumphant way. Lyall spotted Dable in the crowd and immediately invited him onto the bus, "You've earned this Tony – get on the bus." According to Dable this was typical of Lyall. He was an absolute gentleman and had tremendous respect from everybody at the club.

The second story concerns young goalkeeper, Richard Wright, then an outstanding prospect in the Ipswich youth team. Wright was on a two-year YTS scheme when Lyall arrived at Portman Road. At the end of the scheme, Lyall invited Wright and his father to his office to discuss professional terms. The Ipswich manager set out the terms of the proposed contract and, just as young Wright was about to ask a question, Lyall turned to him and said, "Don't say anything – you need to go home and discuss the offer with your dad. Come back and give me your decision in a few days."

Most managers would have asked for a decision there and then, afraid that there was another club waiting around the corner. But that was not Lyall's way. The young goalkeeper was also regularly invited onto the first team coach for away games – another subtle man-management ploy. Of course, Wright duly signed his new contract and became a full-time professional at the age of 17. As Dable said, "With John it was often the small things that made the difference." Tony Dable was reasonably close to Lyall and we should respect his opinion and accept his view of events.

Good man-management skills are a vital prerequisite for the

manager of a top football club. Motivating individual players, building team spirit and energising everyone at the club are all priorities for a good leader. There is no room in Lyall's model for dissent or group factions.

Mick McGiven provides a further example of Lyall's approach to management. When Ipswich was romping through the old 2nd Division, one particular player thought he would test the manager's resolve. One evening in the team hotel the night before an away match, Lyall and McGiven noticed that one of the squad hadn't made it back to the hotel at the agreed time. A couple of hours passed and the miscreant had still not appeared. Next day Town lost heavily and Lyall had all the players in the following day for a team meeting. He called in the captain, Dave Linighan and told him:

'We need to set some ground rules. We are going to London on Saturday and if we don't get the right response from the players today, Mick and I are walking away from this club and we won't be back. And let us know if you want our troublemaker to play. Go and ask the players what they want to do.'

Linighan returned from players' meeting and said to his manager:

'The players want all of us involved on Saturday – everybody, and we want you there John. You must be there.'

That was the response Lyall was looking for and the squad left for London determined to put things right. The match was tight and at the final whistle every player was out on their feet, particularly our miscreant. He had run his heart out and the rest of the players refused to have him substituted. As McGiven said: "The rest of the team pushed him to the limit. It was like getting life out of a dead horse."

In January 1994 the chairman asked Lyall if the team would object to playing two games in three days. Ipswich had a League Cup tie against Liverpool on the Wednesday and Sky TV asked if they could play Wimbledon in front of the cameras on the previous Monday evening. Once again, Lyall called in Linighan, explained the financial benefit to the club of the Sky offer, and informed him the whole squad would receive an additional bonus if they played the two games. He then asked his skipper to go away and talk to the players. Linighan returned from his meeting and told him:

'No problem John – it's unanimous. What I mean is there were only a couple of players who said they didn't like it.'

The day after the players' met to discuss the issue of the Monday night televised game the local press ran a highly disingenuous story under a MUTINY-type headline. A reporter had been informed there were one or two dissenting voices in the squad and turned this into a full-scale players' revolt. McGiven challenged the reporter at training the next day to justify his story. He was probably wasting his breath – his complaint would have fallen on deaf ears.

The missing player incident and the Sky TV issue, as recalled by McGiven, are two further examples of Lyall's man-management style and illustrate his effectiveness at dealing with potentially tricky situations. He always consulted the players and gave them responsibility. This is the way he earned their respect and support. They would run through a brick wall for him.

There is no question that the management team at Ipswich clearly enjoyed the full support of the board, the players and the fans. For reasons of their own the local press never accepted Lyall and McGiven, as the latter recalls:

'They didn't like us. They tried, but the local press couldn't break the bond between John and myself. Our relationship was too strong.'

A call from Sir Alex

During our interview in the Director's Box at Portman Road in August 2012, Charlie Woods told a fascinating story which clarifies once and for all Lyall's commitment to Ipswich Town at this time.

One afternoon Woods was sitting with his boss in the boot room upstairs at the training ground when the telephone rang. The caller was none other than the Manchester United manager, Sir Alex Ferguson. Woods assumed Ferguson was calling Lyall to ask his advice about something, as he often did. But the Old Trafford boss had other things on his mind that day, as Woods revealed:

'I can tell you – Sir Alex called that day to offer John the job of Assistant Manager at Old Trafford.'

At once surprised and flattered, Lyall eventually turned down the United manager's interesting offer. He had no wish to move north and, in any case, it was probably too late in his career to take on a key job at one of the world's biggest clubs. But Lyall also knew that he owed Ipswich Town some loyalty. He had behaved impeccably when West Ham blocked his proposed move to QPR in the mid-1980s and stayed loyal to Ipswich when the United manager came calling. There are few people in football that could resist the opportunity to work with Sir Alex at Old Trafford. John Lyall was one of them.

Frankly, I found only affection and respect for Lyall at Ipswich and gratitude for what he achieved in his four years at the club. That is the simple truth of the matter. And, in any case the journey by car up the A12 from Ongar to Ipswich takes no longer than 50 minutes, hardly a matter of distance. Just to put this issue to rest, we know that Lyall used his own car for 12 months before he moved to Suffolk and in that time never once claimed expenses. It doesn't sound like the actions of a man not fully committed to the job.

Life without Jason
Local boy Jason Dozzell joined the Suffolk club as a schoolboy in the winter of 1984. In February of that year he made his first team debut at the tender age of 16 years and 57 days. Named as substitute in the game against Coventry, the Chantry School pupil came off the bench just 30 minutes into the game. He then proceeded to rewrite the record books when, in the 89th minute, he scored his side's third goal in a 3-1 victory. Dozzell became the club's youngest ever first team player that day and when his shot

hit the back of the Coventry net, the youngest to score a goal in the old 1st Division. The following day he was back in school.

Dozzell had been a key player for Lyall in the promotion season and in their first year in the Premier League. His scintillating partnership with Chris Kiwomya provided sufficient goals to keep Ipswich in the top flight. But he was more than just a centre-forward. His adaptability meant that Lyall could deploy his key player in a number of different roles. But after so many years at his home club, it was probably the right time to move. Still only 25-years-old, Dozzell needed a new challenge to rejuvenate his career. In the summer of 1993 he moved to Tottenham for a fee of £1.75 million, which represented good business for Ipswich and an excellent move for the player.

In the summer of '93, following Dozzell's departure, Lyall brought Paul Mason from Aberdeen for £400,000 and paid £750,000 to Oldham Athletic for Ian Marshall, who Lyall turned from a rather ordinary defender into a dangerous forward – much like Ron Greenwood did with Geoff Hurst many years before. Lyall was also delighted to bring to Portman Road one of the most promising young wingers of his generation, Suffolk-born, Stuart Slater. Of course, he was very familiar with Slater's ability from his West Ham days, but the talented outside-left's move from West Ham to Celtic was not a great success and this wonderfully gifted footballer had somewhat lost his way in the game.

The additions to the squad had an immediate impact in the new campaign. Three matches into their second season in the Premier League, Town were sitting at the top of the table having beaten Oldham, Southampton and Chelsea in their first three games. Marshall had scored in all three games and suddenly the Portman Road faithful had forgotten the loss of their local hero, Jason Dozzell. Expectations were suddenly sky high for the second time in two seasons. Sadly the bubble soon burst and by the end of December Lyall's men had managed just seven wins in their first 21 matches. A hard-fought 0-0 draw at Old Trafford was evidence of the team's fighting spirit, but the lack of quality and depth was all too clear. Heavy defeats against Arsenal, Queen Park Rangers and

Sheffield Wednesday (twice) damaged morale among the players and altered the mood of the fans. A 2-1 win over Norwich City in mid-December brought some Christmas cheer to Portman Road, but this was short-lived. The side's poor form continued and they managed just two wins in the second half of the season.

A 2-1 away win against Aston Villa in March brought renewed hope of survival, but with four points from their last 11 League matches, relegation remained a real possibility. Nerves were definitely jangling in Suffolk as Lyall prepared his players for their last game of the season – away to Blackburn Rovers. Henderson and Voller described the mood among the faithful:

'Ipswich went into their final game at Blackburn with their Premiership status hanging by a thread and later, with emotions running high up and down the country, it seemed they were actually down.'

A win at Ewood Park would have ensured Town's survival. But the teams played out a dour 0-0 draw. Fortunately, a late Mark Stein goal for Chelsea against Town's relegation rivals, Sheffield United, saved Ipswich at the 11th hour and sent the Yorkshire club down. Town's supporters went into raptures as the news filtered through that their team had escaped relegation by a whisker. The away supporters danced with delight and Lyall's players ran to embrace their manager in sheer relief.

A total of 43 points would usually be enough to avoid relegation with something to spare, but in the season before Lyall's team had accumulated an impressive 52 points and a 16th place League finish. This represents a considerable decline in Ipswich's performance. The hard facts are that Town were the lowest scorers in the Premier League in 1993/94 and the Marshall/Kiwomya partnership failed to spark, with the latter managing a disappointing five League goals all season. The defence was generally sound and conceded fewer goals than any team in the lower half of the table. But the simple truth is that Lyall's team lacked the quality required to compete at this level. Little Ipswich could not expect to match millionaire clubs like champions Manchester United and runners-up, Blackburn Rovers. However, they could legitimately expect to compete with the likes of QPR,

Norwich and Coventry for a mid-table position – even with their meagre resources. So what went wrong?

Taking a step back

Sometime early in 1994, Lyall took Mick McGiven to one side and told him: "I'm going to step back a bit and I want you to take over running the first team. You will have sole responsibility for picking the team and preparing them for games."

These words came as a shock to McGiven, but he was ambitious and keen to accept. However, he did have one or two reservations. Lyall reassured his friend, "Mick, don't worry. I'll still be here for you."

Lyall had cleared this important change with the Ipswich board and the new arrangements remained in place for the rest of the season. The manager remained in overall charge and had complete trust in his assistant to run the first team. McGiven was a talented coach who enjoyed the respect of the players. He sat on the bench during matches, while Lyall retreated to the comparative safety of the Director's Box. As the season developed the manager rarely attended away games, preferring to spend his Saturdays spying on Ipswich's next opponents. The board's decision to allow Lyall to step back and promote McGiven appeared justified as Town, operating on relatively scarce resources, managed to avoid relegation. But as McGiven said recently:

'It was an extremely daunting task. But John never scaled down his commitment to the job. We continued to travel up the A12 together every day just as we did in our first year at Ipswich.'

Why would Lyall want to step back from a job he loved so much? How could he leave the club's future in the hands of his assistant? It was just not like him. The answer to these questions stems from two things. Firstly, he planned to retire from football as the earliest opportunity – no later than 55. He was simply planning his retirement just like any other professional at his time of life. Despite his deep love for the game he knew there was a life outside of football. But, things didn't quite go to plan. Lacking Lyall's powerful leadership and sheer presence, the team staggered rudderless from one defeat to another. Simon Milton spoke recently of the effect on the players of Lyall's decision to take a step back:

'Mick was a great coach – no question, and he was popular with the players, but when John turned up at training the players immediately gave 20% more effort. He had that aura about him. But he never discussed why he decided to step back.'

The players were confused and disappointed, which showed in their hesitant performances in the second half of the season. John Wark expressed the view of most of the players when he said:

'Our form dipped when John went 'upstairs'. Mick was a very good coach but couldn't expect to command the same respect as John and didn't have John's presence.'

There is little question that Lyall believed the new regime would work. McGiven was a top coach, Charlie Woods was a loyal assistant and John Wark and Paul Goddard were coming to the end of their careers and keen to help out with some coaching. But the decision to drop down was almost certainly a mistake. Yvonne Lyall admitted recently that it was probably impossible to manage a Premier League club on a part-time basis, no matter how good the first team coach. She said recently, "It was never going to work. My father tried to run his building business on the same basis later in his life, but it never worked."

The second reason Lyall decided to step back at Ipswich was the faith he had in Mick McGiven. He would have remembered how Ron Greenwood moved upstairs at West Ham in the mid-'70s to allow his assistant to take full control of the team. The succession worked beautifully at Upton Park with Lyall winning two FA Cup triumphs in five years. But that was Greenwood and Lyall, two of the most highly respected men in football. Despite his excellence as a coach and reputation in the game, McGiven was no John Lyall.

What worked at West Ham was unlikely to work at Ipswich Town and so it proved. Under the new arrangements the team lurched from one crisis to another. It was not McGiven's fault. With Lyall a looming presence, he never enjoyed the ultimate authority of a full-blown manager.

Lyall shuffle's his pack

For the start of the 1994/95 season Lyall decided on a staff reshuffle to halt the slide. He put Paul Goddard and John Wark in charge of the first team, while Mick McGiven was invited to take responsibility for the club's new Academy. From the outside this might seem like demotion for the first team coach, but the future of clubs like Ipswich Town is dependent on producing outstanding young talent. In 1992 Premier League clubs began the task of transforming their old Centres of Excellence into modern Academies. At West Ham, McGiven and Lyall always spent two or three evenings a week at Chadwell Heath working with the club's youngsters. McGiven had a wealth of experience of coaching youngsters and was the ideal man for this important job. He threw himself into his new role with characteristic enthusiasm as he remembers: "I loved working with young players and gave 100% to the new job."

When McGiven stepped down from his first team duties, Goddard and Wark ran the team, although Lyall continued to manage from a distance. This disappointed the Ipswich fans who wanted their manager back full guns blazing. Goddard and Wark shared responsibilities with the former taking the training while Wark looked after the office and travelled to watch the opposition. Wark didn't enjoy the increased responsibility:

'It was an eye-opener for me. It was a proper job. I had years of training in the mornings and going home in the afternoon. It put me off managing for good.'

Despite a few decent results, the Goddard/Wark experiment failed to halt the decline – both were highly respected as players, but lacked managerial experience at any level. By Christmas,

Ipswich looked certain for the drop. Injuries didn't help, as Mick McGiven remembers:

'We had a horrendous injury list. Both Johnson and Whelan were out for long periods. These were key players. We were stretched to the limit.'

After narrowly surviving two seasons in the Premier League, the winter of 1994 was a turbulent time for Ipswich Town and their fans. Paul Goddard had retired as a player in the close season, while Lyall brought in utility player, Steve Sedgely from Tottenham for £1 million. Aarhus Danish international midfielder, Claus Thomsen joined Sedgely as a new arrival, but Lyall trumped these two rather modest signings with what appeared a considerable coup.

We know that Lyall had long admired the skill and inventiveness of foreign footballers. As ever, he was ahead of his time in searching far and wide for the best players. But when Lyall and Charlie Woods ventured as far as South America on a scouting trip, eyebrows were well and truly raised among the Portman Road faithful. But Lyall's initiative was rewarded when Uruguayan striker Adrian Paz and Argentinian full-back Mauricio Taricco agreed to join the Suffolk club. Lyall had high expectations of his two foreign signings. Had he found the new Muhren and Thijssen? Unfortunately, neither Paz nor Taricco made much of an impact at the club and the extravagant looking signings simply added to the fans' frustrations.

With Lyall more hands-on in pre-season training, his reshaped team got off to a decent start. The first three games brought four points from six and a tentative rise in expectations. But three defeats in succession quickly brought the fans down to earth. On the 24 September, Manchester United arrived at Portman Road fully expecting to leave with their customary three points. Lyall and his team had other ideas. Two goals from Paul Mason and a third from Steve Sedgely gave the Tractor Boys a well-deserved 3-2 victory. In front of over 22,000 delirious fans, they had triumphed over the Premier League champions. If they could beat Manchester United, anything was possible. But hopes were soon dashed as the victory over the Red Devils proved a false dawn.

A disappointing run of five defeats followed the heroics against Alex Ferguson's side. A solitary win against Leeds United brought temporary relief for Lyall's beleaguered team, before a run of nine games without a win left Ipswich firmly at the foot of the Premier League. There was a real sense of crisis around Portman Road as the manager and his staff worked desperately to turn things around. The local press began baying for blood. But much worse, the fans began to turn on Lyall and it was not pretty.

The Evening Star spoke for most Town supporters at this difficult time. Under the headline, 'WHAT A MESS', their football reporter wrote:

'Ipswich Town are not just in a crisis situation, they are in a mega crisis.'

A disastrous run of just three wins in 16 games preceded Manchester City's visit to Portman Road on Saturday, 3 December. An indication of the fans dwindling support for their team was the worryingly low attendance. Only 13,504 fans turned up that day to watch the match against City, one of the top clubs in the country. A Paul Mason goal was not enough to deny the Mancunians their victory, further cementing Town's place at the foot of the table. It was a bleak day for everyone at the club. What followed next was a huge shock to everyone associated with Ipswich Town FC.

Football followers are notoriously fickle and Ipswich fans are no exception. After all, Bobby Robson was continually booed at Portman Road in his early days. When their team hit rock bottom in December 1994, the glory days of promotion to the Premier League in 1992, wonderful results against Manchester United and Tottenham were quickly forgotten. As were headlines comparing Lyall's team with the great Ramsey side of 1962. Both the fans and the local press turned on Lyall with a vengeance. Subdued chants of 'Lyall Out' were first heard on the terraces in November, but those faint cries of frustration turned to orchestrated abuse at the end of the Manchester City home game in early December.

After the final whistle against City, Lyall waited at the players' tunnel to commiserate with his team and shake hands with the opposition. A group of youths gathered nearby – one of them turned to Lyall and screamed: "You're rubbish. I hope your car crashes and you get killed on the way home."

Lyall was visibly shaken and turned to Charlie Woods and said: "Did you hear that?"

"I did," replied Woods, "but John, look – it's just a few stroppy kids – take no notice."

Sitting in the stands that day, as he did for all home matches, was Tony Dable. The former Youth Development Officer, who was appalled by the 'Lyall Out' chanting, turned to his friend and said, "John doesn't deserve this and he won't put up with any of it." He was right.

Lyall leaves Town in shock

Lyall drove back down the A137 to Tattingstone that evening deep in thought. He spent Sunday at home with his family and the evening in quiet reflection. He didn't really need to discuss the situation with Yvonne at any great length – his mind was made up. Later that evening Lyall called Charlie Woods: "Hello Charlie, I'd like you to be in first thing in the morning, if that's OK?"

"Of course, what's up John?" replied the intrigued Woods.

"I've got something to tell you, see you in the morning Charlie," replied his boss.

Lyall arrived at the training ground early on Monday, took Woods to one side and told him, "Charlie – I'm resigning, I've had enough mate. Saturday was the last straw."

Woods knew there was little point in trying to change Lyall's mind. John informed the chairman of his decision, who in turn broke the news to the players and everyone at the club. The media were informed at a press conference later that day. Lyall not only walked away from Portman Road that December morning, he turned his back on professional football for good.

Later that day the local Evening Star carried this banner headline on its front page, 'LYALL LEAVES TOWN IN SHOCK'. The article began:

'Portman Road was in a state of shock today as John Lyall

297

sensationally quit the club.'

A stunned Mick McGiven heard the news on his car radio and drove straight round to Tattingstone. He remembers:

'I couldn't believe it. I was shocked. But when I got round to the house, there was John, covered in creosote with a huge smile on his face. He was fixing up the garage loft. It was typical John. There was never any animosity with the Ipswich board and John walked away with his head held high.'

John Lyall's long love affair with football was over.

Highs and lows at Portman Road

Lyall's appointment as Ipswich manager in the summer of 1990 was greeted with unanimous delight at Portman Road. Staff, players and fans alike were genuinely excited by the arrival at the club of someone of Lyall's stature. Promotion in Lyall's second season brought back memories of the achievements of the great Ipswich sides under Ramsey and Robson. Lyall transformed a group of decent players and one or two astute signings into a winning team. Promotion and three seasons in the Premier League were achieved on a shoestring budget, in stark contrast to the limitless wealth available to the likes of Manchester United and Blackburn Rovers. There is only so much a manager can do, even one as gifted as John Lyall, against the ever- increasing riches of the top Premier League clubs.

The tetchy provincial press whipped up the fans with their callous criticism and downright lies, for example:

'Lyall continued to live in London during his reign at Portman Road.'

This is a cruel and unfair verdict on Lyall's time at Ipswich. When he joined Ipswich, Lyall was asked by a local pressman what he should do to win the new manager's trust. Lyall replied: "You have my trust now, you can only lose it."

The Suffolk press wasted no time in losing John Lyall's trust. Murray Lyall witnessed at first hand the bond his father enjoyed with the London media:

'Vic Railton, Denis Signy, Reg Drury and Michael Hart were very close friends. Dad would regularly be on the phone to them for over an hour in his busy schedule. Despite the close friendship they all knew their boundaries and when JL said 'off the record' they would never betray the trust he had in them and the matter stayed in strict confidence. He had a similar rapport and understanding with the East London press.'

Lyall largely ignored the excesses of the local press. The players and staff put things in proper perspective. Chris Kiwomya was devastated to hear of Lyall's resignation,

'...he was the best thing that ever happened to Ipswich. I'll miss my daily private tutorials and our chats about football and life in general.'

Kiwomya benefitted more than most from Lyall's teaching and soon left Ipswich for the richer pastures of Highbury. Disappointingly, his career never quite took off at Arsenal as he explains:

'I never fulfilled my promise because I lacked the daily contact. I really missed him. John was very good at encouraging black players as he did at West Ham. Ron Greenwood's wife told me that Clyde Best stayed with the Greenwoods when he first arrived from Bermuda. He was also very good with Paul Ince as a youngster. John understood. He had a big impact on my life.'

Simon Milton spoke for most of the players:

'We missed him. It was never the same.'

John Wark, Ipswich Player of the Year on four occasions, played over 600 games in the top flight. The Ipswich legend who played in Jock Stein's 1982 World Cup side, and gained 29 caps for his country, had the greatest respect for Lyall:

'I played under Sir Bobby Robson, Joe Fagan and Jock Stein and John was right up there with these great managers. He had a real presence – when he entered a room people took notice.'

The irrepressible and highly experienced Charlie Woods has worked with some of the best managers in the game and had no doubts that:

'John was up there as one of the three best managers I ever worked with – the other two were Sir Bobby Robson and George

Graham.'

Henderson and Voller in their Essential History of Ipswich Town, although often critical, acknowledged Lyall's good work at Portman Road,

'... he could retire in the knowledge that Ipswich, despite their precarious position in the Premier League, were in far better health than before his appointment.'

The genuine affection shown to Lyall by his players and colleagues sits in stark contrast to the treatment he received from the press and ungrateful fans during his time at Ipswich. In fairness to the irritable media men and disgruntled supporters, promotion had raised unrealistic expectations of further glory. These people vented their disappointment in the only way they knew how. In fairness to Lyall's critics, the Ipswich board should probably not have sanctioned their manager taking a back seat in 1994 – the consequences for the club were disastrous. Lyall continued to work hard looking for new players and casting his expert eye over the opposition as he did when he first arrived at the club. But did Lyall really think he could head up a Premier League club from a distance? Perhaps, as Charlie Woods intimated, he was tired and disillusioned with the game he had been involved with on a day-to-day basis for nearly 40 years. The gross commercial world of modern football, with huge player salaries, aggressive agents and constant media attention would have been distasteful to someone with Lyall's values. But I don't think this was the reason he decided to take things down a notch or two at Ipswich. For some time he had struggled to reconcile the pull of family life with the pressures of a high profile job in professional football. In the end he chose his family over football, a wise choice and one he never regretted.

Chapter 16
A life away from football

On Monday, 6 December 1994, John kept his promise to Yvonne and retired to his Suffolk farmhouse with its well-stocked fishing lake and lovely gardens. He had finished with football for good. After 40 years of long working days, weeks away from home and constant media attention, John Lyall walked away from the game he loved so much. He'd simply had enough. Former player, Paul Goddard admired John's resolve in turning his back on the game:

'One of the great things he managed to do was retire and he did actually retire. He didn't do TV work, even though there were plenty of offers. He decided to change his lifestyle, which is incredibly difficult, and he totally devoted his life to his wife Yvonne. There are not many football people who do that.'

Lyall's love of fishing, his enjoyment of the countryside and delight in rural tranquillity can be traced to his Scottish roots and wonderful family holidays in the Highlands. Work kept him away from Scotland for years, but he never forgot his background as his Gaelic-speaking brother, Jim reminds us:

"Although we were brought up in East London... the Highlands are in our blood."

In case there was any doubt about the East London boy's ancestral roots, the playing of Scotland the Brave at his funeral would have settled the issue. Like his brothers, John also inherited his parents' profound faith in family life. Combined with his love of the countryside, it was not difficult for John to say goodbye to the gruelling responsibilities of managing a top football club. After all, nobody had done more for the game – after 40 years at the top, his job was complete.

The Lyalls began to make up for lost time. The couple spent many happy hours together fishing in the grounds of Wallers Farm, their peace only disrupted by the grandchildren pleading for John to join them in a kick-about. Murray, now a successful construction manager, lived next door with Samantha and their children, providing John and Yvonne with constant company and support. With the enthusiastic assistance of his dad, Murray lovingly restored the old farmhouse and its spacious garden. The move to Suffolk had been a great success.

The Lyalls loved to spend long days together at Tattingstone away from media attention and the tyranny of needing to win football matches. One of the most interesting things about Lyall was that he seemed to enjoy both the hustle and bustle of running a professional football club and the peace he found in his home life. Lyall loved dealing with players, fans, directors and the press, but had the rare ability to shut out this public world as soon as he got home. Whether his team won or lost, when he arrived home he kept his emotions in check. It requires a special person to balance the relentless demands of public life with running a family. John Lyall was that kind of person, but after a lifetime in the public eye, he had earned the right to relax and enjoy life.

The couple had some wonderful memories of their time in football, particularly at West Ham where they both had local roots. Relationships with the press were not always as fraught as they became during his time at Ipswich. Yvonne recently recalled that John always enjoyed a very good rapport with the media. Among their personal friends were distinguished journalists, Vic Railton, Reg Drury, Bernard Joy, Denis Signy, Michael Hart, Jim Gaines, Steve Stammers and his old neighbour, Peter Lorenzo. They trusted John and knew if there was a story they would be the first to hear.

A particular fond memory for Yvonne was the special invitation dinner parties hosted by Bernard Joy. It was an honour to be invited to Joy's soirées in the distinguished company of Signy, Bill

Nicholson, Jimmy Hill, Alex Stock, Brian Moore and Sir Stanley Rous and their wives, where Chatham House rules were rigidly applied. Relations between managers, players and the press have deteriorated over the years and it is difficult to imagine these kinds of events happening today.

The Lyall's enjoyed 12 years of peaceful retirement together; fishing, visiting friends and working in their garden. With the grandchildren on their doorstep to keep John fit and active, the couple delighted in their well-earned rest. Charlie, Scott and Sam helped around the grounds, driving the tractor and generally keeping things under control. Life at Tattingstone was good and football became a fond, but receding memory.

Since he retired from football in the winter of 1994 many of Lyall's old players and colleagues kept in touch and remained friends. Simon Milton, Chris Kiwomya and Charlie Woods lived locally and were regular visitors to Tattingstone. Billy Bonds, Patsy Holland, Trevor Brooking, Phil Parkes, David Cross, Ray Stewart, Paul Goddard and many others from the West Ham days, kept in regular contact with John and Yvonne.

Tragedy strikes
On the evening of 18 April 2006, the Lyalls' well-earned peace and serenity was shattered forever. John and Yvonne had spent the morning shopping and the afternoon pottering in the garden and playing with their grandsons – a typical day in the Lyall household. That evening Yvonne decided to retire early, leaving John downstairs in his favourite chair watching football on TV. As she got into bed, Yvonne was disturbed by what she described as a terrible noise. Thinking intruders had entered the house, she rushed downstairs only to find John collapsed in his chair, clearly in great distress. Yvonne dialled 999 and somehow dragged her husband onto the floor as instructed by the telephone operator. When the ambulance arrived the paramedics worked furiously to save John's life, but to no avail. Like his father before him, John had suffered a massive rupture in his heart and died within minutes.

Yvonne was stunned and inconsolable and had the dreadful task of breaking the tragic news to Murray and Samantha, who were awakened by Yvonne shouting into the answerphone. The grandchildren were heartbroken and were kept away from school for days. Murray took two months' leave from work and threw himself into organising the funeral and memorial service, taking care of his mother and dealing with all the complex and upsetting legal business which follows the sudden death of a parent. Mercifully for Murray, this unenviable task was made considerably easier by the typically meticulous manner in which his father arranged his affairs. As for Yvonne, she could not face the prospect of going back in the main house and chose to stay with Murray and Samantha, before summoning the courage to return. Understandably, the family was devastated as they struggled to cope with their tragic loss. John's death threw a dark shadow over Wallers Farm which took years to lift.

Epilogue

The news of John Lyall's death spread quickly across the world of football. Murray and Samantha tried desperately to contact the rest of the family before they heard the news on the radio or television. Members of John's great West Ham team of the 1980s called to offer their condolences, as did many of his old friends in the game. Stunned West Ham supporters travelled up the A12 to drape claret and blue shirts on the main gates at Portman Road, while down in the East End, grateful Hammers' fans paid their own quiet tribute at Upton Park. Yvonne has kept the Hammers' shirts, many carrying heart-felt messages, left as a reminder of the great affection in which John was held at the club he served for 34 years.

The tributes were many and provided the family with some comfort in their grief. Ipswich Town FC issued a statement saying:

'It is with deep regret that Ipswich Town has learned of the death of John Lyall. John… took the team into the new Premier League in 1992. We extend our sympathies and condolences to his family.'

The club held a minute's silence before its next home match and the Ipswich players wore black arm bands in memory of their former manager. People connected with the Suffolk club were swift to pay their respects to their friend and colleague. The man who succeeded Lyall as manager, George Burley, spoke for many when he said:

'Although I didn't know him personally very well, he was highly respected in the world of football. He was tactically a very good coach and his teams always played very good football. I remember many battles with his West Ham teams during my playing days.'

Lyall was clearly welcomed by the Suffolk football public, as

Burley confirms:

'He was also very well thought of at Ipswich. When I came to the club the players really respected what he had achieved and the work he had done there. As an incoming manager you tend to bring in your own ideas and your own people, but I could see how highly he was thought of.'

The former England centre-forward and former Ipswich manager, Joe Royle, offered this moving tribute:

'I am shocked. He was a first class football coach and a first class man. He almost signed me once in 1977. I sometimes wondered what would have happened if things had turned out differently. I know that people who did work with him, like Keith Robson, Graham Paddon and Mark Ward always had the greatest respect and affection for him. This is a very sad day.'

Mike Noye, Ipswich Town's commercial manager during John Lyall's time at Portman Road, added his own, very personal tribute:

'We were quite close when he was at the club, he had a good sense of humour and we got on very well. And he got on very well with the players – he really brought out the best in them. When we were promoted in 1992 he managed to knit together a team that didn't have any real stars but all played for each other.'
'People like Chris Kiwomya really responded to him. I always thought it was a shame that he walked away from football when he left Ipswich but his other great love was fishing and he enjoyed that in retirement.'

Phil Ham, Evening Star columnist and editor of Ipswich Town fanzine Those Were the Days, provided a fan's perspective on Lyall's time at the club which runs counter to some of the unwarranted abuse he received at Portman Road in his last few weeks at the club:

'What fans will remember is the 1991/92 season when he did a fantastic job to take a team which the previous year had finished 14th and put

them into the first ever Premiership. He turned ordinary players into a side which beat Kenny Dalglish's Blackburn, took the old Division Two title and fans won't forget that. Then, on limited funds, he kept them there for three seasons.'

Former Ipswich players lined up to pay their respects. Club legend, Kevin Beattie, spoke for many:

'I will never forget him. He was such a nice man, so much so you would never imagine he was a football manager. He wanted to get in with the players unlike other managers and was very dedicated to the club.'

Paul Goddard, former Ipswich and West Ham striker, knew Lyall better than most and paid this very personal tribute:

'The news is a real shock. He was, without doubt, the best coach I have ever had the privilege to work with and without a doubt one of the most knowledgeable footballing people I have ever been in contact with in my career.'

Sir Bobby Robson said of his old friend:

'He (is) a very knowledgeable and well-informed manager and one of the best readers of the game that I know.'

One of the Boys of '86, Tony Gale, wrote:

'John was a man of strong morals, both on and off the pitch and I don't know of any player who had a bad word to say about him.' (West Ham official programme, 28 April 2006)

Gale was very clear about Lyall's influence as a coach:

'Much is talked about football coaching, but I can assure everyone that most of its origins come from Greenwood and Lyall.'

Long-time friend and colleague, Mick McGiven who shared most of Lyall's career ups and downs, was characteristically forthright:

'John was highly intelligent, a man of genius – I miss him terribly.'

Fellow Ilford boy and claret and blue legend, Sir Trevor Brooking described his former manager as, 'a modest man and unbelievable coach.'

The tributes from the national press were equally moving. The Guardian's Julie Welch wrote this moving passage:

'The former West Ham United and Ipswich Town manager John Lyall, who has died of a heart attack aged 66, was an affable man, an almost complete contrast to the brooding, preening, haunted characters in charge of teams today.'

The family were overwhelmed by the response to John's death. When Ron Greenwood died in February 2006, just two months before John, his family decided on a very quiet, family service. But Yvonne and Murray felt they could not exclude ex-players, managers and colleagues who desperately wanted to pay their final respects to their great friend. The family agreed on a morning cremation at nearby Weeley for close friends and family, followed in the afternoon by a Memorial Service at St Mary le Tower in Ipswich. The funeral was followed by a Celebration of John`s Life in the Galleria Suite at Ipswich Town Football Club, organised by John's former secretary, Pat Godbold.

Among those who attended the funeral were many ex-West Ham and Ipswich players including Patsy Holland – who asked Yvonne to place a letter in the coffin. As Trevor Brooking reminds us in the Foreword to this book, Sir Alex Ferguson chartered a private jet to Suffolk and spoke at the service, a typically generous act which meant a great deal to the family. Picking up on Lyall's love of DIY and famed sense of humour, Ferguson recalled repeatedly trying to contact John to ask his advice, only to be told by Yvonne, "I'm sorry Alex he's up a ladder."

The United manager replied with typical candour, "Every time I call him Yvonne, he's up a bloody ladder."

Ferguson's quiet humour was well-appreciated by everyone at the service.

Mark Ward, the Hammers' former winger, sent flowers from his prison cell, while people like Terry Venables and Billy Bonds proved reliable sources of comfort for the family. A few weeks later John's ashes were placed in the local church at Tattingstone, a short walk from the Lyall home. Paul Goddard and Simon Milton live locally and keep in contact, while Chris Kiwomya, who to this day refers to Yvonne as Mrs Lyall, is a regular visitor and every year leaves flowers in the little Suffolk church on the anniversary of John's death.

For Yvonne, life in Tattingstone would never be the same again. Despite having Murray and his family close by, she found living alone in the isolated farmhouse extremely difficult. The wonderful memories only seemed to make things worse. In retirement, the couple attended an evening class in Bury St Edmunds – a 60 mile round trip from their home in Tattingstone. John learnt upholstery, while Yvonne sat at the other end of the room making curtains. John was the only man in the class, a source of great delight to his female classmates. The couple spent many of their winter evenings in the workshop at the top of the Suffolk house, Von running up curtains and John upholstering one of the many chairs neatly placed around their lovely home.

For Yvonne and the family, the loss of John remains extremely hard to bear. Christmas and anniversaries have a particular poignancy. John, Yvonne, Murray, Samantha and the children decamped to Centre Parcs for Christmas every year after John retired and continued going for four years after his death. The Lyalls were a close knit family. This closeness helped the family wounds to heal as they began to rebuild their lives in the years following the shock of John's sudden death.

Early in 2012 Yvonne sold Wallers Farm and moved to a smaller house in the heart of a nearby Suffolk village where the great painter, John Constable produced his magnificent depictions of the Suffolk countryside. She loves the closeness and warmth of her new community and keeps in regular contact with old friends from West Ham and Ipswich, including Jean Musgrove, Susan Dick and Vic Keeble. One of Yvonne's closest friends is Pat Godbold, who worked with nine managers during her long career at Ipswich Town. Her friends and family have been a real source of comfort to Yvonne who has shown great courage in rebuilding her life after the tragic loss of her husband – one of the most loved and respected figures in professional football.

At last, a fitting tribute

At the end of this story of John Lyall's life in football, it is fitting to return to the place where it all began. Lyall's death created a hole at the heart of West Ham United that has never been filled. A minute's silence was held in his honour before the 2006 FA Cup semi-final against Middlesborough. A lone supporter, who understood what Lyall achieved at the club, started the chant of 'John Lyall's claret and blue army', 30 seconds into the minute's silence. Soon thousands of Hammers' supporters joined in and the familiar chant echoed around the stadium. It was entirely appropriate that the fans broke the silence – it just felt right, and the spontaneous tribute was of great comfort to the Lyall family, watching at home on television.

Murray Lyall reveals that the club telephoned him the following day to apologise for the appalling behaviour of the fans. As Murray recalls:

'The representative of the Board was both stunned and relieved when I explained how terrific and poignant the family thought it was.'

The West Ham players paid their own tribute to the club's most successful manager that day, winning 1-0 to reach the FA Cup Final for the first time since Lyall's team beat Arsenal at Wembley in 1980. West Ham fans and former players will remember John Lyall for his integrity, leadership and inspirational coaching. His death was truly the end of an era.

On 5 December, 2007 a blue plaque was erected at the Boleyn by the Heritage Foundation in memory of Lyall's contribution to the history of the old East London club. The plaque is placed on the left hand side of the main entrance to the ground in Green Street. To the right of the entrance are memorial plaques for Ron

Greenwood and Bobby Moore. Two years later West Ham finally provided their own tribute to their former manager when they renamed the main gates at Upton Park, the John Lyall gates. An emotional unveiling ceremony was attended by many of Lyall's players and friends, including Sir Trevor Brooking, Alvin Martin, Ray Stewart, Alan Devonshire, Tony Cottee and Terry Venables. Billy Bonds was closer to Lyall than most:

'As coaches Ron and John were geniuses... As people they were exceptional. Every player who came through the youth set-up became a proper person too. I was lucky to be part of the proper football club they built.'

The most moving tribute on the day came from Lyall's son, Murray who admitted, "Dad didn't like a fuss and would probably be squirming a bit with all this attention on him, but also deep down, very proud as are all of us."

There is no question that West Ham took their time in providing a permanent tribute to John Lyall, despite continual pressure from friends and family. Tony Cottee, among others, helped to convince the club that they should show some respect to their tradition, as Ipswich Town did when they erected statues to Bobby Robson and Alf Ramsey. Yvonne and Murray were also upset by the manner in which the family was treated by the new Board in the years following John's death. Writing in the Hammers' fanzine Ex, Yvonne wrote:

'After my husband's 34 years' loyal service to the club in a playing, coaching and managerial capacity, I feel my family should have been shown greater respect and understanding, given our tragic loss four years ago and the legacy he left behind.'

The PA to CEO, Karren Brady, rang Murray to apologise for their oversight in withdrawing the Lyall family season tickets issued by the previous regime. The family are now invited by the club to attend three matches each season, providing complimentary hospitality in the corporate lounges, described by Murray as, "A wonderful gesture, much appreciated by the family."

There is better news for the future. If the club achieves its ambition in moving to Stratford as is looking likely at the time of writing, fans will insist that the Lyall Gates are taken down and re-erected at the new Olympic Stadium to ensure John's memory endures. They will be encouraged by this statement from Karren Brady, published in The Sun newspaper:

'West Ham fans will be able to pass through the John Lyall gates as they approach the new stadium.'

This will help, but the club's behaviour towards highly-respected club servants is probably symptomatic of the ethics of the commercial environment of the English Premier League – ethics which are in stark contrast to those which made West Ham a special club.

Brian Clough was a great friend of Lyall and always insisted John sat next to him at Football League meetings. "Come on young man, sit next to me," demanded the outspoken Clough, who once said, "What the hell do directors know about football?" It is to be hoped that providing a lasting tribute to their most successful manager has taught the club hierarchy something about the value of its heritage and proud traditions.

Last word

'He was a great coach. But it's the man you're going to miss more.'
- Sir Trevor Brooking

It is not difficult to assess Lyall's contribution to the history of West Ham United. His team played exquisite football in great style and became one of the most respected teams in Europe. Younger Hammers' fans can only look back in wonder at the golden age. With his great friends Ron Greenwood and Bobby Moore, John Lyall created a brand that today's so-called business gurus can only dream about. But all is not lost. It is encouraging to hear of innovations like the Greenwood and Lyall Legacy Fund, set up to ensure the old West Ham values survive and prosper.

Like most people in professional sport, Lyall had his share of disappointment and defeat. In 1989, relegation from the top flight cost him his job at West Ham. But he'll be remembered more for his considerable achievements. Perhaps the most impressive of these was recovering from a career-ending injury at the age of 23 to become one of the most respected coaches in the game. More tangible rewards came in the form of two FA Cup final wins for the Hammers, the club's highest ever top flight finish, and electrifying European nights at Upton Park. Promotion to the new Premier League in only his second season at Ipswich Town was an outstanding achievement. But, much more than trophies, his legacy stems from the wonderful football his teams played and the testimony of his players as to the kind of man he was.

Lyall's character was forged from a combination of Scottish steel and a Londoner's charm. He had a gentle sense of humour and a remarkable flair for dealing with people. In addition, Lyall was a compassionate and considerate man, but with a difference. He had a great big lump of steel inside him which, together with his more insightful qualities, made him a formidable manager. The crude excesses of today's Premier League cry out for the leadership and guiding hand of a John Lyall. But his legacy endures and Lyall's name continues to resonate down the years at Upton Park, as it will if the club moves to the new Olympic Stadium.

John Lyall was of a generation that spanned acute social change. They lived through the austerity of the 1950s, which shaped the steady, stoical values of Lyall's parents. The 1960s were colourful and liberating in comparison. Suddenly, football became fashionable with Bobby Moore and George Best leading the way. The appalling violence of the 1970s was in direct contrast to its freewheeling predecessor, while the final years of Lyall's managerial career were set within the excesses of the Thatcher era. Throughout 40 years of social instability, Lyall remained unflustered, trusting his better instincts. Individual lives do not generally make a major difference to us. But the real value Lyall saw in his work was the good it might do for others – players, colleagues and fans alike. Few are fortunate to leave behind a footprint from which the rest of us draw strength. John Angus Lyall was such a man.

Chronology

1940 Born on 24 February in Ilford, Essex, one of three sons to Scottish parents, James and Catherine Lyall

1945-55 Parkhill Primary School and Ilford County High School

1955 Signed professional forms for West Ham United at the age of 15

1960 First team debut at left-back against Chelsea

1961 Married Yvonne Webb in Ilford, Essex

1962 Murray Lyall born on 17 April, 1962

1964 Retired as a player due to a serious knee injury, aged 23

1964 Appointed part-time youth team coach at Upton Park

1971 Appointed Assistant Manager to Ron Greenwood

1975 Appointed Manager at West Ham in succession to Ron Greenwood

1975 West Ham beat Fulham 2-0 in the FA Cup Final

1980 West Ham beat Arsenal 1-0 in the FA Cup Final

1986 West Ham third in the 1st Division – the club's highest ever League finish in the top flight of English football

1989 West Ham relegated from the 1st Division at the end of the 1988/89 season

1989 Sacked after 14 years as manager of West Ham and a total of 34 years' service at the club

1989 Appointed part-time coach at Tottenham Hotspur by Terry Venables

1990 Appointed Manager of Ipswich Town FC

1992 Ipswich 2nd Division Champions – promoted to the new Premier League

1994 Resigned as manager of Ipswich Town and retired from football

2006 Died on 18 April 2006, aged 66

2009 Main gates at Upton Park renamed, The John Lyall Gates

Bibliography

Books

Bacon, Steve, Hammers in Focus: A Photographic History over Three Decades, 1998, Hallamshire Press

Bonds, Billy, Bonzo: An Autobiography, 1988, Weidenfield and Nicholson

Bose, Mihir, False Messiah: The Life and Times of Terry Venables, Andre Deutsch, 1996

Blows & Hogg, The Essential History of West Ham United, 2000, Headline Book Publishing

Fenton, Ted, At Home with the Hammers, 1960, Nicholas Kaye

Henderson & Voller, The Essential History of Ipswich Town, 2001, Headline Book Publishing

Goldleman, Martin, Hammers Through the Looking Glass, An Alternative History of West Ham United, 2006, Desert Island Books

Godleman, Martin, West Ham United: 101 Beautiful Games, 2008, Desert Island Books

Greenwood, Ron, Yours Sincerely, 1984, Willow Books

Harris, Harry, West Ham United 1982 Annual, Maybank Press

Hogg, Tony, Who's Who of West Ham United 1895-2005, 2005, Profile Sports Media

Lyall, John, Just Like My Dreams: My Life with West Ham, 1990, Penguin

Press

Moore, Tina, Bobby Moore: By the Person Who Knew Him Best, 2006, Harper Sport

McDonald, Tony, West Ham United: The Managers, 2007, Football World

McDonald, Tony & Francis, Danny, Boys of '86: The Untold Story of West Ham's Greatest Season, 2001, Mainstream Publishing

Northcutt, John, The Claret & Blue Book of West Ham United, 2007, Pitch Publishing

Northcutt, John, The Definitive West Ham United, 2004, Soccer Data Publications

Powell, Jeff, Bobby Moore: The Life and Times of a Sporting Hero, 1994, Robson Books

Redknapp, Harry, My Autobiography, 1998, Collins Willow

Stevens, Philip, Sporting Heroes of East London and Essex: Bobby Moore & Graham Gooch, 2010, Apex Publishing

Stevens, Philip, Pioneers of West Ham United, 2011, Derby Books

Ward, Mark, Hammered, 2010, John Blake

Wilson, Jonathan, Brian Clough: Nobody Ever Says Thank You – The Biography, 2011, Orion Books

Newspapers

Ipswich Evening Star, Match Reports and Articles

Stratford Express, Match Reports

Ilford Recorder, Match Reports

Websites

www.theyflysohigh.co.uk

www.whufc.co.uk

www.wikipedia.com

www.itfc.co.uk

www.ex-hammers.com

www.journeysthroughsport.com

Name Index

Dunmore, Dave – 40-1, 44, 46

Eastham, George – 27, 65, 69

Eustace, Peter – 107, 114

Fenton, Ted – 1, 22-30, 31-42, 44-6, 48-50, 70, 78, 83, 86, 103-4, 116, 138, 216-7, 241

Ferdinand, Rio – 183, 235

Ferguson, Alex – 10, 12, 14, 116, 125, 166, 197, 206, 219, 239, 243-4, 259, 279, 282, 289, 296, 308

Ferguson, Bobby (goalkeeper) – 105, 113, 196

Ferguson, Bobby (Manager) - 261

Finn, Tom – 239

Finney, Tom – 27, 60

Forrest, Craig – 269, 276

Francis, Danny – 217, 226-7

Francis, Trevor – 205-6

Fry, Barry - 225

Gaines, Jim - 302

Gascoigne, Paul - 256

Gale, Tony – 203, 226, 229, 233, 242, 307

Gerrard, Steven – 225, 227

Giggs, Ryan – 279, 282

Gillam, Eddie - 242

Godbold, Pat – 7, 260, 263, 308-9

Goddard, Paul – 164, 184-6, 190-1, 203, 207, 213, 220, 237, 265, 269, 293-5, 301, 303, 307, 309

Gooch, Graham – 15, 26

Gould, Bobby – 114, 123-4, 130, 132

Goulden, Len – 32, 216

Graham, George – 227

Greaves, Jimmy – 21, 29, 39, 59, 64, 73, 107-8

Greenhoff, Jimmy - 154

Gregory, Ernie – 31, 41, 60, 94, 118, 180, 239

Gregory, Jim – 202, 213

Green, Bill – 153, 162

Johnson, Gavin – 269, 272, 295

Johnson, Glen - 183

Jones, Ken – 95, 98

Joy, Bernard - 302

Kanchelskis, Andrei - 279

Keeble, Vic – 30-32, 309

Keen, Kevin - 233

Kendall, Howard – 88-9, 92, 225

Kennedy, Alan – 186-9

Kennedy, Ray - 186

Kerr, John - 271

Kidd, Brian - 172

King, Syd – 1, 56, 108, 116, 216, 241-2

Kingston, Dave – 7, 19-20

Kirkup, Joe – 33, 35-6, 47, 48, 67-8, 98, 100, 103

Kiwomya, Chris – 7, 137, 265-80, 282, 290-1, 299, 303, 306, 309

Lacy, John – 129

Lampard, Frank, Jnr – 102, 183, 235

Lampard, Frank, Snr – 113, 123, 130-1, 143, 146-7, 172, 174, 181, 186, 207, 218, 240

Lawton, Nobby – 88

Lawton, Tommy – 58

Leach, Mick - 21

Lee, Sammy – 186-7

Leslie, Lawrie – 67, 69

Lineker, Gary – 222, 256

Linighan, David – 268, 274, 287-8

Lock, Kevin – 123, 131-2, 136, 162

Lorenzo, Peter- 2-9, 13-17, 181, 302

Lyall, Catherine – 2, 22, 181

Lyall, James, Snr – 2-18

Lyall, James, Jnr – 7-9, 16, 21, 168, 301

Lyall, Murray – 8-9, 53, 55, 77, 117, 138-40, 151, 167, 203, 239, 244, 251, 257, 298, 302-11, 315

Lyall, Samantha – 302-09

Moss, Pauline – 24-5, 66, 78, 85, 93, 247

Morley, Trevor - 225

Motson, John - 273

Muhren, Arnold – 251, 285, 295

Musgrove, Malcolm – 2, 31, 38, 40, 44-5, 47-8, 66, 70-3, 84, 217,309

Musgrove, Jean - 309

Neighbour, Jimmy – 184-89

Neil, Terry – 175, 181

Nicholas, Charlie - 224

Nicholson, Bill – 10, 17, 21-2, 60, 73, 80, 151, 169, 303

Northcutt, John – 7, 245, 248, 250

Noye, Mike - 306

O'Hare, John - 171

O'Leary, David – 176-7

O'Neil, Martin - 171

Orr, Neil – 197, 204, 230

Paddon, Graham – 114, 123, 129-34, 143-6, 151, 153

Pallister, Gary - 279

Parkboo, Jaywat - 245

Parkes, Phil – 7, 137, 162, 171, 174, 181-4, 201, 203, 220, 241, 243, 264, 303

Parkes, Lavinia – 202-3

Parris, George - 220

Partridge, Pat – 128

Paz, Adrian - 295

Pearson, Stuart – 1154, 164-5, 172, 176-82, 184, 186-7, 191-3, 208

Perchey, Jack - 193

Peters, Martin- 1, 28, 31, 45, 62-3, 68-71, 84, 88, 95, 99, 101-7, 109-10, 114, 124, 135, 137, 141, 169, 217, 231, 277

Pike, Geoff – 137, 154, 167, 178, 180-2, 186, 191, 193, 201, 204, 208-11, 230

Pratt, Reg – 45, 49, 56, 116-7, 153, 170

Potts, Steve – 233

Puddefoot, Syd - 216

Puskas, Ferenc - 89

Smith, John - 40

Smith, Trevor – 159, 285

Spavin, Alan - 88

Spitz, Mark - 119

Souness, Graham – 186, 189, 228

St Pier, Wally – 22, 26, 33, 60, 71, 80

Stammers, Steve - 302

Standen, Jim – 63, 71-2, 83, 89, 95, 97, 103

Stapleton, Frank - 175

Stephenson, Alan - 105

Stewart, Micky - 26

Stewart, Ray – 7, 10, 137, 165, 167-71, 181, 222, 228-9, 243, 264, 273, 303, 311

Stock, Alex – 126, 129, 303

Stockwell, Michael – 269, 279, 282

Strodder, Gary - 277

Sunderland, Alan – 177-8

Swindon, George – 46, 56

Tanner, Adam - 285

Taricco, Mauricio - 295

Taylor, Alan – 123-5, 130-1, 147, 151, 165

Taylor, Tommy - 108, 143, 146, 161, 165, 169

Taylor, Gordon – 208, 231

Taylor, Graham - 233

Thatcher, Margaret – 119, 173, 313

Thijssen, Franz – 285, 295

Thomas, Clive – 186, 189

Thomas, Mitchell - 256

Thompson, Neil – 267, 273, 278, 280

Thompson, Phil – 189

Toshack, John - 171

Trevivian, Peter – 259, 271

Trinder, Tommy – 126

Van der Elst, Francois – 147, 196, 207

Venables, Terry – 7, 10, 13-4, 25-6, 39, 85, 111-2, 213, 239, 255-9, 309, 311, 315

Villa, Ricardo - 251

Other books by the author

Sporting Heroes of East London and Essex:
Bobby Moore and Graham Gooch

West Ham's 30 Greatest Matches

Pioneers of West Ham United

Left: The promising full-back emerging from the tunnel at Upton Park

Below: Lyall pictured with the 1962-63 Hammers (back row, far left)

Left: A proud young professional at the start of his career

Below: Supporting a young John Charles against Blackburn Rovers

Above: Defending against a lively Wolves attack

Bottom left: Keeping an eye on Spur's Terry Dyson in front of the 'Chicken Run' at Upton Park

Above: Lyall helping to clear the snow from the West Ham car park during the 'big freeze' of 1963 - note the players' cars

Below: With Bobby Moore and John Dick before Lyall's Testimonial Match in 1964

Left: Programme cover from Lyall's 1964 testimonial match

Above: Working with the Hammers' youth team

Left: Warming up the reserves at Chadwell Heath

Right: Ted Fenton's great 2nd Division Championship winning side of 1957-58. Lyall served his apprenticeship alongside such Hammers' legends as Malcolm Allison, Noel Cantwell, John Dick and Malcolm Musgrove

Right: The Lyall and Greenwood brains trust in action - with Mick McGiven seated in the background

Below: Lyall enjoying the sunshine with Rob Jenkins, Albert Walker and reserves Bobby Ferguson and Ray Stewart

Above: Lyall on the bench feeling every kick with Boyce, Jenkins, Walker and a young Trevor Brooking

Right: Wrapped up well against the cold, with trademark overcoat, escorted by Hammers' physio, Rob Jenkins

Left: Lyall in conversation
with one of West Ham's
greatest signings,
Alan Devonshire

Below: Enjoying a joke with
Ted MacDougall

Left: Posing with the 1975
FA Cup final goal-scorer,
Alan Taylor

Below: Pictured with the
FA Cup at Wally St Pier's
testimonial match

Above: Pictured with West
Ham's Billy Jennings and
all-time great, Billy Bonds

Below: Smiling through the
good times at Upton Park

Above: A smiling John Lyall -
one of the wisest and most
honourable men in football

Below: Lyall with Hammers'
historian John Northcutt at
Chadwell Heath in 1987

Left: With chairman, Len Cearns and Phil Parkes in happier times

Below: The 'Boys of 86' - one of West Ham's all-time greatest teams

Left: A very contented looking West Ham manager

Below: Blue plaque sited at the entrance to Upton Park in memory of West Ham's most successful manager

John Lyall
1940-2006

Manager of
West Ham United
1974-1989

SPORTS HERITAGE

Left: Pat Godbolt and Charlie Woods - two of Lyall's loyal staff at Ipswich Town

Right: May 1992 - scenes of celebration at Portman Road as Ipswich end the season with a 3-1 win over Brighton

Left: Lyall's tractor boys celebrate winning the 2nd Division championship at Oxford in 1992

Right: An angry Lyall trudges off the Portman Road pitch following the disastrous home defeat against Manchester City in December 1994

www.apexpublishing.co.uk

CPSIA information can be obtained
at www.ICGtesting.com
Printed in the USA
LVOW11s0648011216

515162LV00001B/33/P

9 781785 384929